PENGUIN BOOKS

ASYLUMS

Erving Goffman graduated from the University of Toronto in 1945, gaining his M.A. in sociology from the University of Chicago in 1949. He carried out field research in the Shetland Islands while a member of the department of social anthropology at Edinburgh University from 1949 to 1951, then worked on two projects in the division of social sciences, University of Chicago. His doctoral dissertation, *Communication Conduct in an Island Community*, gained him his Ph.D. in sociology from the University of Chicago in 1953, then from 1954 until 1957 he served as a visiting scientist in the laboratory of socio-environmental studies at the National Institute of Mental Health. In 1962 he became professor of sociology at the University of California, Berkeley, and transferred in September 1968 to the Departments of Anthropology and Sociology at the University of Pennsylvania.

Erving Goffman contributed to various specialized journals; he was also the author of *Presentation of Self in Everyday Life* (1956; Penguin 1990), which won the MacIver Award in 1961, *Encounters* (1961), *Behaviour in Public Places* (1963), *Stigma* (1963; reissued in Penguin 1990), *Interaction Ritual* (1967), *Strategic Interaction* (1970), *Asylums* (1974), *Frame Analysis* (1975), *Gender Advertisements* (1979), and *Forms of Talk* (1981). Professor Goffman died in 1983.

D1102615

ERVING GOFFMAN

ASYLUMS

ESSAYS ON THE
SOCIAL SITUATION OF
MENTAL PATIENTS AND
OTHER INMATES

PENGUIN BOOKS

PENGUIN BOOKS

Published by the Penguin Group
Penguin Books Ltd, 27 Wrights Lane, London W8 5TZ, England
Penguin Books USA Inc., 375 Hudson Street, New York, New York 10014, USA
Penguin Books Australia Ltd, Ringwood, Victoria, Australia
Penguin Books Canada Ltd, 10 Alcorn Avenue, Toronto, Ontario, Canada M4V 3B2
Penguin Books (NZ) Ltd, 182–190 Wairau Road, Auckland 10, New Zealand

Penguin Books Ltd, Registered Offices: Harmondsworth, Middlesex, England

First published by Anchor Books, Doubleday & Co. 1961
Published in Pelican Books 1968
Reprinted in Peregrine Books 1987
Reprinted in Penguin Books 1991
3 5 7 9 10 8 6 4

Printed in England by Clays Ltd, St Ives plc
Set in Monotype Times

CONTENTS

PREFACE

FROM Autumn 1954 to the end of 1957 I was a visiting member of the Laboratory of Socio-environmental Studies of the National Institute of Mental Health in Bethesda, Maryland. During those three years I did some brief studies of ward behaviour in the National Institutes of Health Clinical Center. In 1955–6 I did a year's field work at St Elizabeth's Hospital, Washington, D.C., a federal institution of somewhat over 7,000 inmates that draws three-quarters of its patients from the District of Columbia. Later additional time for writing up the material was made possible by an NIMH grant, M-4111(A), and through participation in the Center for the Integration of Social Science Theory at the University of California at Berkeley.

My immediate object in doing field work at St Elizabeth's was to try to learn about the social world of the hospital inmate, as this world is subjectively experienced by him. I started out in the role of an assistant to the athletic director, when pressed avowing to be a student of recreation and community life, and I passed the day with patients, avoiding sociable contact with the staff and the carrying of a key. I did not sleep in the wards, and the top hospital management knew what my aims were.

It was then and still is my belief that any group of persons – prisoners, primitives, pilots, or patients – develop a life of their own that becomes meaningful, reasonable, and normal once you get close to it, and that a good way to learn about any of these worlds is to submit oneself in the company of the members to the daily round of petty contingencies to which they are subject.

The limits, of both my method and my application of it, are obvious: I did not allow myself to be committed even nominally, and had I done so my range of movements and roles, and hence my data, would have been restricted even more than they were. Desiring to obtain ethnographic detail regarding selected aspects of patient social life, I did not employ usual kinds of measurements and controls. I assumed that the role and time required to gather statistical evidence for a few statements would preclude my gathering data on the tissue and fabric of patient life. My method has other limits, too. The world view of a group functions to sustain its members and expectedly provides them with a self-justifying definition of their own situation and a prejudiced view of non-members, in this case, doctors, nurses, attendants, and relatives. To describe the patient's situation faithfully is necessarily to present a partisan view. (For this last bias I partly excuse myself by arguing that the imbalance is at least on the right side of the scale, since almost all professional literature on mental patients is written from the point of view of the psychiatrist, and he, socially speaking, is on the other side.) Further, I want to warn that my view is probably too much that of a middle-class male; perhaps I suffered vicariously about conditions that lower-class patients handled with little pain. Finally, unlike some patients, I came to the hospital with no great respect for the discipline of psychiatry nor for agencies content with its current practice.

I would like to acknowledge in a special way the support I was given by the sponsoring agencies. Permission to study St Elizabeth's was negotiated through the then First Assistant Physician, the late Dr Jay Hoffman. He agreed that the hospital would expect pre-publication criticism rights but exert no final censorship or clearance privileges, these being lodged in N I M H in Bethesda. He agreed to the understanding that no observation made about any identified staff person or inmate would be reported to him or to anyone else, and that as an observer I was not obliged to interfere in any way whatsoever with what I could observe going on. He agreed to open any door in the hospital to me, and throughout the study did so when asked with a courtesy, speed, and effectiveness that I will never forget. Later, when the Superintendent of the hospital, Dr Winifred Overholser, reviewed drafts of my papers, he made helpful corrections regarding some outright errors of fact, along with a useful suggestion that my point of view and method be made explicit. During the study, the Laboratory of Socio-environmental Studies, then headed by its originating director, John Clausen, provided my salary, secretarial help, collegial criticism, and encouragement to look at the hospital with sociology in mind, not junior psychiatry. The clearance rights possessed by the Laboratory and its parent body, NIMH, were exercised, the only consequence I am aware of being that on one occasion I was asked to consider a substitute for one or two impolite adjectives.

The point I want to make is that this freedom and opportunity to engage in pure research was afforded me in regard to a government agency, through the financial support of another government agency, both of which were required to operate in the presumably delicate atmosphere of Washington, and this was done at a time when some universities in this country, the traditional bastions of free inquiry, would have put more restrictions on my efforts. For this I must thank the open- and fair-mindedness of psychiatrists and social scientists in government.

ERVING GOFFMAN
Berkeley, California, 1961

INTRODUCTION

A TOTAL institution may be defined as a place of residence and work where a large number of like-situated individuals, cut off from the wider society for an appreciable period of time, together lead an enclosed, formally administered round of life. Prisons serve as a clear example, providing we appreciate that what is prison-like about prisons is found in institutions whose members have broken no laws. This volume deals with total institutions in general and one example, mental hospitals, in particular. The main focus is on the world of the inmate, not the world of the staff. A chief concern is to develop a sociological version of the structure of the self.

Each of the four essays in this book was written to stand by itself, the first two having been separately published. All were intended to focus on the same issue – the inmate's situation. Some repetition is therefore involved. On the other hand, each paper approaches the central issue from a different vantage point, each introduction drawing upon a different source in sociology and having little relation to the other papers.

This method of presenting material may be irksome to the reader, but it allows me to pursue the main theme of each paper analytically and comparatively past the point that would be allowable in chapters of an integrated book. I plead the state of our discipline. I think that at present, if sociological concepts are to be treated with affection, each must be traced back to where it best applies, followed from there wherever it seems to lead, and pressed to disclose the rest of its family. Better, perhaps, different coats to clothe the children well than a single splendid tent in which they all shiver.

The first paper, 'On the Characteristics of Total Institutions', is a general examination of social life in these establishments, drawing heavily on two examples that feature involuntary membership – mental hospitals and prisons. There the schemes developed in detail in the remaining papers are stated and their place in the broader whole suggested. The second paper, 'The

Moral Career of the Mental Patient', considers the initial effects of institutionalization on the social relationships the individual possessed before he became an inmate. The third paper, 'The Underlife of a Public Institution', is concerned with the attach- ment the inmate is expected to manifest to his iron home and, in detail, with the way in which inmates can introduce some distance between themselves and these expectations. The final paper, 'The Medical Model and Mental Hospitalization', turns attention back to the professional staffs to consider, in the case of mental hospitals, the role of the medical perspective in presenting to the inmate the facts of his situation.

ON THE CHARACTERISTICS
OF TOTAL INSTITUTIONS

A shorter version of this paper appears in the *Symposium on Preventive and Social Psychiatry*, Walter Reed Army Institute of Research, Washington, D.C. (15–17 April 1957), pp. 43–84. The present version is reprinted from *The Prison*, edited by Donald R. Cressey, copyright © 1961 by Holt, Rinehart and Winston, Inc.

INTRODUCTION

I

SOCIAL establishments – institutions in the everyday sense of that term – are places such as rooms, suites of rooms, buildings, or plants in which activity of a particular kind regularly goes on. In sociology we do not have a very apt way of classifying them. Some establishments, like Grand Central Station, are open to anyone who is decently behaved; others, like the Union League Club of New York or the laboratories at Los Alamos, are felt to be somewhat snippy about who is let in. Some, like shops and post offices, have a few fixed members who provide a service and a continuous flow of members who receive it. Others, like homes and factories, involve a less changing set of participants. Some institutions provide the place for activities from which the individual is felt to draw his social status, however enjoyable or lax these pursuits may be; other institutions, in contrast, provide a place for associations felt to be elective and unserious, calling for a contribution of time left over from more serious demands. In this book another category of institutions is singled out and claimed as a natural and fruitful one because its members appear to have so much in common – so much, in fact, that to learn about one of these institutions we would be well advised to look at the others.

II

Every institution captures something of the time and interest of its members and provides something of a world for them; in brief, every institution has encompassing tendencies. When we review the different institutions in our Western society, we find some that are encompassing to a degree discontinuously greater than the ones next in line. Their encompassing or total character is symbolized by the barrier to social intercourse with the outside and to departure that is often built right into the physical plant, such as locked doors, high walls, barbed wire, cliffs, water, forests, or moors. These establishments I am calling *total institutions*, and it is their general characteristics I want to explore.[1]

The total institutions of our society can be listed in five rough groupings. First, there are institutions established to care for persons felt to be both incapable and harmless; these are the homes for the blind, the aged, the orphaned, and the indigent. Second, there are places established to care for persons felt to be both incapable of looking after themselves and a threat to the community, albeit an unintended one: T B sanitaria, mental hospitals, and leprosaria. A third type of total institution is organized to protect the community against what are felt to be intentional dangers to it, with the welfare of the persons thus sequestered not the immediate issue: jails, penitentiaries, P.O.W. camps, and concentration camps. Fourth, there are institutions purportedly established the better to pursue some worklike task and justifying themselves only on these instrumental grounds: army barracks, ships, boarding schools, work camps, colonial compounds, and large mansions from the point of view of those who live in the servants' quarters. Finally, there are those establishments designed as retreats from the world even while often serving also as training stations for the religious; examples are abbeys, monasteries, convents, and other cloisters. This classification of total institutions is not neat, exhaustive, nor of immediate analytical use, but it does provide a purely denotative definition of the category as a concrete starting point. By anchoring the initial definition of total institutions in this way, I hope to be able to discuss the general characteristics of the type without becoming tautological.

Before I attempt to extract a general profile from this list of

1. The category of total institutions has been pointed out from time to time in the sociological literature under a variety of names, and some of the characteristics of the class have been suggested, most notably perhaps in Howard Rowland's neglected paper, 'Segregated Communities and Mental Health', in *Mental Health Publication of the American Association for the Advancement of Science*, No. 9, edited by F. R. Moulton, 1939. A preliminary statement of the present paper is reported in *Group Processes*, Transactions of the Third (1956) Conference, edited by Bertram Schaffner (New York) Josiah Macy, Jr, Foundation, 1957). The term 'total' has also been used in its present context in Amitai Etzioni, 'The Organizational Structure of "Closed" Educational Institutions in Israel', *Harvard Educational Review*, XXVII (1957), p. 115.

establishments, I would like to mention one conceptual problem: none of the elements I will describe seems peculiar to total institutions, and none seems to be shared by every one of them; what is distinctive about total institutions is that each exhibits to an intense degree many items in this family of attributes. In speaking of 'common characteristics', I will be using this phrase in a way that is restricted but I think logically defensible. At the same time this permits using the method of ideal types, establishing common features with the hope of highlighting significant differences later.

III

A basic social arrangement in modern society is that the individual tends to sleep, play, and work in different places, with different co-participants, under different authorities, and without an over-all rational plan. The central feature of total institutions can be described as a breakdown of the barriers ordinarily separating these three spheres of life. First, all aspects of life are conducted in the same place and under the same single authority. Second, each phase of the member's daily activity is carried on in the immediate company of a large batch of others, all of whom are treated alike and required to do the same thing together. Third, all phases of the day's activities are tightly scheduled, with one activity leading at a prearranged time into the next, the whole sequence of activities being imposed from above by a system of explicit formal rulings and a body of officials. Finally, the various enforced activities are brought together into a single rational plan purportedly designed to fulfil the official aims of the institution.

Individually, these features are found in places other than total institutions. For example, our large commercial, industrial, and educational establishments are increasingly providing cafeterias and free-time recreation for their members; use of these extended facilities remains voluntary in many particulars, however, and special care is taken to see that the ordinary line of authority does not extend to them. Similarly, housewives or farm families may have all their major spheres of life within the same fenced-in area, but these persons are not collectively regimented and do not march through the day's activities in the immediate company of a batch of similar others.

The handling of many human needs by the bureaucratic organization of whole blocks of people – whether or not this is a necessary or effective means of social organization in the circumstances – is the key fact of total institutions. From this follow certain important implications.

When persons are moved in blocks, they can be supervised by personnel whose chief activity is not guidance or periodic inspection (as in many employer-employee relations) but rather surveillance – a seeing to it that everyone does what he has been clearly told is required of him, under conditions where one person's infraction is likely to stand out in relief against the visible, constantly examined compliance of the others. Which comes first, the large blocks of managed people, or the small supervisory staff, is not here at issue; the point is that each is made for the other.

In total institutions there is a basic split between a large managed group, conveniently called inmates, and a small supervisory staff. Inmates typically live in the institution and have restricted contact with the world outside the walls; staff often operate on an eight-hour day and are socially integrated into the outside world.[2] Each grouping tends to conceive of the other in terms of narrow hostile stereotypes, staff often seeing inmates as bitter, secretive, and untrustworthy, while inmates often see staff as condescending, highhanded, and mean. Staff tends to feel superior and righteous; inmates tend, in some ways at least, to feel inferior, weak, blameworthy, and guilty.[3]

2. The binary character of total institutions was pointed out to me by Gregory Bateson, and has been noted in the literature. See, for example, Lloyd E. Ohlin, *Sociology and the Field of Corrections* (New York: Russell Sage Foundation, 1956), pp. 14, 20. In those situations where staff are also required to live in, we may expect staff to feel they are suffering special hardships and to have brought home to them a status dependency on life on the inside which they did not expect. See Jane Cassels Record, 'The Marine Radioman's Struggle for Status', *American Journal of Sociology*, LXII (1957), p. 359.

3. For the prison version, see S. Kirson Weinberg, 'Aspects of the Prison's Social Structure', *American Journal of Sociology*, XLVII (1942), pp. 717–26.

Social mobility between the two strata is grossly restricted; social distance is typically great and often formally prescribed. Even talk across the boundaries may be conducted in a special tone of voice, as illustrated in a fictionalized record of an actual sojourn in a mental hospital:

'I tell you what,' said Miss Hart when they were crossing the day-room. 'You do everything Miss Davis says. Don't think about it, just do it. You'll get along all right.'

As soon as she heard the name Virginia knew what was terrible about Ward One. Miss Davis. 'Is she the head nurse?'

'And how,' muttered Miss Hart. And then she raised her voice. The nurses had a way of acting as if the patients were unable to hear anything that was not shouted. Frequently they said things in normal voices that the ladies were not supposed to hear; if they had not been nurses you would have said they frequently talked to themselves. 'A most competent and efficient person, Miss Davis,' announced Miss Hart.[4]

Although some communication between inmates and the staff guarding them is necessary, one of the guard's functions is the control of communication from inmates to higher staff levels. A student of mental hospitals provides an illustration:

Since many of the patients are anxious to see the doctor on his rounds, the attendants must act as mediators between the patients and the physician if the latter is not to be swamped. On Ward 30, it seemed to be generally true that patients without physical symptoms who fell into the two lower privilege groups were almost never permitted to talk to the physician unless Dr Baker himself asked for them. The per-severing, nagging delusional group – who were termed 'worry warts', 'nuisances', 'bird dogs', in the attendants' slang – often tried to break through the attendant-mediator but were always quite summarily dealt with when they tried.[5]

Just as talk across the boundary is restricted, so, too, is the passage of information, especially information about the staff's plans for inmates. Characteristically, the inmate is excluded from knowledge of the decisions taken regarding his fate. Whether the

4. Mary Jane Ward, *The Snake Pit* (New York: New American Library, 1955), p. 72.

5. Ivan Belknap, *Human Problems of a State Mental Hospital* (New York: McGraw-Hill, 1956), p. 177.

official grounds are military, as in concealing travel destination from enlisted men, or medical, as in concealing diagnosis, plan of treatment, and approximate length of stay from tuberculosis patients,[6] such exclusion gives staff a special basis of distance from and control over inmates.

All these restrictions of contact presumably help to maintain the antagonistic stereotypes.[7] Two different social and cultural worlds develop, jogging alongside each other with points of official contact but little mutual penetration. Significantly, the institutional plant and name come to be identified by both staff and inmates as somehow belonging to staff, so that when either grouping refers to the views or interests of 'the institution', by implication they are referring (as I shall also) to the views and concerns of the staff.

The staff-inmate split is one major implication of the bureau-cratic management of large blocks of persons; a second pertains to work.

In the ordinary arrangements of living in our society, the authority of the work place stops with the worker's receipt of a money payment; the spending of this in a domestic and recrea-tional setting is the worker's private affair and constitutes a mechanism through which the authority of the work place is kept within strict bounds. But to say that inmates of total institutions have their full day scheduled for them is to say that all their essential needs will have to be planned for. Whatever the incentive given for work, then, this incentive will not have the structural significance it has on the outside. There will have to be different motives for work and different attitudes towards it. This is a basic adjustment required of the inmates and of those who must induce them to work.

Sometimes so little work is required that inmates, often un-

6. A very full case report on this matter is provided in a chapter titled 'Information and the Control of Treatment', in Julius A. Roth's forth-coming monograph on the tuberculosis hospital. His work promises to be a model study of a total institution. Preliminary statements may be found in his articles, 'What is an Activity?' *Etc.*, XIV (Autumn 1956), pp. 54–6, and 'Ritual and Magic in the Control of Contagion', *American Sociological Review*, XXII (1957), pp. 310–14.

7. Suggested in Ohlin, op. cit., p. 20.

trained in leisurely pursuits, suffer extremes of boredom. Work that is required may be carried on at a very slow pace and may be geared into a system of minor, often ceremonial payments, such as the weekly tobacco ration and the Christmas presents that lead some mental patients to stay on their jobs. In other cases, of course, more than a full day's hard labour is required, induced not by reward but by threat of physical punishment. In some total institutions, such as logging camps and merchant ships, the practice of forced saving postpones the usual relation to the world that money can buy; all needs are organized by the institution and payment is given only when a work season is over and the men leave the premises. In some institutions there is a kind of slavery, with the inmate's full time placed at the convenience of staff; here the inmate's sense of self and sense of possession can become alienated from his work capacity. T. E. Lawrence gives an illustration in his record of service in an R.A.F. training depot:

The six-weeks men we meet on fatigues shock our moral sense by their easy-going. 'You're silly —, you rookies, to sweat yourselves' they say. Is it our new keenness, or a relic of civility in us? For by the R.A.F. we shall be paid all the twenty-four hours a day, at three half-pence an hour; paid to work, paid to eat, paid to sleep: always those halfpence are adding up. Impossible, therefore, to dignify a job by doing it well. It must take as much time as it can for afterwards there is not a fireside waiting, but another job.[8]

Whether there is too much work or too little, the individual who was work-oriented on the outside tends to become demoralized by the work system of the total institution. An example of such demoralization is the practice in state mental hospitals of 'bumming' or 'working someone for' a nickel or dime to spend in the canteen. Persons do this – often with some defiance – who on the outside would consider such actions beneath their self-respect. (Staff members, interpreting this begging pattern in terms of their own civilian orientation to earning, tend to see it as a symptom of mental illness and one further bit of evidence that inmates really are unwell.)

There is an incompatibility, then, between total institutions and the basic work-payment structure of our society. Total

8. T. E. Lawrence, *The Mint* (London: Jonathan Cape, 1955), p. 40.

institutions are also incompatible with another crucial element of our society, the family. Family life is sometimes contrasted with solitary living, but in fact the more pertinent contrast is with batch living, for those who eat and sleep at work, with a group of fellow workers, can hardly sustain a meaningful domestic existence.[9] Conversely, maintaining families off the grounds often permits staff members to remain integrated with the outside community and to escape the encompassing tendency of the total institution.

Whether a particular total institution acts as a good or bad force in civil society, force it will have, and this will in part depend on the suppression of a whole circle of actual or potential households. Conversely, the formation of households provides a structural guarantee that total institutions will not be without resistance. The incompatibility of these two forms of social organization should tell us something about the wider social functions of them both.

The total institution is a social hybrid, part residential community, part formal organization; therein lies its special sociological interest. There are other reasons for being interested in these establishments, too. In our society, they are the forcing houses for changing persons; each is a natural experiment on what can be done to the self.

Some of the key features of total institutions have been suggested. I want now to consider these establishments from two perspectives: first, the inmate world; then the staff world. Finally, I want to say something about contacts between the two.

9. An interesting marginal case here is the Israeli *kibbutz*. See Melford E. Spiro, *Kibbutz, Venture in Utopia*, (Cambridge: Harvard University Press, 1956), and Etzioni, op. cit.

THE INMATE WORLD

IT is characteristic of inmates that they come to the institution with a 'presenting culture' (to modify a psychiatric phrase) derived from a 'home world' – a way of life and a round of activities taken for granted until the point of admission to the institution. (There is reason, then, to exclude orphanages and foundling homes from the list of total institutions, except in so far as the orphan comes to be socialized into the outside world by some process of cultural osmosis even while this world is being systematically denied him.) Whatever the stability of the recruit's personal organization, it was part of a wider framework lodged in his civil environment – a round of experience that confirmed a tolerable conception of self and allowed for a set of defensive manoeuvres, exercised at his own discretion, for coping with conflicts, discreditings, and failures.

Now it appears that total institutions do not substitute their own unique culture for something already formed; we deal with something more restricted than acculturation or assimilation. If cultural change does occur, it has to do, perhaps, with the removal of certain behaviour opportunities and with failure to keep pace with recent social changes on the outside. Thus, if the inmate's stay is long, what has been called 'disculturation'[10] may occur – that is, an 'untraining' which renders him temporarily incapable of managing certain features of daily life on the outside, if and when he gets back to it.

The full meaning for the inmate of being 'in' or 'on the inside' does not exist apart from the special meaning to him of 'getting out' or 'getting on the outside'. In this sense, total institutions do not really look for cultural victory. They create and sustain a

10. A term employed by Robert Sommer, 'Patients who grow old in a mental hospital', *Geriatrics*, XIV (1959), pp. 586–7. The term 'desocialization', sometimes used in this context, would seem to be too strong, implying loss of fundamental capacities to communicate and cooperate.

particular kind of tension between the home world and the institutional world and use this persistent tension as strategic leverage in the management of men.

II

The recruit comes into the establishment with a conception of himself made possible by certain stable social arrangements in his home world. Upon entrance, he is immediately stripped of the support provided by these arrangements. In the accurate language of some of our oldest total institutions, he begins a series of abasements, degradations, humiliations, and profanations of self. His self is systematically, if often unintentionally, mortified. He begins some radical shifts in his *moral career*, a career composed of the progressive changes that occur in the beliefs that he has concerning himself and significant others.

The processes by which a person's self is mortified are fairly standard in total institutions;[11] analysis of these processes can help us to see the arrangements that ordinary establishments must guarantee if members are to preserve their civilian selves.

The barrier that total institutions place between the inmate and the wider world marks the first curtailment of self. In civil life, the sequential scheduling of the individual's roles, both in the life cycle and in the repeated daily round, ensures that no one role he plays will block his performance and ties in another. In total institutions, in contrast, membership automatically disrupts role scheduling, since the inmate's separation from the wider world lasts around the clock and may continue for years. Role dispossession therefore occurs. In many total institutions the privilege of having visitors or of visiting away from the establishment is completely withheld at first, ensuring a deep initial break with past roles and an appreciation of role dispossession. A report on cadet life in a military academy provides an illustration:

This clean break with the past must be achieved in a relatively short period. For two months, therefore, the swab is not allowed to leave the

11. An example of the description of these processes may be found in Gresham M. Sykes, *The Society of Captives* (Princeton: Princeton University Press, 1958), ch. iv, 'The Pains of Imprisonment', pp. 63–83.

base or to engage in social intercourse with non-cadets. This complete isolation helps to produce a unified group of swabs, rather than a heterogeneous collection of persons of high and low status. Uniforms are issued on the first day, and discussions of wealth and family background are taboo. Although the pay of the cadet is very low, he is not permitted to receive money from home. The role of the cadet must supersede other roles the individual has been accustomed to play. There are few clues left which will reveal social status in the outside world.[12]

I might add that when entrance is voluntary, the recruit has already partially withdrawn from his home world; what is cleanly severed by the institution is something that had already started to decay.

Although some roles can be re-established by the inmate if and when he returns to the world, it is plain that other losses are irrevocable and may be painfully experienced as such. It may not be possible to make up, at a later phase of the life cycle, the time not now spent in educational or job advancement, in courting, or in rearing one's children. A legal aspect of this permanent dispossession is found in the concept of 'civil death'; prison inmates may face not only a temporary loss of the rights to will money and write cheques, to contest divorce or adoption proceedings, and to vote but may have some of these rights permanently abrogated.[13]

The inmate, then, finds certain roles are lost to him by virtue of the barrier that separates him from the outside world. The process of entrance typically brings other kinds of loss and mortification as well. We very generally find staff employing what are called admission procedures, such as taking a life history, photographing, weighing, fingerprinting, assigning numbers, searching, listing personal possessions for storage,

12. Sanford M. Dornbusch, 'The Military Academy as an Assimilating Institution', *Social Forces*, XXXIII (1955), p. 317. For an example of initial visiting restrictions in a mental hospital, see D. McI. Johnson and N. Dodds, eds., *The Plea for the Silent* (London: Christopher Johnson, 1957), p. 16. Compare the rule against having visitors which has often bound domestic servants to their total institution. See J. Jean Hecht, *The Domestic Servant Class in Eighteenth-Century England* (London: Routledge and Kegan Paul, 1956), pp. 127–8.

13. A useful review in the case of American prisons may be found in Paul W. Tappan, 'The Legal Rights of Prisoners', *The Annals*, CCXCIII (May 1954), pp. 99–111.

undressing, bathing, disinfecting, haircutting, issuing institutional clothing, instructing as to rules, and assigning to quarters.[14] Admission procedures might better be called 'trimming' or 'programming' because in thus being squared away the new arrival allows himself to be shaped and coded into an object that can be fed into the administrative machinery of the establishment, to be worked on smoothly by routine operations. Many of these procedures depend upon attributes such as weight or fingerprints that the individual possesses merely because he is a member of the largest and most abstract of social categories, that of human beings. Action taken on the basis of such attributes necessarily ignores most of his previous bases of self-identification.

Because a total institution deals with so many aspects of its inmates' lives, with the consequent complex squaring away at admission, there is a special need to obtain initial cooperativeness from the recruit. Staff often feel that a recruit's readiness to be appropriately deferential in his initial face-to-face encounters with them is a sign that he will take the role of the routinely pliant inmate. The occasion on which staff members first tell the inmate of his deference obligations may be structured to challenge the inmate to balk or to hold his peace forever. Thus these initial moments of socialization may involve an 'obedience test' and even a will-breaking contest: an inmate who shows defiance receives immediate visible punishment, which increases until he openly 'cries uncle' and humbles himself.

An engaging illustration is provided by Brendan Behan in reviewing his contest with two warders upon his admission to Walton prison:

'And 'old up your 'ead, when I speak to you.'
' 'Old up your 'ead, when Mr Whitbread speaks to you,' said Mr Holmes.

14. See, for example, J. Kerkhoff, *How Thin the Veil: A Newspaperman's Story of His Own Mental Crack-up and Recovery* (New York: Greenberg, 1952), p. 110; Elie A. Cohen, *Human Behaviour in the Concentration Camp*, (London: Jonathan Cape, 1954), pp. 118–22; Eugen Kogon, *The Theory and Practice of Hell* (New York: Berkley Publishing Corp., n.d.), pp. 63–8.

I looked round at Charlie. His eyes met mine and he quickly lowered them to the ground.

'What are you looking round at, Behan? Look at me.'

. . . .

I looked at Mr Whitbread. 'I am looking at you,' I said.

'You are looking at Mr Whitbread – what?' said Mr Holmes.

'I am looking at Mr Whitbread.'

Mr Holmes looked gravely at Mr Whitbread, drew back his open hand, and struck me on the face, held me with his other hand and struck me again.

My head spun and burned and pained and I wondered would it happen again. I forgot and felt another smack, and forgot, and another, and moved, and was held by a steadying, almost kindly hand, and another, and my sight was a vision of red and white and pity-coloured flashes.

'You are looking at Mr Whitbread – what, Behan?'

I gulped and got together my voice and tried again till I got it out. 'I, sir, please, sir, I am looking at you, I mean, I am looking at Mr Whitbread, sir.'[15]

Admission procedures and obedience tests may be elaborated into a form of initiation that has been called 'the welcome', where staff or inmates, or both, go out of their way to give the recruit a clear notion of his plight.[16] As part of this rite of passage he may be called by a term such as 'fish' or 'swab', which tells him that he is merely an inmate, and, what is more, that he has a special low status even in this low group.

The admission procedure can be characterized as a leaving off and a taking on, with the midpoint marked by physical nakedness. Leaving off of course entails a dispossession of property, important because persons invest self feelings in their possessions. Perhaps the most significant of these possessions is not physical

15. Brendan Behan, *Borstal Boy* (London: Hutchinson, 1958), p. 40. See also Anthony Heckstall-Smith, *Eighteen Months* (London: Allan Wingate, 1954), p. 26.

16. For a version of this process in concentration camps, see Cohen, op. cit., p. 120, and Kogon, op. cit., pp. 64–5. For a fictionalized treatment of the welcome in a girls' reformatory see, Sara Harris, *The Wayward Ones* (New York: New American Library, 1952), pp. 31–4. A prison version, less explicit, is found in George Dendrickson and Frederick Thomas, *The Truth About Dartmoor* (London: Gollancz, 1954), pp. 42–57.

at all, one's full name; whatever one is thereafter called, loss of one's name can be a great curtailment of the self.[17]

Once the inmate is stripped of his possessions, at least some replacements must be made by the establishment, but these take the form of standard issue, uniform in character and uniformly distributed. These substitute possessions are clearly marked as really belonging to the institution and in some cases are recalled at regular intervals to be, as it were, disinfected of identifications. With objects that can be used up – for example, pencils – the inmate may be required to return the remnants before obtaining a reissue.[18] Failure to provide inmates with individual lockers and periodic searches and confiscations of accumulated personal property[19] reinforce property dispossession. Religious orders have appreciated the implications for self of such separation from belongings. Inmates may be required to change their cells once a year so as not to become attached to them. The Benedictine Rule is explicit:

> For their bedding let a mattress, a blanket, a coverlet, and a pillow suffice. These beds must be frequently inspected by the Abbot, because of private property which may be found therein. If anyone be discovered to have what he has not received from the Abbot, let him be most severely punished. And in order that this vice of private ownership may be completely rooted out, let all things that are necessary be supplied by the Abbot: that is, cowl, tunic, stockings, shoes, girdle, knife, pen, needle, handkerchief, and tablets; so that all plea of necessity may be taken away. And let the Abbot always consider that passage in the Acts of the Apostles: 'Distribution was made to each according as anyone had need.'[20]

One set of the individual's possessions has a special relation to self. The individual ordinarily expects to exert some control over the guise in which he appears before others. For this he needs

17. For example, Thomas Merton, *The Seven Storey Mountain* (New York: Harcourt, Brace and Company, 1948), pp. 290–91; Cohen, op. cit., pp. 145–7.

18. Dendrickson and Thomas, op. cit., pp. 83–4, also *The Holy Rule of Saint Benedict*, Ch. 55.

19. Kogon, op. cit., p. 69.

20. *The Holy Rule of Saint Benedict*, Ch. 55.

cosmetic and clothing supplies, tools for applying, arranging, and repairing them, and an accessible, secure place to store these supplies and tools – in short, the individual will need an 'identity kit' for the management of his personal front. He will also need access to decoration specialists such as barbers and clothiers.

On admission to a total institution, however, the individual is likely to be stripped of his usual appearance and of the equipment and services by which he maintains it, thus suffering a personal defacement. Clothing, combs, needle and thread, cosmetics, towels, soap, shaving sets, bathing facilities – all these may be taken away or denied him, although some may be kept in inaccessible storage, to be returned if and when he leaves. In the words of St Benedict's Holy Rule:

Then forthwith he shall, there in the oratory, be divested of his own garments with which he is clothed and be clad in those of the monastery. Those garments of which he is divested shall be placed in the wardrobe, there to be kept, so that if, perchance, he should ever be persuaded by the devil to leave the monastery (which God forbid), he may be stripped of the monastic habit and cast forth.[21]

As suggested, the institutional issue provided as a substitute for what has been taken away is typically of a 'coarse' variety, ill-suited, often old, and the same for large categories of inmates. The impact of this substitution is described in a report on imprisoned prostitutes:

First, there is the shower officer who forces them to undress, takes their own clothes away, sees to it that they take showers and get their prison clothes – one pair of black oxfords with cuban heels, two pairs of much-mended ankle socks, three cotton dresses, two cotton slips, two pairs of panties, and a couple of bras. Practically all the bras are flat and useless. No corsets or girdles are issued.

There is not a sadder sight than some of the obese prisoners, who, if nothing else, have been managing to keep themselves looking decent on the outside, confronted by the first sight of themselves in prison issue.[22]

21. *The Holy Rule of Saint Benedict*, Ch. 58.

22. John M. Murtagh and Sara Harris, *Cast the First Stone* (New York: Pocket Books, 1958), pp. 239–40. On mental hospitals see, for example, Kerkhoff, op. cit., p. 10. Ward, op. cit., p. 60, makes the reasonable suggestion that men in our society suffer less defacement in total institutions than do women.

In addition to personal defacement that comes from being stripped of one's identity kit, there is personal disfigurement that comes from direct and permanent mutilations of the body such as brands or loss of limbs. Although this mortification of the self by way of the body is found in few total institutions, still, loss of a sense of personal safety is common and provides a basis for anxieties about disfigurement. Beatings, shock therapy, or, in mental hospitals, surgery – whatever the intent of staff in providing these services for some inmates – may lead many inmates to feel that they are in an environment that does not guarantee their physical integrity.

At admission, loss of identity equipment can prevent the individual from presenting his usual image of himself to others. After admission, the image of himself he presents is attacked in another way. Given the expressive idiom of a particular civil society, certain movements, postures, and stances will convey lowly images of the individual and be avoided as demeaning. Any regulation, command, or task that forces the individual to adopt these movements or postures may mortify his self. In total institutions, such physical indignities abound. In mental hospitals, for example, patients may be forced to eat all food with a spoon.[23] In military prisons, inmates may be required to stand at attention whenever an officer enters the compound.[24] In religious institutions, there are such classic gestures of penance as the kissing of feet,[25] and the posture recommended to an erring monk that he

... lie prostrate at the door of the oratory in silence; and thus, with his face to the ground and his body prone, let him cast himself at the feet of all as they go forth from the oratory.[26]

In some penal institutions we find the humiliation of bending over to receive a birching.[27]

23. Johnson and Dodds, op. cit., p. 15; for a prison version see Alfred Hassler, *Diary of a Self-Made Convict* (Chicago: Regnery, 1954), p. 33.
24. L. D. Hankoff, 'Interaction Patterns Among Military Prison Personnel', *U.S. Armed Forces Medical Journal*, X (1959), p. 1419.
25. Kathryn Hulme, *The Nun's Story* (London: Muller, 1957), p. 52.
26. *The Holy Rule of Saint Benedict*, Ch. 44.
27. Dendrickson and Thomas, op. cit., p. 76.

Just as the individual can be required to hold his body in a humiliating pose, so he may have to provide humiliating verbal responses. An important instance of this is the forced deference pattern of total institutions; inmates are often required to punctuate their social interaction with staff by verbal acts of deference, such as saying 'sir'. Another instance is the necessity to beg, importune, or humbly ask for little things such as a light for a cigarette, a drink of water, or permission to use the telephone.

Corresponding to the indignities of speech and action required of the inmate are the indignities of treatment others accord him. The standard examples here are verbal or gestural profanations: staff or fellow inmates call the individual obscene names, curse him, point out his negative attributes, tease him, or talk about him or his fellow inmates as if he were not present.

Whatever the form or the source of these various indignities, the individual has to engage in activity whose symbolic implications are incompatible with his conception of self. A more diffuse example of this kind of mortification occurs when the individual is required to undertake a daily round of life that he considers alien to him – to take on a disidentifying role. In prisons, denial of heterosexual opportunities can induce fear of losing one's masculinity.[28] In military establishments, the patently useless make-work forced on fatigue details can make men feel their time and effort are worthless.[29] In religious institutions there are special arrangements to ensure that all inmates take a turn performing the more menial aspects of the servant role.[30] An extreme is the concentration-camp practice requiring prisoners to administer whippings to other prisoners.[31]

There is another form of mortification in total institutions; beginning with admission a kind of contaminative exposure occurs. On the outside, the individual can hold objects of self-feeling – such as his body, his immediate actions, his thoughts, and some of his possessions – clear of contact with alien and

28. Sykes, op. cit., pp. 70–72.
29. For example, Lawrence, op. cit., pp. 34–5.
30. *The Holy Rule of Saint Benedict*, Ch. 35.
31. Kogon, op. cit., p. 102.

contaminating things. But in total institutions these territories of the self are violated; the boundary that the individual places between his being and the environment is invaded and the embodiments of self profaned.

There is, first, a violation of one's informational preserve regarding self. During admission, facts about the inmate's social statuses and past behaviour - especially discreditable facts - are collected and recorded in a dossier available to staff. Later, in so far as the establishment officially expects to alter the self-regulating inner tendencies of the inmate, there may be group or individual confession - psychiatric, political, military, or religious, according to the type of institution. On these occasions the inmate has to expose facts and feelings about self to new kinds of audiences. The most spectacular examples of such exposure come to us from Communist confession camps and from the *culpa* sessions that form part of the routine of Catholic religious institutions.[32] The dynamics of the process have been explicitly considered by those engaged in so-called milieu therapy.

New audiences not only learn discreditable facts about oneself that are ordinarily concealed but are also in a position to perceive some of these facts directly. Prisoners and mental patients cannot prevent their visitors from seeing them in humiliating circumstances.[33] Another example is the shoulder patch of ethnic identification worn by concentration-camp inmates.[34] Medical and security examinations often expose the inmate physically, sometimes to persons of both sexes; a similar exposure follows from collective sleeping arrangements and doorless toilets.[35] An extreme here, perhaps, is the situation of a self-destructive mental patient who is stripped naked for what is felt to be his own protection and placed in a constantly lit seclusion room, into whose Judas window any person passing on the ward can peer. In

32. Hulme, op. cit., pp. 48–51.

33. Wider communities in Western society, of course, have employed this technique too, in the form of public floggings and public hangings, the pillory and stocks. Functionally correlated with the public emphasis on mortifications in total institutions is the commonly found strict ruling that staff is not to be humiliated by staff in the presence of inmates.

34. Kogon, op. cit., pp. 41–2.

35. Behan, op. cit., p. 23.

general, of course, the inmate is never fully alone; he is always within sight and often earshot of someone, if only his fellow inmates.[36] Prison cages with bars for walls fully realize such exposure.

Perhaps the most obvious type of contaminative exposure is the directly physical kind – the besmearing and defiling of the body or of other objects closely identified with the self. Sometimes this involves a breakdown of the usual environmental arrangements for insulating oneself from one's own source of contamination, as in having to empty one's own slops[37] or having to subject one's evacuation to regimentation, as reported from Chinese political prisons:

An aspect of their isolation regimen which is especially onerous to Western prisoners is the arrangement for the elimination of urine and feces. The 'slop jar' that is usually present in Russian cells is often absent in China. It is a Chinese custom to allow defecation and urination only at one or two specified times each day – usually in the morning after breakfast. The prisoner is hustled from his cell by a guard, double-timed down a long corridor, and given approximately two minutes to squat over an open Chinese latrine and attend to all his wants. The haste and the public scrutiny are especially difficult for women to tolerate. If the prisoners cannot complete their action in about two minutes, they are abruptly dragged away and back to their cells.[38]

A very common form of physical contamination is reflected in complaints about unclean food, messy quarters, soiled towels, shoes and clothing impregnated with previous users' sweat,

36. For example, Kogon, op. cit., p. 128; Hassler, op. cit., p. 16. For the situation in a religious institution, see Hulme, op. cit., p. 48. She also describes a lack of aural privacy since thin cotton hangings are used as the only door closing off the individual sleeping cells (p. 20).

37. Heckstall-Smith, op. cit., p. 21; Dendrickson and Thomas, op. cit., p. 53.

38. L. E. Hinkle, Jr., and H. G. Wolff, 'Communist Interrogation and Indoctrination of "Enemies of the State"', *A.M.A. Archives of Neurology and Psychiatry*, LXXVI (1956), p. 153. An extremely useful report on the profanizing role of faecal matter, and the social necessity of personal as well as environmental control, is provided in C. E. Orbach, *et al.*, 'Fears and Defensive Adaptations to the Loss of Anal Sphincter Control', *The Psychoanalytic Review*, XLIV (1957), pp. 121–75.

toilets without seats, and dirty bath facilities.[39] Orwell's comments on his boarding school may be taken as illustrative:

For example, there were the pewter bowls out of which we had our porridge. They had overhanging rims, and under the rims there were accumulations of sour porridge, which could be flaked off in long strips. The porridge itself, too, contained more lumps, hairs and un-explained black things than one would have thought possible, unless someone were putting them there on purpose. It was never safe to start on that porridge without investigating it first. And there was the slimy water of the plunge bath – it was twelve or fifteen feet long, the whole school was supposed to go into it every morning, and I doubt whether the water was changed at all frequently – and the always-damp towels with their cheesy smell: . . . And the sweaty smell of the changing-room with its greasy basins, and, giving on this, the row of filthy, dilapidated lavatories, which had no fastenings of any kind on the doors, so that whenever you were sitting there someone was sure to come crashing in. It is not easy for me to think of my school days without seeming to breathe in a whiff of something cold and evil-smelling – a sort of com-pound of sweaty stockings, dirty towels, fecal smells blowing along corridors, forks with old food between the prongs, neck-of-mutton stew, and the banging doors of the lavatories and the echoing chamber pots in the dormitories.[40]

There are still other sources of physical contamination, as an interviewee suggests in describing a concentration-camp hospital:

We were lying two in each bed. And it was very unpleasant. For example, if a man died he would not be removed before twenty-four hours had elapsed because the block trusty wanted, of course, to get the bread ration and the soup which was allotted to this person. For this reason the dead person would be reported dead twenty-four hours later so that his ration would still be allotted. And so we had to lie all that time in bed together with the dead person.[41]

We were on the middle level. And that was a very gruesome situation, especially at night. First of all, the dead men were badly emaciated and they looked terrible. In most cases they would soil themselves at the moment of death and that was not a very esthetic event. I saw such

39. For example, Johnson and Dodds, op. cit., p. 75; Heckstall-Smith, op. cit., p. 15.

40. George Orwell, 'Such, Such Were the Joys', *Partisan Review* XIX, (September–October 1952), p. 523.

41. David P. Boder, *I Did Not Interview the Dead* (Urbana: University of Illinois Press, 1949), p. 50.

cases very frequently in the lager, in the sick people's barracks. People who died from phlegmonous, suppurative wounds, with their beds overflowing with pus would be lying together with somebody whose illness was possibly more benign, who had possibly just a small wound which now would become infected.[42]

The contamination of lying near the dying has also been cited in mental-hospital reports,[43] and surgical contamination has been cited in prison documents:

Surgical instruments and bandages in the dressing-room lie exposed to the air and dust. George, attending for the treatment, by a medical orderly, of a boil on his neck, had it lanced with a scalpel that had been used a moment before on a man's foot, and had not been sterilized in the meantime.[44]

Finally, in some total institutions the inmate is obliged to take oral or intravenous medications, whether desired or not, and to eat his food, however unpalatable. When an inmate refuses to eat, there may be forcible contamination of his innards by 'forced feeding.'

I have suggested that the inmate undergoes mortification of the self by contaminative exposure of a physical kind, but this must be amplified: when the agency of contamination is another human being, the inmate is in addition contaminated by forced interpersonal contact and, in consequence, a forced social relationship. (Similarly, when the inmate loses control over who observes him in his predicament or knows about his past, he is being contaminated by a forced relationship to these people – for it is through such perception and knowledge that relations are expressed.)

The model for interpersonal contamination in our society is presumably rape; although sexual molestation certainly occurs in total institutions, there are many other less dramatic examples. Upon admission, one's on-person possessions are pawed and fingered by an official as he itemizes and prepares them for storage. The inmate himself may be frisked and searched to the extent – often reported in the literature – of a rectal examination.[45]

42. ibid., p. 50.   43. Johnson and Dodds, op. cit., p. 16.

44. Dendrickson and Thomas, op. cit., p. 122.

45. For example, Lowell Naeve, *A Field of Broken Stones* (Glen Gardner, New Jersey: Libertarian Press, 1950), p. 17; Kogon, op. cit., p. 67;

Later in his stay he may be required to undergo searchings of his person and of his sleeping quarters, either routinely or when trouble arises. In all these cases it is the searcher as well as the search that penetrates the private reserve of the individual and violates the territories of his self. Even routine inspections can have this effect, as Lawrence suggests:

In the old days men had weekly to strip off boots and socks, and expose their feet for an officer's inspection. An ex-boy'd kick you in the mouth, as you bent down to look. So with the bath-rolls, a certificate from your N.C.O. that you'd had a bath during the week. One bath! And with the kit inspections, and room inspections, and equipment inspections, all excuses for the dogmatists among the officers to blunder, and for the nosy-parkers to make beasts of themselves. Oh, you require the gentlest touch to interfere with a poor man's person, and not give offence.[46]

Further, the practice of mixing age, ethnic, and racial groups in prisons and mental hospitals can lead an inmate to feel he is being contaminated by contact with undesirable fellow inmates. A public-school prisoner, describing his admission to prison, provides an example:

Another warder came up with a pair of handcuffs and coupled me to the little Jew, who moaned softly to himself in Yiddish.[47] . . .

Suddenly, the awful thought occurred to me that I might have to share a cell with the little Jew and I was seized with panic. The thought obsessed me to the exclusion of all else.[48]

Obviously, group living will necessitate mutual contact and exposure among inmates. At the extreme, as in cells for Chinese political prisoners, mutual contact may be very great:

At some stage in his imprisonment the prisoner can expect to find himself placed in a cell with about eight other prisoners. If he was initially isolated and interrogated, this may be shortly after his first 'confession' is accepted; but many prisoners are placed in group cells from the outset of their imprisonment. The cell is usually barren, and scarcely large enough to hold the group it contains. There may be a

---

Holley Cantine and Dachine Rainer, *Prison Etiquette* (Bearsville, N.Y.: Retort Press, 1950), p. 46.

46. Lawrence, op. cit., p. 196.
47. Heckstall-Smith, op. cit., p. 14.
48. ibid., p. 17.

sleeping platform, but all of the prisoners sleep on the floor; and when all lie down, every inch of floor space may be taken up. The atmosphere is extremely intimate. Privacy is entirely nonexistent.[49]

Lawrence provides a military illustration in discussing his difficulties in merging with fellow airmen in the barracks hut:

> You see, I cannot play at anything with anyone: and a native shyness shuts me out from their freemasonry of — and blinding, pinching, borrowing, and talking dirty: this despite my sympathy for the abandon of functional frankness in which they wallow. Inevitably, in our crowded lodging, we must communicate just those physical modesties which polite life keeps veiled. Sexual activity's a naïve boast, and any abnormalities of appetite or organ are curiously displayed. The Powers encourage this behaviour. All latrines in camp have lost their doors. 'Make the little — sleep and — and eat together,' grinned old Jock Mackay, senior instructor, 'and we'll have 'em drilling together, naturally.'[50]

One routine instance of this contaminative contact is the naming system for inmates. Staff and fellow inmates automatically assume the right to employ an intimate form of address or a truncated formal one; for a middle-class person, at least, this denies the right to hold oneself off from others through a formal style of address.[51] When the individual has to eat food he considers alien and polluted, this contamination sometimes derives from other persons' connexion with the food, as is nicely illustrated in the penance of 'begging soup' practised in some nunneries:

> ... she placed her pottery bowl on the left of the Mother Superior, knelt, clasped her hands and waited until two spoonfuls of soup had been put into her beggar's bowl, then on to the next oldest and the next, until the bowl was filled.... When at last her bowl was filled, she returned to her place and swallowed the soup, as she knew she must, down to the last drop. She tried not to think how it had been tossed into her bowl from a dozen other bowls that had already been eaten from....[52]

49. Hinkle and Wolff, op. cit., p. 156.
50. Lawrence, op. cit., p. 91.
51. For example, see Hassler, op. cit., p. 104.
52. Hulme, op. cit., pp. 52–3.

Another kind of contaminative exposure brings an outsider into contact with the individual's close relationship to significant others. For example, an inmate may have his personal mail read and censored, and even made fun of to his face.[53] Another example is the enforced public character of visits, as reports from prisons suggest:

> But what a sadistic kind of arrangement they have for these visits! One hour a month – or two half-hours – in a big room with perhaps a score of other couples, with guards prowling about to make sure you exchange neither the plans nor the implements of escape! We met across a six-foot-wide table, down the middle of which a sort of bundling-board six inches high presumably prevents even our germs from intermingling. We were permitted one sanitary handshake at the beginning of the visit and one at the end; for the rest of the time we could only sit and look at each other while we called across that vast expanse![54]

> Visits take place in a room by the main gate. There is a wooden table, at one side of which sits the prisoner and at the other side his visitors. The warder sits at the head; he hears every word that is spoken, watches every gesture and nuance of expression. There is no privacy at all – and this when a man is meeting his wife whom he may not have seen for years. Nor is any contact allowed between prisoner and visitor, and, of course, no articles are allowed to change hands.[55]

A more thoroughgoing version of this type of contaminative exposure occurs, as already implied, in institutionally arranged confessions. When a significant other must be denounced, and especially when this other is physically present, confession of the relationship to outsiders can mean an intense contamination of the relationship and, through this, of the self. A description of practices in a nunnery provides an illustration:

> The bravest of the emotionally vulnerable were the sisters who stood up together in the culpa and proclaimed each other – for having gone out of their way to be near to one another, or perhaps for having talked together in recreation in a way that excluded others. Their tormented but clearly spoken disclosures of a nascent affinity gave it the *coup de grâce* which they themselves might not have been able to do,

53. Dendrickson and Thomas, op. cit., p. 128.
54. Hassler, op. cit., pp. 62–3.
55. Dendrickson and Thomas, op. cit., p. 175.

for the entire community would henceforth see to it that these two would be kept far apart. The pair would be helped to detach themselves from one of those spontaneous personal attachments which often sprang to life in the body of the community as unexpectedly as wildflowers appeared, now and again, in the formal geometric patterns of the cloister gardens.[56]

A parallel example can be found in mental hospitals devoted to intensive milieu therapy, where patient pairs conducting an affair may be obliged to discuss their relationship during group meetings.

In total institutions, exposure of one's relationships can occur in even more drastic forms, for there may be occasions when an individual witnesses a physical assault upon someone to whom he has ties and suffers the permanent mortification of having (and being known to have) taken no action. Thus we learn of a mental hospital:

This knowledge [of shock therapy] is based on the fact that some of the patients in Ward 30 have assisted the shock team in the administration of therapy to patients, holding them down, and helping to strap them in bed, or watching them after they have quieted. The administration of shock on the ward is often carried out in full sight of a group of interested onlookers. The patient's convulsions often resemble those of an accident victim in death agony and are accompanied by choking gasps and at times by a foaming overflow of saliva from the mouth. The patient slowly recovers without memory of the occurrence, but he has served the others as a frightful spectacle of what may be done to them.[57]

Melville's report on flogging aboard a nineteenth-century man-of-war provides another example:

However much you may desire to absent yourself from the scene that ensues, yet behold it you must; or, at least, stand near it you must; for the regulations enjoin the attendance of almost the entire ship's company, from the corpulent captain himself to the smallest boy who strikes the bell.[58]

And the inevitableness of his own presence at the scene: the strong arm that drags him in view of the scourge, and holds him there till all is over: forcing upon his loathing eye and soul the sufferings and groans

56. Hulme, op. cit., pp. 50–51.
57. Belknap, op. cit., p. 194.
58. Herman Melville, *White Jacket* (New York: Grove Press, n.d.), p. 135.

of men who have familiarly consorted with him, eaten with him, battled out watches with him – men of his own type and badge – all this conveys a terrible hint of the omnipotent authority under which he lives.[59]

Lawrence offers a military example:

Tonight's crash of the stick on the hut door at roll call was terrific; and the door slammed back nearly off its hinges. Into the light strode Baker, V.C., a corporal who assumed great licence in the camp because of his war decoration. He marched down my side of the hut, checking the beds. Little Nobby, taken by surprise, had one boot on and another off. Corporal Baker stopped. 'What's the matter with YOU?' 'I was knocking out a nail which hurts my foot.' 'Put your boot on at once. Your name?' He passed on to the end door and there whirled round, snorting, 'Clarke.' Nobby properly cried, 'Corporal' and limped down the alley at a run (we must always run when called) to bring up stiffly at attention before him. A pause, and then curtly, 'Get back to your bed.'

Still the Corporal waited and so must we, lined up by our beds. Again, sharply, 'Clarke.' The performance was repeated, over and over, while the four files of us looked on, bound fast by shame and discipline. We were men, and a man over there was degrading himself and his species, in degrading another. Baker was lusting for trouble and hoped to provoke one of us into some act or word on which to base a charge.[60]

The extreme of this kind of experiential mortification is found, of course, in the concentration-camp literature:

A Jew from Breslau named Silbermann had to stand by idly as SS Sergeant Hoppe brutally tortured his brother to death. Silbermann went mad at the sight, and late at night he precipitated a panic with his frantic cries that the barracks was on fire.[61]

III

I have considered some of the more elementary and direct assaults upon the self – various forms of disfigurement and defilement through which the symbolic meaning of events in the inmate's immediate presence dramatically fails to corroborate his prior conception of self. I would now like to consider a source

59. ibid., p. 135.
60. Lawrence, op. cit., p. 62.
61. Kogon, op. cit., p. 160.

of mortification that is less direct in its effect, with a significance for the individual that is less easy to assess: a disruption of the usual relationship between the individual actor and his acts.

The first disruption to consider here is 'looping': an agency that creates a defensive response on the part of the inmate takes this very response as the target of its next attack. The individual finds that his protective response to an assault upon self is collapsed into the situation; he cannot defend himself in the usual way by establishing distance between the mortifying situation and himself.

Deference patterns in total institutions provide one illustration of the looping effect. In civil society, when an individual must accept circumstances and commands that affront his conception of self, he is allowed a margin of face-saving reactive expression – sullenness, failure to offer usual signs of deference, *sotto voce* profaning asides, or fugitive expressions of contempt, irony, and derision. Compliance, then, is likely to be associated with an expressed attitude to it that is not itself subject to the same degree of pressure for compliance. Although such self-protective expressive response to humiliating demands does occur in total institutions, the staff may directly penalize inmates for such activity, citing sullenness or insolence explicitly as grounds for further punishment. Thus, in describing the contamination of self resulting from having to drink soup from the beggar's bowl, Kathryn Hulme says of her subject that she

... blanked out from her facial expression the revolt that rose up in her fastidious soul as she drank her dregs. One look of rebellion, she knew, would be enough to invite a repetition of the awful abasement which she was sure she could never go through again, not even for the sake of the Blessed Lord Himself.[62]

The desegregating process in total institutions creates other instances of looping. In the normal course of affairs in civil society, audience and role segregation keep one's avowals and implicit claims regarding self made in one physical scene of activity from being tested against conduct in other settings.[63] In

62. Hulme, op. cit., p. 53.

63. In civil society, crimes and certain other forms of deviance affect the way in which the offender is received in all areas of life, but this breakdown

total institutions spheres of life are desegregated, so that an inmate's conduct in one scene of activity is thrown up to him by staff as a comment and check upon his conduct in another context. A mental patient's effort to present himself in a well-oriented, unantagonistic manner during a diagnostic or treatment conference may be directly embarrassed by evidence introduced concerning his apathy during recreation or the bitter comments he made in a letter to a sibling – a letter which the recipient has forwarded to the hospital administrator, to be added to the patient's dossier and brought along to the conference.

Psychiatric establishments of the advanced type provide excellent illustrations of the looping process, since in them didactic feedback may be erected into a basic therapeutic doctrine. A 'permissive' atmosphere is felt to encourage the inmate to 'project' or 'act out' his typical difficulties in living, which can then be brought to his attention during group-therapy sessions.[64]

Through the process of looping, then, the inmate's reaction to his own situation is collapsed back into this situation itself, and he is not allowed to retain the usual segregation of these phases of action. A second assault upon the inmate's status as an actor may now be cited, one that has been loosely described under the categories of regimentation and tyrannization.

In civil society, by the time the individual is an adult he has incorporated socially acceptable standards for the performance of most of his activity, so that the issue of the correctness of his action arises only at certain points, as when his productivity is judged. Beyond this, he is allowed to go at his own pace.[65] He

---

of spheres applies mainly to offenders, not to the bulk of the population that does not offend in these ways or offends without being caught.

64. A clear statement may be found in R. Rapoport and E. Skellern, 'Some Therapeutic Functions of Administrative Disturbance', *Administrative Science Quarterly*, II (1957), pp. 84–5.

65. The span of time over which an employee works at his own discretion without supervision can in fact be taken as a measure of his pay and status in an organization. See Elliott Jaques, *The Measurement of Responsibility: A Study of Work, Payment and Individual Capacity* (Cambridge: Harvard University Press, 1956). And just as 'time-span of responsibility' is an index of position, so a long span of freedom from inspection is a reward of position.

need not constantly look over his shoulder to see if criticism or other sanctions are coming. In addition, many actions will be defined as matters of personal taste, with choice from a range of possibilities specifically allowed. For much activity the judgement and action of authority are held off and one is on one's own. Under such circumstances, one can with over-all profit schedule one's activities to fit into one another – a kind of 'personal economy of action', as when an individual postpones eating for a few minutes in order to finish a task, or lays aside a task a little early in order to join a friend for dinner. In a total institution, however, minute segments of a person's line of activity may be subjected to regulations and judgements by staff; the inmate's life is penetrated by constant sanctioning interaction from above, especially during the initial period of stay before the inmate accepts the regulations unthinkingly. Each specification robs the individual of an opportunity to balance his needs and objectives in a personally efficient way and opens up his line of action to sanctions. The autonomy of the act itself is violated.

Although this process of social control is in effect in all organized society, we tend to forget how detailed and closely restrictive it can become in total institutions. The routine reported for one jail for youthful offenders provides a striking example:

At 5:30 we were wakened and had to jump out of bed and stand at attention. When the guard shouted 'One!' you removed your night shirt; at 'Two!' you folded it; at 'Three!' you made your bed. (Only two minutes to make the bed in a difficult and complicated manner.) All the while three monitors would shout at us: 'Hurry it up!' and 'Make it snappy!'

We also dressed by numbers: shirts on at 'One!'; pants at 'Two!'; socks at 'Three!'; shoes at 'Four!' Any noise, like dropping a shoe or even scraping it along the floor, was enough to send you to the line.

... Once downstairs everyone faced the wall at strict attention, hands at side, thumbs even with trouser seams, head up, shoulders back, stomach in, heels together, eyes straight ahead, no scratching or putting hands to face or head, no moving even the fingers.[66]

A jail for adults provides another example:

The silence system was enforced. No talking outside the cell, at meals or at work.

66. Hassler, op. cit., p. 155, quoting Robert McCreery.

No pictures were allowed in the cell. No gazing about at meals. Bread crusts were allowed to be left only on the left side of the plate. Inmates were required to stand at attention, cap in hand, until any official, visitor or guard moved beyond sight.[67]

And a concentration camp:

In the barracks a wealth of new and confusing impressions overwhelmed the prisoners. Making up beds was a particular source of SS chicanery. Shapeless and matted straw pallets had to be made as even as a board, the pattern of the sheets parallel to the edges, head bolsters set up at right angles....[68]

... the SS seized on the most trifling offenses as occasions for punishment: keeping hands in pockets in cold weather; turning up the coat collar in rain or wind; missing buttons; the tiniest tear or speck of dirt on the clothing; unshined shoes ...; shoes that were too well shined – indicating that the wearer was shirking work; failure to salute, including so-called 'sloppy posture'; ... The slightest deviation in dressing ranks and files, or arranging the prisoners in the order of size, or any swaying, coughing, sneezing – any of these might provoke a savage outburst from the SS.[69]

From the military comes an example of the specifications possible in kit laying:

Now the tunic, so folded that the belt made it a straight edge. Covering it, the breeches, squared to the exact area of the tunic, with four concertina-folds facing forward. Towels were doubled once, twice, thrice, and flanked the blue tower. In front of the blue sat a rectangular cardigan. To each side a rolled puttee. Shirts were packed and laid in pairs like flannel bricks. Before them, pants. Between them, neat balls of socks, wedged in. Our holdalls were stretched wide, with knife, fork, spoon, razor, comb, toothbrush, lather brush, button-stick, in that order, ranged across them.[70]

67. T. E. Gaddis, *Birdman of Alcatraz* (New York: New American Library, 1958), p. 25. For a similar rule of silence in a British prison, see Frank Norman, *Bang to Rights* (London: Secker and Warburg, 1958), p. 27

68. Kogon, op. cit., p. 68.

69. ibid., pp. 99–100.

70. Lawrence, op. cit., p. 83. In this connexion see the comments by M. Brewster Smith on the concept of 'chicken' in Samuel Stouffer *et al.*, *The American Soldier* (4 vols.; Princeton: Princeton University Press, 1949), Vol. I, p. 390.

Similarly, an ex-nun is reported as having to learn to keep her hands still[71] and hidden and to accept the fact that only six specified items were permitted in one's pockets.[72] An ex-mental patient speaks of the humiliation of being doled out limited toilet paper at each request.[73]

As suggested earlier, one of the most telling ways in which one's economy of action can be disrupted is the obligation to request permission or supplies for minor activities that one can execute on one's own on the outside, such as smoking, shaving, going to the toilet, telephoning, spending money, or mailing letters. This obligation not only puts the individual in a submissive or suppliant role 'unnatural' for an adult but also opens up his line of action to interceptions by staff. Instead of having his request immediately and automatically granted, the inmate may be teased, denied, questioned at length, not noticed, or, as an ex-mental patient suggests, merely put off:

Probably anyone who has never been in a similarly helpless position cannot realize the humiliation to anyone able bodied yet lacking authority to do the simplest offices for herself of having to beg repeatedly for even such small necessities as clean linen or a light for her cigarette from nurses who constantly brush her aside with, 'I'll give it to you in a minute, dear', and go off leaving her unsupplied. Even the canteen staff seemed to share the opinion that civility was wasted upon lunatics, and would keep a patient waiting indefinitely, while they gossiped with their friends.[74]

I have suggested that authority in total institutions is directed to a multitude of items of conduct – dress, deportment, manners – that constantly occur and constantly come up for judgement. The inmate cannot easily escape from the press of judgemental officials and from the enveloping tissue of constraint. A total institution is like a finishing school, but one that has many refinements and is little refined. I would like to comment on two aspects of this tendency towards a multiplication of actively enforced rulings.

71. Hulme, op. cit., p. 3.
72. ibid., p. 39.
73. Ward, op. cit., p. 23.
74. Johnson and Dodds, op. cit., p. 39.

First, these rulings are often geared in with an obligation to perform the regulated activity in unison with blocks of fellow inmates. This is what is sometimes called regimentation.

Second, these diffuse rulings occur in an authority system of the *echelon* kind: *any* member of the staff class has certain rights to discipline *any* member of the inmate class, thereby markedly increasing the probability of sanction. (This arrangement, it may be noted, is similar to the one that gives any adult in some small American towns certain rights to correct any child not in the immediate presence of his parents and to demand small services from him.) On the outside, the adult in our society is typically under the authority of a *single* immediate superior in connexion with his work, or the authority of one spouse in connexion with domestic duties; the only echelon authority he must face – the police – is typically not constantly or relevantly present, except perhaps in the case of traffic-law enforcement.

Given echelon authority and regulations that are diffuse, novel, and strictly enforced, we may expect inmates, especially new ones, to live with chronic anxiety about breaking the rules and the consequence of breaking them – physical injury or death in a concentration camp, being 'washed out' in an officer's training school, or demotion in a mental hospital:

Yet, even in the apparent liberty and friendliness of an 'open' ward, I still found a background of threats that made me feel something between a prisoner and a pauper. The smallest offence, from a nervous symptom to displeasing a sister personally, was met by the suggestion of removing the offender to a closed ward. The idea of a return to 'J' ward, if I did not eat my food, was brandished at me so constantly that it became an obsession and even such meals as I was able to swallow disagreed with me physically, while other patients were impelled to do unnecessary or uncongenial work by a similar fear.[75]

In total institutions staying out of trouble is likely to require persistent conscious effort. The inmate may forgo certain levels of sociability with his fellows to avoid possible incidents.

75. Johnson and Dodds, op. cit., p. 36.

IV

In concluding this description of the processes of mortification, three general issues must be raised.

First, total institutions disrupt or defile precisely those actions that in civil society have the role of attesting to the actor and those in his presence that he has some command over his world – that he is a person with 'adult' self-determination, autonomy, and freedom of action. A failure to retain this kind of adult executive competency, or at least the symbols of it, can produce in the inmate the terror of feeling radically demoted in the age-grading system.[76]

A margin of self-selected expressive behaviour – whether of antagonism, affection, or unconcern – is one symbol of self-determination. This evidence of one's autonomy is weakened by such specific obligations as having to write one letter home a week, or having to refrain from expressing sullenness. It is further weakened when this margin of behaviour is used as evidence concerning the state of one's psychiatric, religious, or political conscience.

There are certain bodily comforts significant to the individual that tend to be lost upon entrance into a total institution – for example, a soft bed[77] or quietness at night.[78] Loss of this set of comforts is apt to reflect a loss of self-determination, too, for the individual tends to ensure these comforts the moment he has resources to expend.[79]

Loss of self-determination seems to have been ceremonialized in concentration camps; thus we have atrocity tales of prisoners being forced to roll in the mud,[80] stand on their heads in the snow, work at ludicrously useless tasks, swear at themselves,[81]

76. Cf. Sykes, op. cit., pp. 73–6, 'The Deprivation of Autonomy'.

77. Hulme, op. cit., p. 18; Orwell, op. cit., p. 521.

78. Hassler, op. cit., p. 78; Johnson and Dodds, op. cit., p. 17.

79. This is one source of mortification that civilians practise on themselves during camping vacations, perhaps on the assumption that a new sense of self can be obtained by voluntarily forgoing some of one's previous self-impregnated comforts.

80. Kogon, op. cit., p. 66.

81. ibid., p. 61.

or, in the case of Jewish prisoners, sing anti-Semitic songs.[82] A milder version is found in mental hospitals where attendants have been reported forcing a patient who wanted a cigarette to say 'pretty please' or jump up for it. In all such cases the inmate is made to display a giving up of his will. Less ceremonialized, but just as extreme, is the embarrassment to one's autonomy that comes from being locked in a ward, placed in a tight wet pack, or tied in a camisole, and thereby denied the liberty of making small adjustive movements.

Another clear-cut expression of personal inefficacy in total institutions is found in inmates' use of speech. One implication of using words to convey decisions about action is that the recipient of an order is seen as capable of receiving a message and acting under his own power to complete the suggestion or command. Executing the act himself, he can sustain some vestige of the notion that he is self-determining. Responding to the question in his own words, he can sustain the notion that he is somebody to be considered, however slightly. And since it is only words that pass between himself and the others, he succeeds in retaining at least physical distance from them, however unpalatable the command or statement.

The inmate in a total institution can find himself denied even this kind of protective distance and self-action. Especially in mental hospitals and political training prisons, the statements he makes may be discounted as mere symptoms, with staff giving attention to non-verbal aspects of his reply.[83] Often he is considered to be of insufficient ritual status to be given even minor greetings, let alone listened to.[84] Or the inmate may find that a kind of rhetorical use of language occurs: questions such as, 'Have you washed yet?' or, 'Have you got both socks on?' may be accompanied by simultaneous searching by the staff which physically discloses the facts, making these verbal questions superfluous. And instead of being told to move in a particular

82. ibid., p. 78.

83. See Alfred H. Stanton and Morris S. Schwartz, *The Mental Hospital* (New York: Basic Books, 1954), pp. 200, 203, 205–6.

84. For an example of this non-person treatment, see Johnson and Dodds, op. cit., p. 122.

direction at a particular rate, he may find himself pushed along by the guard, or pulled (in the case of overalled mental patients), or frog-marched. And finally, as will be discussed later, the inmate may find that a dual language exists, with the disciplinary facts of his life given a translated ideal phrasing by the staff that mocks the normal use of language.

The second general consideration is the rationale that is employed for assaults upon the self. This issue tends to place total institutions and their inmates into three different groupings.

In religious institutions the implications environmental arrangements have for the self are explicitly recognized:

> That is the meaning of the contemplative life, and the sense of all the apparently meaningless little rules and observances and fasts and obediences and penances and humiliations and labors that go to make up the routine of existence in a contemplative monastery: they all serve to remind us of what we are and Who God is – that we may get sick of the sight of ourselves and turn to Him: and in the end, we will find Him in ourselves, in our own purified natures which have become the mirror of His tremendous Goodness and of His endless love. . . .[85]

The inmates, as well as the staff, actively seek out these curtailments of the self, so that mortification is complemented by self-mortification, restrictions by renunciations, beatings by self-flagellations, inquisition by confession. Because religious establishments are explicitly concerned with the processes of mortification, they have a special value for the student.

In concentration camps and, to a lesser extent, prisons, some mortifications seem to be arranged solely or mainly for their mortifying power, as when a prisoner is urinated on, but here the inmate does not embrace and facilitate his own destruction of self.

In many of the remaining total institutions, mortifications are officially rationalized on other grounds, such as sanitation (in connexion with latrine duty), responsibility for life (in connexion with forced feeding), combat capacity (in connexion with Army rules for personal appearance), 'security' (in connexion with restrictive prison regulations).

In total institutions of all three varieties, however, the various

85. Merton, op. cit., p. 372.

rationales for mortifying the self are very often merely rationalizations, generated by efforts to manage the daily activity of a
large number of persons in a restricted space with a small
expenditure of resources. Further, curtailments of the self occur
in all three, even where the inmate is willing and the management
has ideal concerns for his well-being.

Two issues have been considered: the inmate's sense of personal inefficacy and the relation of his own desires to the ideal
interests of the establishment. The connexion between these two
issues is variable. Persons can voluntarily elect to enter a total
institution and cease thereafter, to their regret, to be able to
make such important decisions. In other cases, notably the
religious, inmates may begin with and sustain a wilful desire to
be stripped and cleansed of personal will. Total institutions are
fateful for the inmate's civilian self, although the attachment of
the inmate to this civilian self can vary considerably.

The processes of mortification I have been considering have to
do with the implications for self that persons oriented to a particular expressive idiom might draw from an individual's appearance, conduct, and general situation. In this context I want to
consider a third and final issue: the relation between this
symbolic-interaction framework for considering the fate of the
self and the conventional psycho-physiological one centred on
the concept of stress.

The basic facts about self in this report are phrased in a sociological perspective, always leading back to a description of the
institutional arrangements which delineate the personal prerogatives of a member. Of course, a psychological assumption is
also implied; cognitive processes are invariably involved, for the
social arrangements must be 'read' by the individual and others
for the image of himself that they imply. But, as I have argued,
the relation of this cognitive process to other psychological processes is quite variable; according to the general expressive idiom
of our society, having one's head shaved is easily perceived as a
curtailment of the self, but while this mortification may enrage a
mental patient, it may please a monk.

Mortification or curtailment of the self is very likely to involve
acute psychological stress for the individual, but for an individual

sick with his world or guilt-ridden in it mortification may bring psychological relief. Further, the psychological stress often created by assaults on the self can also be produced by matters not perceived as related to the territories of the self – such as loss of sleep, insufficient food, or protracted decision-making. So, too, a high level of anxiety, or the unavailability of fantasy materials such as movies and books, may greatly increase the psychological effect of a violation of the self's boundaries, but in themselves these facilitating factors have nothing to do with the mortification of the self. Empirically, then, the study of stress and of encroachments on the self will often be tied together, but, analytically, two different frameworks are involved.

V

While the process of mortification goes on, the inmate begins to receive formal and informal instruction in what will here be called the privilege system. In so far as the inmate's attachment to his civilian self has been shaken by the stripping processes of the institution, it is largely the privilege system that provides a framework for personal reorganization. Three basic elements of the system may be mentioned.

First, there are the 'house rules', a relatively explicit and formal set of prescriptions and proscriptions that lays out the main requirements of inmate conduct. These rules spell out the austere round of life of the inmate. Admission procedures, which strip the recruit of his past supports, can be seen as the institution's way of getting him ready to start living by house rules.

Secondly, against this stark background, a small number of clearly defined rewards or privileges are held out in exchange for obedience to staff in action and spirit. It is important to see that many of these potential gratifications are carved out of the flow of support that the inmate had previously taken for granted. On the outside, for example, the inmate probably could unthinkingly decide how he wanted his coffee, whether to light a cigarette, or when to talk; on the inside, such rights may become problematic. Held up to the inmate as possibilities, these few recapturings seem to have a reintegrative effect, re-establishing relationships with the whole lost world and assuaging withdrawal symptoms from it and from one's lost self. The inmate's attention, especially at first, comes to be fixed on these supplies and obsessed with them. He can spend the day, like a fanatic, in devoted thoughts about the possibility of acquiring these gratifications or in contemplation of the approaching hour at which they are scheduled to be granted. Melville's report on navy life contains a typical example:

In the American Navy the law allows one gill of spirits per day to every seaman. In two portions, it is served out just previous to breakfast and dinner. At the roll of the drum, the sailors assemble round a large tub, or cask, filled with the liquid; and, as their names are called off by a midshipman, they step up and regale themselves from a little tin measure called a 'tot'. No high-liver helping himself to Tokay off a well-polished sideboard smacks his lips with more mighty satisfaction than the sailor does over his tot. To many of them, indeed, the thought of their daily tots forms a perpetual perspective of ravishing landscapes, indefinitely receding in the distance. It is their great 'prospect in life'.

Take away their grog, and life possesses no further charms for them.[86]

It is one of the most common punishments for very trivial offences in the Navy, to 'stop' a seaman's grog for a day or a week. And as most seamen so cling to their grog, the loss of it is generally deemed by them a very serious penalty. You will sometimes hear them say, 'I would rather have my wind *stopped* than my grog!'[87]

The building of a world around these minor privileges is perhaps the most important feature of inmate culture, and yet it is something that cannot easily be appreciated by an outsider, even one who has previously lived through the experience himself. This concern with privileges sometimes leads to generous sharing; it almost always leads to a willingness to beg for such things as cigarettes, candy, and newspapers. Understandably, inmate conversation often revolves around a 'release binge fantasy', namely, a recital of what one will do during leave or upon release from the institution. This fantasy is related to a feeling that civilians do not appreciate how wonderful their life is.[88]

86. Melville, op. cit., pp. 62–3.

87. ibid., p. 140. For examples of the same process in P.O.W. camps, see Edgar H. Schein, 'The Chinese Indoctrination Program for Prisoners of War', *Psychiatry*, XIX (1956), pp. 160–61.

88. Interestingly enough, there is sometimes a corresponding pre-entrance binge, during which the inmate-to-be indulges in activity he feels

The third element in the privilege system is punishments; these are designated as the consequence of breaking the rules. One set of these punishments consists of the temporary or permanent withdrawal of privileges or the abrogation of the right to try to earn them. In general, the punishments meted out in total institutions are more severe than anything encountered by the inmate in his home world. In any case, conditions in which a few easily controlled privileges are so important are the same conditions in which their withdrawal has a terrible significance.

There are some special features of the privilege system which should be noted.

First, punishments and privileges are themselves modes of organization peculiar to total institutions. Whatever their severity, punishments are largely known in the inmate's home world as something applied to animals and children; this conditioning, behaviouristic model is not widely applied to adults, since failure to maintain required standards typically leads to indirect disadvantageous consequences and not to specific immediate punishment at all.[89] And privileges in the total institution, it should be emphasized, are not the same as perquisites, indulgences, or values, but merely the absence of deprivations one ordinarily expects not to have to sustain. The very notions of punishments and privileges are not ones that are cut from civilian cloth.

Second, the question of release from the total institution is elaborated into the privilege system. Some acts become known as ones that mean an increase, or no decrease, in length of stay, while others become known as means for shortening the sentence.

Third, punishments and privileges come to be geared into a residential work system. Places to work and places to sleep become clearly defined as places where certain kinds and levels of privilege obtain, and inmates are shifted very frequently and visibly from one place to another as the administrative device for giving them the punishment or reward their cooperativeness

will soon be quite unavailable to him. For an example regarding nuns, see Hulme, op. cit., p. 7.

89. See S. F. Nadel, 'Social Control and Self-Regulation', *Social Forces*, XXXI (1953), pp. 265–73.

warrants. The inmates are moved, the system is not. We can therefore expect some spatial specialization, with one ward or hut acquiring the reputation of a punishment place for especially recalcitrant inmates, while certain guard assignments become recognized as punishments for staff.

The privilege system consists of a relatively few components, put together with some rational intent, and clearly proclaimed to the participants. The over-all consequence is that cooperativeness is obtained from persons who often have cause to be uncooperative.[90] An illustration of this model universe may be taken from a recent study of a state mental hospital:

> The authority of the attendant in the operation of his control system is backed up by both positive and negative power. This power is an essential element in his control of the ward. He can give the patient privileges, and he can punish the patient. The privileges consist of having the best job, better rooms and beds, minor luxuries like coffee on the ward, a little more privacy than the average patient, going outside the ward without supervision, having more access than the average patient to the attendant's companionship or to professional personnel like the physicians, and enjoying such intangible but vital things as being treated with personal kindness and respect.

> The punishments which can be applied by the ward attendant are suspension of all privileges, psychological mistreatment, such as ridicule, vicious ribbing, moderate and sometimes severe corporal punishment, or the threat of such punishment, locking up the patient in an isolated room, denial or distortion of access to the professional personnel, threatening to put, or putting, the patient on the list for electroshock therapy, transfer of the patient to undesirable wards, and regular assignment of the patient to unpleasant tasks such as cleaning up after the soilers.[91]

90. As a qualification it has been argued that in some cases this sytem is either not very effective or not much relied upon. In some prisons, the rewards that are carved out of usual expectations are granted upon entrance, and little official betterment of position is apparently possible – the only change in status possible involving a loss of privileges (Sykes, op. cit., pp. 51–2). It has been further argued that if the inmate is stripped of enough, then instead of cherishing what remains he can come to see little remaining difference between this and complete expropriation, and so cease to be subject to the power of staff to motivate him to obedience, especially when disobedience may bring prestige among the inmate group (ibid.).

91. Belknap, op. cit., p. 164.

A parallel may be found in British prisons in which the 'four-stage system' is employed, with an increase at each stage of payment for labour, 'association' time with other prisoners, access to newspapers, group eating, and recreation periods.[92]

Associated with the privilege system are certain processes important in the life of total institutions.

An 'institutional lingo' develops through which inmates describe the events that are crucial in their particular world. The staff, especially its lower levels, will know this language, too, and use it when talking to inmates, reverting to more standardized speech when talking to superiors and outsiders. Along with a lingo, inmates acquire knowledge of the various ranks and officials, an accumulation of lore about the establishment, and some comparative information about life in other similar total institutions.

Furthermore, the staff and inmates will be clearly aware of what, in mental hospitals, prisons, and barracks, is called 'messing up'. Messing up involves a complex process of engaging in forbidden activity (including sometimes an effort at escape), getting caught, and receiving something like full punishment. There is usually an alteration in privilege status, categorized by a phrase such as 'getting busted'. Typical infractions involved in messing up are: fights, drunkenness, attempted suicide, failure at examinations, gambling, insubordination, homosexuality, improper leave-taking, and participation in collective riots. Although these infractions are typically ascribed to the offender's cussedness, villainy, or 'sickness', they do in fact constitute a vocabulary of institutionalized actions, but a limited one, so that the same messing up may occur for quite different reasons. Inmates and staff may tacitly agree, for example, that a given messing up is a way for inmates to show resentment against a situation felt to be unjust in terms of the informal agreements between staff and inmates,[93] or a way of postponing release without having to admit to one's fellow inmates that one does not really want to go. Whatever the meaning imputed to them, messings up have

92. For example, Dendrickson and Thomas, op. cit., pp. 99–100.

93. For bibliography, see Morris G. Caldwell, 'Group Dynamics in the Prison Community', *Journal of Criminal Law, Criminology and Police Science*, XLVI (1956), p. 656.

some important social functions for the institution. They tend to limit rigidities which would occur were seniority the only means of mobility in the privilege system; further, demotion through messing up brings old-time inmates into contact with new inmates in unprivileged positions, assuring a flow of information concerning the system and the people in it.

In total institutions there will also be a system of what might be called secondary adjustments, namely, practices that do not directly challenge staff but allow inmates to obtain forbidden satisfactions or to obtain permitted ones by forbidden means. These practices are variously referred to as 'the angles', 'knowing the ropes', 'conniving', 'gimmicks', 'deals', or 'ins'. Such adaptations apparently reach their finest flower in prisons, but of course other total institutions are overrun with them, too.[94] Secondary adjustments provide the inmate with important evidence that he is still his own man, with some control of his environment; sometimes a secondary adjustment becomes almost a kind of lodgement for the self, a *churinga* in which the soul is felt to reside.[95]

We can predict from the presence of secondary adjustments that the inmate group will have evolved some kind of code and some means of informal social control to prevent one inmate from informing staff about the secondary adjustments of another. On the same ground, we can expect that one dimension of social typing of and among inmates will be this question of security, leading to definitions of persons as 'squealers', 'finks', 'rats', or 'stoolies' on one hand, and 'right guys' on the other.[96] When new inmates can play a role in the system of secondary adjustments, as by providing new faction members or new sexual objects, then their 'welcome' may indeed be a sequence of initial indulgences and enticements instead of exaggerated depriva-

94. For example, see Norman S. Hayner and Ellis Ash, 'The Prisoner Community as a Social Group', *American Sociological Review*, IV (1939), p. 364 ff, under 'conniving' processes; also Caldwell, op. cit., pp. 650–51.

95. See, for example, Melville's extended description of the fight his fellow seamen put up to prevent the clipping of their beards, the clipping being in accordance with full navy regulations. Melville, op. cit., pp. 333–47.

96. See, for example, Donald Clemmer, 'Leadership Phenomena in a Prison Community', *Journal of Criminal Law and Criminology*, XXVIII (1938), p. 868.

tions.[97] Because of secondary adjustments we also find 'kitchen strata', a kind of rudimentary, largely informal stratification of inmates on the basis of differential access to disposable illicit commodities; again, too, we find social typing to designate the powerful persons in the informal market system.[98]

While the privilege system seems to provide the chief framework within which reassembly of the self takes place, there are other factors that characteristically lead by different routes in the same general direction. Relief from economic and social responsibilities – much touted as part of the therapy of mental hospitals – is one, although in many cases it seems that the disorganizing effect of this moratorium is more significant than its organizing effect. More important as a reorganizing influence is the fraternalization process, through which socially distant persons find themselves developing mutual support and common countermores in opposition to a system that has forced them into intimacy and into a single, equalitarian community of fate.[99] The new recruit frequently starts out with something like the staff's popular misconceptions of the character of the inmates; he comes to find that most of his fellows have all the properties of ordinary, occasionally decent human beings worthy of sympathy and support. The offences that inmates are known to have committed on the outside cease to provide an effective means for judging their personal qualities – a lesson that conscientious objectors, for example, seem to have learned in prison.[1] Further, if the inmates are persons who are accused of having committed a crime

97. See, for example, Ida Ann Harper, 'The Role of the "Fringer" in a State Prison for Women', *Social Forces*, XXXI (1952), pp. 53–60.

98. For concentration camps, see the discussion of 'prominents' throughout Cohen, op. cit.; for mental hospitals, see Belknap, op. cit., p. 189; for prisons, see the discussion of 'Politicians' in Donald Clemmer, *The Prison Community* (Boston: Christopher Publishing House, 1940), pp. 277–9 and 298–309; also Hayner and Ash, op. cit., p. 367; and Caldwell, op. cit., pp. 651–3.

99. For the version of this inmate solidarity to be found in military academies, see Dornbusch, op. cit., p. 318.

1. See Hassler, op. cit., pp. 74, 117. In mental hospitals, of course, the patient's antagonism to staff obtains one of its supports from the discovery that, like himself, many other patients are more like ordinary persons than like anything else.

of some kind against society, then the new inmate, even though sometimes in fact quite guiltless, may come to share both the guilty feelings of his fellows and their well-elaborated defences against these feelings. A sense of common injustice and a sense of bitterness against the outside world tend to develop, marking an important movement in the inmate's moral career. This response to felt guilt and massive deprivation is most clearly illustrated, perhaps, in prison life:

By their reasoning, after an offender has been subjected to unfair or excessive punishment and treatment more degrading than that prescribed by law, he comes to justify his act which he could not have justified when he committed it. He decides to 'get even' for his unjust treatment in prison and take reprisals through further crime at the first opportunity. *With that decision he becomes a criminal.*[2]

An imprisoned conscientious objector provides a similar statement from his own experience:

A point I want to record here is the curious difficulty I have in feeling innocent, myself. I find it very easy to accept the notion that I am paying for the same kind of misdeeds as those charged to the other men in here, and I must remind myself from time to time that a government that actually believes in freedom of conscience should not put men in prison for practicing it. Consequently, what indignation I feel toward prison practices is not the indignation of the persecuted innocent or the martyr, but of the guilty who feels his punishment to be beyond his deserts and *inflicted by those who are not themselves free of guilt.* This latter point is one that all the inmates feel strongly, and is the source of the deep cynicism that pervades the prison.[3]

A more general statement may be taken from two other students of the same kind of total institution:

In many ways, the inmate social system may be viewed as providing a way of life which enables the inmate to avoid the devastating psychological effects of internalizing and converting social rejection into self-

2. Richard McCleery, *The Strange Journey*, University of North Carolina Extension Bulletin, XXXII (1953), p. 24. (Italics in the original.) There is a suggestion in Brewster Smith (Stouffer, op. cit.) that with the decision that officer training camp has 'earned' him rights over enlisted men, the officer trainee becomes an officer. The pain suffered in camp can be used as a justification for the pleasures of command.

3. Hassler, op. cit., p. 97. (Italics in the original).

rejection. In effect, it permits the inmate to reject his rejectors rather than himself.[4]

Here of course is one irony of a somewhat therapeutic and permissive policy – the inmate becomes less able to protect his ego by directing hostility to external targets.[5]

There is one secondary adjustment that very clearly reflects the fraternalization process and the rejection of the staff, namely, collective teasing. Although the punishment-reward system can deal with individual infractions that are identifiable as to source, inmate solidarity may be strong enough to support brief gestures of anonymous or mass defiance. Examples are: slogan shouting,[6] booing,[7] tray thumping, mass food rejection, and minor sabotage.[8] These actions tend to take the form of 'rise-getting': a warder, guard, or attendant – or even the staff as a whole – is teased, mocked, or accorded other forms of minor abuse until he loses some measure of self-control and engages in ineffective counteraction.

In addition to fraternalization among all inmates there is likely to be bond formation of a more differentiating kind. Sometimes special solidarities extend throughout a physically closed region, such as a ward or cottage, whose inhabitants perceive they are being administered as a single unit, and hence have a lively sense of common fate. Lawrence provides an illustrative statement concerning air force 'administered groups':

There lies a golden mist of laughter – even if silly laughter – over our hut. Shake together fifty-odd fellows, strangers of every class, in a close room for twenty days: subject them to a new and arbitrary discipline: weary them with dirty, senseless, uncalled for yet arduous fatigues ... but there has not been a sharp word between any two of us. Such liberality of body and spirit, such active vigour, cleanliness and good

4. Lloyd W. McCorkle and Richard Korn, 'Resocialization Within Walls', *The Annals*, CCXCIII (May 1954), p. 88.

5. This issue is incisively treated in ibid., p. 95.

6. Cantine and Rainer, op. cit., p. 59; see also Norman, op. cit., pp. 56–7.

7. Cantine and Rainer, op. cit., pp. 39–40.

8. 'Resistance in Prison', by Clif Bennett, in Cantine and Rainer, op. cit., pp. 3–11, provides a useful review of techniques for collective teasing.

temper would hardly have persisted save in the conditions of a common servitude.[9]

And of course still smaller units are found, too: cliques; more or less stable sexual ties; and, most importantly perhaps, 'buddy formation', whereby a pair of inmates come to be recognized by other inmates as 'buddies' or 'mates' and come to rely on each other for a wide range of assistance and emotional support.[10] Although these friendship pairs may be given quasi-official recognition, as when a bosun on board ship arranges for buddies to take a watch together,[11] deep involvement in the relationship may also meet with a kind of institutional incest taboo functioning to prevent dyads from creating their own world in the institution. In fact, in some total institutions, the staff feel that solidarity among sets of inmates can provide the base for concerted activity forbidden by the rules, and the staff may consciously try to hinder primary group formation.

VI

Although there are solidarizing tendencies such as fraternalization and clique formation, they are limited. Constraints which place inmates in a position to sympathize and communicate with each other do not necessarily lead to high group morale and solidarity. In some concentration camps and prisoner-of-war installations the inmate cannot rely on his fellows, who may steal from him, assault him, and squeal on him, leading to what some students have referred to as anomie.[12] In mental hospitals, dyads and triads may keep secrets from the authorities, but anything known to a whole ward of patients is likely to get to the ear of the attendant. (In prisons, of course, inmate organization has some-

9. Lawrence, op. cit., p. 59. (Ellipsis dots in the original.)

10. For example, Heckstall-Smith, op. cit., p. 30. Behan, op. cit., provides much material throughout on the buddy or mate relation.

11. S. A. Richardson, *The Social Organization of British and United States Merchant Ships*. (Unpublished monograph, available at The New York State School of Industrial and Labor Relations, Cornell University, 1954, p. 17.)

12. A full statement of this theme may be found in D. Cressey and W. Krassowski, 'Inmate Organization and Anomie in American Prisons and Soviet Labor Camps', *Social Problems*, V (Winter 1957-8), pp. 217-30.

times been strong enough to run strikes and short-lived insurrections; in prisoner-of-war camps, it has sometimes been possible to organize sections of the prisoners to operate escape channels;[13] in concentration camps there have been periods of thoroughgoing underground organization;[14] and on ships there have been mutinies; but these concerted actions seem to be the exception, not the rule.) But though there is usually little group loyalty in total institutions, the expectation that group loyalty should prevail forms part of the inmate culture and underlies the hostility accorded those who break inmate solidarity.

The privilege system and the mortifying processes that have been discussed represent the conditions to which the inmate must adapt. These conditions allow for different individualistic ways of meeting them, apart from any effort at collective subversive action. The same inmate will employ different personal lines of adaptation at different phases in his moral career and may even alternate among different tacks at the same time.

First, there is the tack of 'situational withdrawal'. The inmate withdraws apparent attention from everything except events immediately around his body and sees these in a perspective not employed by others present. This drastic curtailment of involvement in interactional events is best known, of course, in mental hospitals, under the title of 'regression'. Aspects of 'prison psychosis' or going 'stir simple' represent the same adjustment,[15] as do some forms of 'acute depersonalization' described in concentration camps and 'tankeritis' apparently found among confirmed merchant mariners.[16] I do not think it is known whether this line of adaptation forms a single continuum of varying degrees of withdrawal or whether there are standard plateaux of disinvolvement. Given the pressures apparently required to dislodge an inmate from this status, as well as the currently limited

13. See, for example, P. R. Reid, *Escape from Colditz* (New York: Berkley Publishing Corp., 1956).

14. See Paul Foreman, 'Buchenwald and Modern Prisoner-of-War Detention Policy', *Social Forces*, XXXVII (1959), pp. 289–98.

15. For an early treatment, see P. Nitsche and K. Wilmanns, *The History of Prison Psychosis*, Nervous and Mental Disease Monograph Series No. 13 (1912).

16. Richardson, op. cit., p. 42.

facilities for doing so, this line of adaptation is often effectively irreversible.

Secondly, there is the 'intransigent line': the inmate intentionally challenges the institution by flagrantly refusing to cooperate with staff.[17] The result is a constantly communicated intransigency and sometimes high individual morale. Many large mental hospitals, for example, have wards where this spirit prevails. Sustained rejection of a total institution often requires sustained orientation to its formal organization, and hence, paradoxically, a deep kind of involvement in the establishment. Similarly, when staff take the line that the intransigent inmate must be broken (as they sometimes do in the case of hospital psychiatrists prescribing electroshock[18] or military tribunals prescribing the stockade), then the institution shows as much special devotion to the rebel as he has shown to it. Finally, although some prisoners of war have been known to take a staunchly intransigent stance throughout their incarceration, intransigence is typically a temporary and initial phase of reaction, with the inmate shifting to situational withdrawal or some other line of adaptation.

A third standard alignment in the institutional world is 'colonization'; the sampling of the outside world provided by the establishment is taken by the inmate as the whole, and a stable, relatively contented existence is built up out of the maximum satisfactions procurable within the institution.[19] Experience of the outside world is used as a point of reference to demonstrate the desirability of life on the inside, and the usual tension between the two worlds is markedly reduced, thwarting the motivational scheme based upon this felt discrepancy which I described as peculiar to total institutions. Characteristically, the individual who too obviously takes this line may be accused by his fellow inmates of 'having found a home' or of 'never having had it so good'. The staff itself may become vaguely embarrassed by this use that is being made of the institution, sensing that the benign

17. See, for example, the discussion of 'The Resisters', in Schein, op. cit., pp. 166–7.

18. Belknap, op. cit., p. 192.

19. In the case of mental hospitals, those who take this line are sometimes called ' institutional cures' or are said to suffer from 'hospitalitis'.

possibilities in the situation are somehow being misused. Colonizers may feel obliged to deny their satisfaction with the institution, if only to sustain the counter-mores supporting inmate solidarity. They may find it necessary to mess up just prior to their slated discharge to provide themselves with an apparently involuntary basis for continued incarceration. Significantly, the staff who try to make life in total institutions more bearable must face the possibility that doing so may increase the attractiveness and likelihood of colonization.

A fourth mode of adaptation to the setting of a total institution is that of 'conversion': the inmate appears to take over the official or staff view of himself and tries to act out the role of the perfect inmate. While the colonized inmate builds as much of a free community for himself as possible by using the limited facilities available, the convert takes a more disciplined, moralistic, monochromatic line, presenting himself as someone whose institutional enthusiasm is always at the disposal of the staff. In Chinese P.O.W. camps, we find Americans who became 'Pros' and fully espoused the Communist view of the world.[20] In army barracks there are enlisted men who give the impression that they are always 'sucking around' and always 'bucking for promotion'. In prisons there are 'square johns'. In German concentration camps, a long-time prisoner sometimes came to adopt the vocabulary, recreation, posture, expressions of aggression, and clothing style of the Gestapo, executing the role of straw boss with military strictness.[21] Some mental hospitals have the distinction of providing two quite different conversion possibilities – one for the new admission, who can see the light after an appropriate inner struggle and adopt the psychiatric view of himself, and another for the chronic patient, who adopts the manner and dress of attendants while helping them to manage the other patients, employing a stringency sometimes excelling that of the attendants themselves. And of course in officer training camps we find

20. Schein, op. cit., pp. 167–9.

21. See Bruno Bettelheim, 'Individual and Mass Behavior in Extreme Situations', *Journal of Abnormal and Social Psychology*, XXXVIII (1943), pp. 447–51. It should be added that in concentration camps, colonization and conversion often seemed to go together. See Cohen, op. cit., pp. 200–203, where the role of the 'Kapo' is discussed.

trainees who quickly become 'G.I.', espousing a torment of themselves that they will soon be able to inflict on others.[22]

Here is a significant way in which total institutions differ: many, like progressive mental hospitals, merchant ships, TB sanitaria, and brainwashing camps, offer the inmate an opportunity to live up to a model of conduct that is at once ideal and staff-sponsored – a model felt by its advocates to be in the best interests of the very persons to whom it is applied; other total institutions, like some concentration camps and some prisons, do not officially sponsor an ideal that the inmate is expected to incorporate.

The alignments that have been mentioned represent coherent courses to pursue, but few inmates seem to pursue any one of them very far. In most total institutions, most inmates take the tack of what some of them call 'playing it cool'. This involves a somewhat opportunistic combination of secondary adjustments, conversion, colonization, and loyalty to the inmate group, so that the inmate will have a maximum chance, in the particular circumstances, of eventually getting out physically and psychologically undamaged.[23] Typically, the inmate when with fellow inmates will support the counter-mores and conceal from them how tractably he acts when alone with the staff.[24] Inmates who play it cool subordinate contacts with their fellows to the higher claim of 'keeping out of trouble'; they tend to volunteer for nothing; and they may learn to cut their ties to the outside world just enough to

22. Brewster Smith (Stouffer, op. cit.), p. 390.

23. See the discussion in Schein, op. cit., pp. 165–6, of the 'Get-Along-ers', and Robert J. Lifton, 'Home by Ship: Reaction Patterns of American Prisoners of War Repatriated from North Korea', *American Journal of Psychiatry*, CX (1954), p. 734.

24. This two-facedness is very commonly found in total institutions. In the state mental hospital studied by the writer, even the few élite patients selected for individual psychotherapy, and hence in the best position to espouse the psychiatric approach to self, tended to present their favourable view of psychotherapy only to the members of their intimate cliques. For a report on the way in which army prisoners concealed from fellow offenders their interest in 'restoration' to the Army, see the comments by Richard Cloward in Session Four of *New Perspectives for Research on Juvenile Delinquency*, eds. Helen L. Witmer and Ruth Kotinsky, U.S. Dept. of Health, Education, and Welfare, Children's Bureau Publication No. 356 (1956), especially p. 90.

give cultural reality to the world inside but not enough to lead to colonization.

I have suggested some of the lines of adaptation that inmates can take to the pressures present in total institutions. Each tack represents a way of managing the tension between the home world and the institutional world. Sometimes, however, the home world of the inmate has been, in fact, such as to immunize him against the bleak world on the inside, and for these persons no particular scheme of adaptation need be carried very far. Some lower-class mental-hospital patients who have lived all their previous lives in orphanages, reformatories, and jails tend to see the hospital as just another total institution, to which they can apply the adaptive techniques learned and perfected in similar institutions. For these persons, playing it cool does not represent a shift in their moral career but an alignment that is already second nature. Similarly, Shetland youths recruited into the British merchant service are apparently not much threatened by the cramped, arduous life on board, because island life is even more stunted; they make uncomplaining sailors because from their point of view they have little to complain about.

Something similar in effect to immunization is achieved by inmates who have special compensations inside the institution or special means of being impervious to its assaults. In the early period of German concentration camps, criminals apparently derived compensative satisfaction from living with middle-class political prisoners.[25] Similarly, the middle-class vocabulary of group psychotherapy and the classless ideology of 'psychodynamics' give to some socially ambitious and socially frustrated lower-class mental patients the closest contact with the polite world that they have ever had. Strong religious and political convictions have served to insulate the true believer against the assaults of a total institution. Failure to speak the staff's language may make the staff give up its efforts at reformation, freeing the non-speaker from certain pressures.[26]

25. Bettelheim, op. cit., p. 425.
26. Thus, Schein, op. cit., p. 165 fn., suggests that the Chinese gave up on Puerto Ricans and other non-English-speaking prisoners of war and allowed them to work out a viable routine of menial chores.

VII

I would now like to consider some of the dominant themes of inmate culture.

First, in many total institutions a peculiar kind and level of self-concern is engendered. The low position of inmates relative to their station on the outside, established initially through the stripping processes, creates a milieu of personal failure in which one's fall from grace is continuously pressed home. In response, the inmate tends to develop a story, a line, a sad tale – a kind of lamentation and apologia – which he constantly tells to his fellows as a means of accounting for his present low estate. In consequence, the inmate's self may become even more a focus of his conversation and concern than it does on the outside, leading to much self-pity.[27] Although the staff constantly discredit these stories, inmate audiences tend to be tactful, suppressing at least some of the disbelief and boredom engendered by these recitations. Thus, an ex-prisoner writes:

Even more impressive is the almost universal delicacy when it comes to inquiring into another man's misdeeds, and the refusal to determine one's relations with another convict on the basis of his record.[28]

Similarly, in American state mental hospitals, inmate etiquette allows one patient to ask another what ward and service he is on, and how long he has been in the hospital; but questions about why the other is in are not quickly asked, and, when asked, the biased version almost inevitably given tends to be accepted.

Second, among inmates in many total institutions there is a strong feeling that time spent in the establishment is time wasted or destroyed or taken from one's life; it is time that must be written off; it is something that must be 'done' or 'marked' or 'put in' or 'pulled'. In prisons and mental hospitals, a general statement of how well one is adapting to the institution may be

27. For prison examples, see Hassler, op. cit., p. 18; Heckstall-Smith, op. cit., pp. 29–30.
28. Hassler, op. cit., p. 116.

phrased in terms of how one is doing time, whether easily or hard.[29] This time is something its doers have bracketed off for constant conscious consideration in a way not quite found on the outside. As a result, the inmate tends to feel that for the duration of his required stay – his sentence – he has been totally exiled from living.[30] It is in this context that we can appreciate something of the demoralizing influence of an indefinite sentence or a very long one.[31]

However harsh the conditions of life in total institutions, harshness alone cannot account for this sense of life wasted; we must rather look to the social disconnexions caused by entrance and to the failure (usually) to acquire within the institution gains that can be transferred to outside life – gains such as money earned, or marital relations formed, or certified training received. One of the virtues of the doctrine that insane asylums are treatment hospitals for sick people is that inmates who have given up three or four years of their life to this kind of exile can try to convince themselves they have been busily working on their cure and that, once cured, the time spent getting cured will have been a reasonable and profitable investment.

This sense of dead and heavy-hanging time probably explains the premium placed on what might be called removal activities, namely, voluntary unserious pursuits which are sufficiently engrossing and exciting to lift the participant out of himself, making him oblivious for the time being to his actual situation. If the ordinary activities in total institutions can be said to torture time, these activities mercifully kill it.

Some removal activities are collective, such as field games, dances, orchestra or band playing, choral singing, lectures, art

29. Much material on the conception of time in total institutions may be found in Maurice L. Farber, 'Suffering and Time Perspective of the Prisoner', Part IV, *Authority and Frustration*, by Kurt Lewin, *et al.*, Studies in Topological and Vector Psychology III, University of Iowa Studies in Child Welfare, Vol. XX (1944).

30. The best description that I know of this feeling of not living is Freud's paper, 'Mourning and Melancholia', where the state is said to come about as a consequence of losing a loved object. See *Collected Papers of Sigmund Freud* (London: Hogarth Press, 1925), Vol. IV, pp. 152–70.

31. See, for example, Cohen, op. cit., p. 128.

classes[32] or woodworking classes, and card playing; some are individual but rely on public materials, such as reading[33] and solitary TV watching.[34] No doubt private fantasy ought to be included, too, as Clemmer suggests in his description of the prisoner's 'reverie-plus'.[35] Some of these activities may be officially sponsored by staff; some, not officially sponsored, will constitute secondary adjustments – for example, gambling, homosexuality, or 'highs' and 'jags' achieved with industrial alcohol, nutmeg, or ginger.[36] Whether officially sponsored or not, whenever any of these removal activities become too engrossing or too continuous, the staff is likely to object – as they often do, for example, to liquor, sex, and gambling – since in their eyes the institution, not some other kind of social entity enclosed within the institution, must possess the inmate.

Every total institution can be seen as a kind of dead sea in which little islands of vivid, encapturing activity appear. Such activity can help the individual withstand the psychological stress usually engendered by assaults upon the self. Yet it is precisely in the insufficiency of these activities that an important deprivational effect of total institutions can be found. In civil society, an individual pushed to the wall in one of his social roles usually has an opportunity to crawl into some protected place where he can indulge in commercialized fantasy – movies, TV, radio, reading – or employ 'relievers' like cigarettes or drink. In total institutions, especially right after admission, these materials may be too little available. At a time when these resting points are most needed, they may be most difficult to obtain.[37]

32. A good prison illustration is provided by Norman, op. cit., p. 71.

33. See, for example, the fine description by Behan, op. cit., pp. 72–5, of the delights of reading in bed in one's cell, and the consequent precaution of rationing one's reading supply.

34. Such activity is, of course, not restricted to total institutions. Thus, we find the classic case of the bored and weary housewife who 'takes a few minutes for herself' to 'put her feet up', removing herself from home by reading the morning paper over a cup of coffee and a cigarette.

35. Clemmer, op. cit., pp. 244–7.

36. Cantine and Rainer, op. cit., pp. 59–60, provide an example.

37. For example, Cantine and Rainer, op. cit., p. 59, quoting James Peck: 'I missed the drinks even more than the women and a number of guys agreed with me. When you get the blues on the outside you can always kill

VIII

In this discussion of the inmate world, I have commented on the mortification processes, the reorganizing influences, the lines of responses inmates take, and the cultural milieu that develops. I would like to add a concluding comment on the processes that generally occur if and when the inmate is released and sent back into the wider society.

Although inmates do plan release binges and may keep an hourly count of the time until their release date, those about to be released very often become anxious at the thought, and, as suggested, some mess up or re-enlist to avoid the issue. The inmate's anxiety about release often seems to take the form of a question put to himself and his friends: 'Can I make it on the outside?' This question brackets all of civil life as something to have conceptions and concerns about. What for outsiders is usually an unperceived ground for perceived figures is for the inmate a figure on a larger ground. Perhaps such a perspective is demoralizing, providing one reason why ex-inmates often think about the possibility of 'going back in' and one reason why an appreciable number do return.

Total institutions frequently claim to be concerned with rehabilitation, that is, with resetting the inmate's self-regulatory mechanisms so that after he leaves he will maintain the standards of the establishment of his own accord. (The staff is expected to be properly self-regulating upon first coming to the total institution, sharing with members of other kinds of establishments the ideal of needing merely to learn procedure.) In fact, this claim of change is seldom realized, and, even when permanent alteration occurs, the changes are often not of the kind intended by the staff. Except in some religious institutions, neither the stripping processes nor the reorganizing processes seem to have a lasting effect,[38] partly because of the availability of secondary adjust-

them with a couple of drinks. But in jail you just have to wait until the blues wear off and that may take a long while.'

38. Important evidence for this comes from our knowledge of the readjustment of repatriated 'brainwashed' prisoners of war. See Hinkle and Wolff, op. cit., p. 174.

ments, the presence of counter-mores, and the tendency for inmates to combine all strategies and play it cool.

Of course, immediately upon release the inmate is likely to be marvellously alive to the liberties and pleasures of civil status that civilians ordinarily do not see as events at all – the sharp smell of fresh air, talking when you want to, using a whole match to light a cigarette, having a solitary snack at a table set for only four people.[39] A mental patient, back at the hospital after a weekend visit home, describes her experience to a circle of closely listening friends:

I got up in the morning, and I went into the kitchen, and I fixed coffee; it was wonderful. And in the evening we had a couple of beers and went and had chili; it was terrific, really delicious. I didn't forget one minute that I was free.[40]

And yet it seems that shortly after release the ex-inmate forgets a great deal of what life was like on the inside and once again begins to take for granted the privileges around which life in the institution was organized. The sense of injustice, bitterness, and alienation, so typically engendered by the inmate's experience and so commonly marking a stage in his moral career, seems to weaken upon graduation.

But what the ex-inmate does retain of his institutional experience tells us important things about total institutions. Very often, entrance means for the recruit that he has taken on what might be called a proactive status: not only is his social position within the walls radically different from what it was on the outside but, as he comes to learn, if and when he gets out, his social position on the outside will never again be quite what it was prior to entrance. Where the proactive status is a relatively favourable one, as it is for those who graduate from officers' training schools, élite boarding schools, ranking monasteries, etc., then jubilant official reunions, announcing pride in one's 'school', can be expected. When the proactive status is unfavourable, as it is for those who graduate from prisons or mental hospitals, we can employ the term 'stigmatization' and expect that the ex-inmate may make an effort to conceal his past and try to 'pass'.

39. Lawrence, op. cit., p. 48.
40. Writer's field notes.

As one student has implied,[41] an important kind of leverage possessed by the staff is their power to give the kind of discharge that reduces stigmatization. Army prison officials can hold out the possibility of the inmate's being restored to active duty and, potentially, an honourable discharge; mental-hospital administrators can hold out the possibility of a 'clean bill of health' (discharged as cured) and also personal recommendations. Here we have one reason why inmates, when with staff, sometimes affect enthusiasm for what the institution is doing for them.

We can now return to a consideration of release anxiety. One explanation offered for it is that the individual is unwilling or too 'sick' to reassume the responsibility from which the total institution freed him. My own experience in the study of one type of total institution, mental hospitals, tends to minimize this factor. A factor likely to be more important is disculturation, the loss or failure to acquire some of the habits currently required in the wider society. Another is stigmatization. When the individual has taken on a low proactive status by becoming an inmate, he finds a cool reception in the wider world – and is likely to experience this at a moment, hard even for those without his stigma, when he must apply to someone for a job and a place to live. Furthermore, release is likely to come just when the inmate has finally learned the ropes on the inside and won privileges that he has painfully learned are very important. In brief, he may find that release means moving from the top of a small world to the bottom of a large one. In addition, when the inmate returns to the free community, he may leave with some limits on his freedom. Some concentration camps required the inmate to sign a release, attesting that he had been treated fairly; he was warned of the consequences of telling tales out of school.[42] In some mental hospitals an inmate being prepared for discharge is interviewed a final time to discover whether or not he harbours resentment against the institution and those who arranged his entrance into it, and he is warned against causing trouble to the latter. Further, the departing inmate must often promise to seek help should he again find himself 'getting sick' or 'getting into trouble'. Often the

41. Cloward, op. cit., pp. 80–83.
42. Cohen, op. cit., p. 7; Kogon, op. cit., p. 72.

ex-mental patient learns his kin and employer have been advised to
get in touch with the authorities should trouble arise again. For to
the man who leaves prison, there may be formal parole, with the
obligation to report regularly and to keep away from the circles
from which he originally entered the institution.

THE STAFF WORLD

I

MANY total institutions, most of the time, seem to function merely as storage dumps for inmates, but, as previously suggested, they usually present themselves to the public as rational organizations designed consciously, through and through, as effective machines for producing a few officially avowed and officially approved ends. It was also suggested that one frequent official objective is the reformation of inmates in the direction of some ideal standard. This contradiction, between what the institution does and what its officials must say it does, forms the basic context of the staff's daily activity.

Within this context, perhaps the first thing to say about the staff is that their work, and hence their world, have uniquely to do with people. This *people-work* is not quite like personnel work or the work of those involved in service relationships; the staff, after all, have objects and products to work upon, not services, but these objects and products are people.

As material upon which to work, people can take on somewhat the same characteristics as inanimate objects. Surgeons prefer to operate on slender patients rather than fat ones, because with fat ones instruments get slippery, and there are the extra layers to cut through. Morticians in mental hospitals sometimes favour thin females over fat men, because heavy 'stiffs' are difficult to move and male stiffs must be dressed in jackets that are hard to pull over stiffened arms and fingers. Also, mismanagement of either animate or inanimate objects may leave tell-tale marks for supervisors to see. And just as an article being processed through an industrial plant must be followed by a paper shadow showing what has been done by whom, what is to be done, and who last had responsibility for it, so a human object, moving, say, through a mental-hospital system, must be followed by a chain of informative receipts detailing what has been done to and by the patient and who had most recent responsibility for him. Even the presence or absence of a particular patient at a given meal or for a given night may have to be recorded, so that cost accounting can be maintained and appropriate adjustments rendered in billing. In the inmate's career from admission suite to burial plot, many different kinds of staff will add their official note to his case file as he temporarily passes under their jurisdiction, and long after he has died physically his marked remains will survive as an actionable entity in the hospital's bureaucratic system.

Given the physiological characteristics of the human organism, it is obvious that certain requirements must be met if any continued use is to be made of people. But this, of course, is the case with inanimate objects, too; the temperature of any storehouse must be regulated, regardless of whether people or things are stored. Also, just as tin mines, paint factories, or chemical plants may involve special work hazards for employees, there are (staffs believe, at least) special dangers in some kinds of people-work. In mental hospitals, the staffs believe that patients may strike out 'for no reason' and injure an official; some attendants feel that prolonged exposure to mental patients can have a contagious effect. In T B sanitaria and in leprosaria, the staff feel they are being specially exposed to dangerous diseases.

While there are these similarities between people-work and object-work, the crucial determinants of the work world of the staff derive from the unique aspects of people as material to work upon.

Persons are almost always considered to be ends in themselves, according to the broad moral principles of a total institution's environing society. Almost always, then, we find that some *technically* unnecessary standards of handling must be maintained with human materials. This maintenance of what we call humane standards comes to be defined as part of the 'responsibility' of the institution and presumably is one of the things the institution guarantees the inmate in exchange for his liberty. Prison officials are obliged to thwart the suicidal efforts of a prisoner and to give him full medical attention, even if this might require postponing his execution. Something similar has been reported in German concentration camps, where inmates were sometimes given medical attention although shortly destined for the gas chamber.

A second special contingency in the work world of the staff is that inmates typically have statuses and relationships in the outside world that must be taken into consideration. This is, of course, related to the previously mentioned fact that the institution must respect some of the rights of inmates *qua* persons. Even with a committed mental patient, whose civil rights are largely taken from him, a large amount of paper work will be involved. Of course, the rights that are denied a mental patient are usually transferred to a relation, a committee, or the superintendent of the hospital itself, who then becomes the legal person whose authorization must be obtained for the many matters originating outside the institution: social-security benefits, income taxes, upkeep of properties, insurance payments, old-age pensions, stock dividends, dental bills, legal obligations incurred prior to commitment, permission to release psychiatric case records to insurance companies or attorneys, permission for special visits from persons other than next of kin, etc. All of these issues have to be dealt with by the institution, even if only to pass the decisions on to those legally empowered to make them.

The staff are reminded of their obligations in these matters of standards and rights not only by their own internal superordinates but also by various watchdog agencies in the wider society and often by the kin of inmates. The material of their work can itself play this role. Some attendants in mental hospitals prefer to work on regressed wards because patients there tend to make fewer time-consuming requests than do patients on better wards who are in good contact. There are even phrases employed by the staff, such as the navy term 'sea lawyer', for denoting an inmate who demands treatment 'by the book'. Kin as critics present a special problem because, while inmates can be educated about the price they will pay for making demands on their own behalf, relations receive less tutoring in this regard and rush in with requests for inmates that inmates would blush to make for themselves.

The multiplicity of ways in which inmates must be considered ends in themselves, and the large number of inmates, forces upon the staff some of the classic dilemmas that must be faced by those who govern men. Since a total institution functions somewhat as a state, its staff suffers somewhat from the tribulations that beset governors.

In the case of any single inmate, the assurance that certain standards will be maintained in his own interests may require sacrifice of other standards; implied in this is a difficult weighing of ends. For example, if a suicidal inmate is to be kept alive, the staff may feel it necessary to keep him under constant surveillance or even tied to a chair in a small locked room. If a mental patient is to be kept from tearing at grossly irritated sores and repeating time and again a cycle of curing and disorder, the staff may feel it necessary to curtail the freedom of his hands. A patient who refuses to eat may have to be humiliated by forced feeding. If inmates of T B sanitaria are to be given an opportunity to recover, freedom of recreation must be curtailed.[43]

The standards of treatment that one inmate has a right to expect may conflict, of course, with the standards desired by another, giving rise to another set of governmental problems. Thus, in mental hospitals, if the grounds gate is to be kept open out of respect for those with town parole, then some other patients who otherwise could have been trusted on the grounds may have to be kept in locked wards. And if a canteen and mailbox are to be freely available to those on the grounds, then patients on a strict diet, or those who write threatening and obscene letters, will have to be denied liberty of the grounds.

The obligation of the staff to maintain certain humane standards of treatment for inmates presents problems in itself, but a further set of characteristic problems is found in the constant conflict between humane standards on one hand and institutional efficiency on the other. I will cite only one example. The personal possessions of an individual are an important part of the materials out of which he builds a self, but as an inmate the ease with which he can be managed by staff is likely to increase with the degree to which he is dispossessed. The remarkable efficiency with which a mental-hospital ward can adjust to a daily shift in number of resident patients is related to the fact that the comers and leavers do not come or leave with any properties but themselves and do not have any right to choose where they will be located.

43. Roth, 'What Is an Activity', op. cit.

Further, the efficiency with which the clothes of these patients can be kept clean and fresh is related to the fact that everyone's soiled clothing can be indiscriminately placed in one bundle, and laundered clothing can be redistributed not according to ownership but according to approximate size. Similarly, the quickest assurance that patients going on the grounds will be warmly dressed is to march them past a pile of the ward's allotment of coats, allowing no choice as to whether to wear one or which to wear, and requiring them for the same purposes of health to give up claim to these collectivized garments on returning to the ward. The very structure of a garment can be determined by the interests of efficiency, not self-enhancement, as the following trade advertisement suggests:

CHEERY, STURDY! SNAP-FASTENED BUILT-IN PANTY All-in-one garment, designed and tested by institutions for mental and retarded patients. Inhibits the exposure impulse, resists tearing. Slips on over head. No brassiere or other undergarment needed. Snap-fasteners at crotch aid toilet training. Pleasing patterns or 2-tones with round, V'or square neckline. Needs no ironing.[44]

Just as personal possessions may interfere with the smooth running of an institutional operation and be removed for this reason, so parts of the body may conflict with efficient management and the conflict may be resolved in favour of efficiency. If the heads of inmates are to be kept clean, and the possessor easily categorized, then a complete head shave is efficacious, despite the damage this does to appearance. On similar grounds, some mental hospitals have found it useful to extract the teeth of 'biters', give hysterectomies to promiscuous female patients, and perform lobotomies on chronic fighters. Flogging as a form of punishment on men-of-war expressed the same issue between organizational and humane interests:

One of the arguments advanced by officers of the Navy in favour of corporal punishment is this: it can be inflicted in a moment; it consumes no valuable time; and when the prisoner's shirt is put on, *that* is the last of it. Whereas, if another punishment were substituted, it would probably occasion a great waste of time and trouble, besides

44. Advertisement in *Mental Hospitals*, VI (1955), p. 20.

thereby begetting in the sailor an undue idea of his importance.[45]

I have suggested that people-work differs from other kinds of work because of the tangle of statuses and relationships that each inmate brings with him to the institution and because of the humane standards that must be maintained with respect to him. Another difference occurs when inmates have rights to visit off the grounds, for then the mischief they may do in civil society becomes something for which the institution has some responsibility. Given this responsibility, it is understandable that many total institutions tend to view off-grounds leave unfavourably. Still another type of difference between people-work and other kinds, and perhaps the most important difference of all, is that by the exercise of threat, reward, or persuasion, human objects can be given instructions and relied upon to carry them out on their own. The span of time during which these objects can be trusted to carry out planned actions without supervision will of course vary a great deal, but, as the social organization of back wards in mental hospitals teaches us, even in the limiting case of catatonic schizophrenics a considerable amount of such reliance is possible. Only the most complicated electronic equipment shares this capacity.

While human materials can never be as refractory as inanimate ones, their very capacity to perceive and follow out the plans of staff ensures that they can hinder the staff more effectively than inanimate objects can, for inanimate objects cannot purposely and intelligently thwart our plans (although we may momentarily react to them as if they had this capacity). Hence in prisons and on 'better' wards of mental hospitals guards have to be ready for organized efforts at escape and must constantly deal with attempts to bait them, 'frame' them, and otherwise get them into trouble; the guard's consequent anxiety is not alleviated by knowledge that the inmate may do these things merely to gain self-respect or to relieve boredom.[46] Even an old, weak mental patient has tremendous power in this regard; for example, by the simple

45. Melville, op. cit., p. 139.
46. For comments on the very difficult role of guard, see McCorkle and Korn, op. cit., pp. 93–4, and Gresham M. Sykes, 'The Corruption of Authority and Rehabilitation', *Social Forces*, XXXIV (1956), pp. 257–62.

expedient of locking his thumbs in his trouser pockets he can remarkably frustrate the efforts of an attendant to undress him. This is one reason why the staff tend to conceal decisions taken regarding the fate of inmates, for were the inmate to know the worst of what was planned for him, he might purposely and openly obstruct the smooth realization of his fate – thus, for example, mental patients being prepared for shock treatment may be told kindly tales and sometimes kept from seeing the room in which they will be treated.

A third general way in which human materials differ from other kinds, and hence present unique problems, is that however distant the staff tries to stay from these materials, such materials can become objects of fellow feeling and even affection. There is always the danger that an inmate will appear human; if what are felt to be hardships must be inflicted on the inmate, then sympathetic staff will suffer. (This, after all, is one rationale officers give for keeping social distance from enlisted men.) And, on the other hand, if an inmate breaks a rule, the staff's conceiving of him as a human being may increase their sense that injury has been done to their moral world: expecting a 'reasonable' response from a reasonable creature, the staff may feel incensed, affronted, and challenged when the inmate does not conduct himself properly.

The capacity of inmates to become objects of staff's sympathetic concern is linked to what might be called an involvement cycle that is sometimes recorded in total institutions. Starting at a point of social distance from inmates, a point from which massive deprivation and institutional trouble cannot easily be seen, the staff person finds he has no reason to refrain from building up a warm involvement in some inmates. This involvement, however, brings the staff member into a position to be hurt by what inmates do and what they suffer, and also brings him to a position from which he is likely to threaten the distant stand from inmates taken by his fellow staff members. In response, the sympathizing staff member may feel he has been 'burnt' and retreat into paper work, committee work, or other staff-enclosed routines. Once removed from the dangers of inmate contact, he may gradually cease to feel he has reason to be wary, and then the cycle of contact and withdrawal may be repeated again.

When we combine the fact that the staff are obliged to maintain certain standards of humane treatment for inmates with the fact that they may come to view inmates as reasonable, responsible creatures who are fitting objects for emotional involvement, we have the context for some of the quite special difficulties of people-work. In mental hospitals, there always seem to be some patients who dramatically act against their own obvious self-interest: they drink water they have themselves first polluted; they overstuff on Thanksgiving and Christmas, so that on these days there are bound to be a few ruptured ulcers and clogged esophagi; they rush headfirst against the wall; they tear out their own sutures after a minor operation; they flush down the toilet false teeth, without which they cannot eat and which take months to obtain; or they smash eyeglasses, without which they cannot see. In an effort to frustrate these visibly self-destructive acts, staff members may find themselves forced to manhandle these patients, creating an image of themselves as harsh and coercive just at the moment when they are attempting to prevent someone from doing to himself what they feel no human being should do to anyone. At such times, understandably, it is extremely difficult for the staff to keep their own emotions in control.

II

The special requirements of people-work establish the day's job for staff; the job itself is carried out in a special moral climate. The staff is charged with meeting the hostility and demands of the inmates, and what it has to meet the inmates with, in general, is the rational perspective espoused by the institution. We must therefore look at these perspectives.

The avowed goals of total institutions are not great in number: accomplishment of some economic goal; education and training; medical or psychiatric treatment; religious purification; protection of the wider community from pollution; and, as a student of prisons suggests, ...'*incapacitation, retribution, deterrence and reformation.*' ...[47] It is widely appreciated that total institutions

47. D. Cressey, 'Achievement of an Unstated Organizational Goal: An Observation on Prisons', *Pacific Sociological Review*, I (1958), p. 43.

typically fall considerably short of their official aims. It is less well appreciated that each of these official goals or charters seems admirably suited to provide a key to meaning – a language of explanation that the staff, and sometimes the inmates, can bring to every crevice of action in the institution. Thus, a medical frame of reference is not merely a perspective through which a decision concerning dosage can be determined and made meaningful; it is a perspective ready to account for all manner of decisions, such as the hours when hospital meals are served or the manner in which hospital linen is folded. Each official goal lets loose a doctrine, with its own inquisitors and its own martyrs, and within institutions there seems to be no natural check on the licence of easy interpretation that results. Every institution must not only make some effort to realize its official aims but must also be protected, somehow, from the tyranny of a diffuse pursuit of them, lest the exercise of authority be turned into a witch hunt. The phantom of 'security' in prisons and the staff actions justified in its name are instances of these dangers. Paradoxically, then, while total institutions seem the least intellectual of places, it is nevertheless here, at least recently, that concern about words and verbalized perspectives has come to play a central and often feverish role.

The interpretative scheme of the total institution automatically begins to operate as soon as the inmate enters, the staff having the notion that entrance is *prima facie* evidence that one must be the kind of person the institution was set up to handle. A man in a political prison must be traitorous; a man in a prison must be a lawbreaker; a man in a mental hospital must be sick. If not traitorous, criminal, or sick, why else would he be there?

This automatic identification of the inmate is not merely name-calling; it is at the centre of a basic means of social control. An illustration is provided in an early community study of a mental hospital:

The chief aim of this attendant culture is to bring about the control of patients – a control which must be maintained irrespective of patient welfare. This aim is sharply illuminated with respect to expressed desires or requests of patients. All such desires and requests, no matter how reasonable, how calmly expressed, or how politely stated, are regarded as evidence of mental disorder. Normality is never recognized by the attendant in a milieu where abnormality is the normal expectancy. Even though most of these behavioral manifestations are reported to the doctors, they, in most cases, merely support the judgments of the attendants. In this way, the doctors themselves help to perpetuate the notion that the essential feature of dealing with mental patients is in their control.[48]

When inmates are allowed to have face-to-face contact with staff, the contact will often take the form of 'gripes' or requests on the part of the inmate and justification for the prevailing restrictive treatment on the part of staff; such, for example, is the general structure of staff-patient interaction in mental hospitals. Having to control inmates and to defend the institution in the name of its avowed aims, the staff resort to the kind of all-embracing identification of the inmates that will make this possible. The staff problem here is to find a crime that will fit the punishment.

Further, the privileges and punishments the staff mete out are often phrased in a language that reflects the legitimated objectives of the institution, as when solitary confinement in prisons is called 'constructive meditation'. Inmates or low-level staff will have the special job of translating these ideological phrasings into the simple language of the privilege system, and vice versa. Belknap's discussion of what happens when a mental patient breaks a rule and is punished provides an illustration:

In the usual case of this kind, such things as impudence, insubordination, and excessive familiarity are translated into more or less professional terms, such as 'disturbed' or 'excited', and presented by the attendant to the physician as a medical status report. The doctor must then officially revoke or modify the patient's privileges on the ward or work out a transfer to another ward where the patient has to begin all over to work up from the lowest group. A 'good' doctor in the attendants' culture is one who does not raise too many questions about these translated medical terms.[49]

The institutional perspective is also applied to actions not clearly

48. J. Bateman and H. Dunham, 'The State Mental Hospital as a Specialized Community Experience', *American Journal of Psychiatry*, CV (1948–9), p. 446.

49. Belknap, op. cit., p. 170.

or usually subject to discipline. Thus Orwell reports that in his boarding school bedwetting was seen as a sign of 'dirtiness' and wickedness,[50] and that a similar perspective applied to disorders even more clearly physical.

I had defective bronchial tubes and a lesion in one lung which was not discovered till many years later. Hence I not only had a chronic cough, but running was a torment to me. In those days however, 'wheeziness', or 'chestiness', as it was called, was either diagnosed as imagination or was looked on as essentially a moral disorder, caused by overeating. 'You wheeze like a concertina,' Sim [the headmaster] would say disapprovingly as he stood behind my chair; 'You're perpetually stuffing yourself with food, that's why.'[51]

Chinese 'thought reform' camps are claimed to have carried this interpretative process to the extreme, translating the innocuous daily events of the prisoner's past into symptoms of counter-revolutionary action.[52]

Although there is a psychiatric view of mental disorder and an environmental view of crime and counter-revolutionary activity, both freeing the offender from moral responsibility for his offence, total institutions can little afford this particular kind of determinism. Inmates must be caused to *self-direct* themselves in a manageable way, and, for this to be promoted, both desired and undesired conduct must be defined as springing from the personal will and character of the individual inmate himself, and defined as something he can himself do something about. In short, each institutional perspective contains a personal morality, and in each total institution we can see in miniature the development of something akin to a functionalist version of moral life.

The translation of inmate behaviour into moralistic terms suited to the institution's avowed perspective will necessarily contain some broad presuppositions as to the character of human beings. Given the inmates of whom they have charge, and the processing that must be done to them, the staff tend to evolve

50. Orwell, op. cit., pp. 506–9.

51. ibid., p. 521.

52. See, for example, R. Lifton, '"Thought Reform" of Western Civilians in Chinese Communist Prisons', *Psychiatry*, XIX (1956), especially pp. 182–4.

what may be thought of as a theory of human nature. As an implicit part of institutional perspective, this theory rationalizes activity, provides a subtle means of maintaining social distance from inmates and a stereotyped view of them, and justifies the treatment accorded them.[53] Typically, the theory covers the 'good' and 'bad' possibilities of inmate conduct, the forms that messing up takes, the instructional value of privileges and punishments, and the 'essential' difference between staff and inmates. In armies, officers will have a theory about the relation between discipline and the obedience of men under fire, the qualities proper to men, the 'breaking point' of men, and the difference between mental sickness and malingering. And they will be trained into a particular conception of their own natures, as one ex-Guardsman suggests in listing the moral qualities expected of officers:

While much of the training was inevitably designed to promote physical fitness, there was nevertheless a strongly held belief that an Officer, whether fit or not, should always have so much in the way of pride (or 'guts') that he would never admit to physical inadequacy until he dropped dead or unconscious. This belief, a very significant one, was mystical both in its nature and intensity. During a crippling exercise at the end of the course two or three Officers fell out complaining of blisters or other mild indispositions. The Chief Instructor, himself a civilized and self-indulgent man, denounced them in round terms. An Officer, he said, simply could not and did not fall out. Willpower, if nothing else, should keep him going for ever. It was all a matter of 'guts'. There was an unspoken implication that, since other ranks could and did fall out, even though they were often physically tougher, the Officer belonged to a superior caste. I found it an accepted belief among Officers later on that they could perform physical feats or endure physical discomforts without it being in the least necessary for them to train or prepare for such things in the manner required of the private soldier. Officers, for example, just did not do P.T.: they did not

53. I derive this from Everett C. Hughes' review of Leopold von Wiese's *Spätlese*, in the *American Journal of Sociology*, LXI (1955), p. 182. A similar area is covered under the current anthropological term 'ethnopsychology', except that the unit to which it applies is a culture, not an institution. It should be added that inmates, too, acquire a theory of human nature, partly taking over the one employed by staff and partly developing a countering one of their own. In this connexion see in McCleery, op. cit., pp. 14–15, the very interesting description of the concept of 'rat' as evolved by prisoners.

need it; they were Officers and would endure to the very end, had they stepped straight on to the field from a sanatorium or a brothel.[54]

In prisons, we find a current conflict between the psychiatric and the moral-weakness theories of crime. In convents, we find theorries about the ways in which the spirit can be weak and strong and the ways in which its defects can be combated. Mental hospitals stand out here because the staff pointedly establish themselves as specialists in the knowledge of human nature, who diagnose and prescribe on the basis of this intelligence. Hence in the standard psychiatric textbooks there are chapters on 'psychodynamics' and 'psychopathology' which provide charmingly explicit formulations of the 'nature' of human nature.[55]

An important part of the theory of human nature in many total institutions is the belief that if the new inmate can be made to show extreme deference to staff immediately upon arrival, he will thereafter be manageable – that in submitting to these initial demands, his 'resistance' or 'spirit' is somehow broken. (This is one reason for the will-breaking ceremonies and welcome practices discussed earlier.) Of course, if inmates adhere to the same theory of human nature, then staff views of character will be confirmed. Recent studies of the conduct of American army personnel taken prisoner in the Korean War provide an example. In America there is a current belief that once a man is brought to the 'breaking point' he will thereafter be unable to show any resistance at all. Apparently this view of human nature, reinforced by training injunctions about the danger of any weakening at all, led some prisoners to give up all resistance once they had made a minor admission.[56]

54. Simon Raven, 'Perish by the Sword', *Encounter*, XII (May 1959), pp. 38–9.

55. The engulfing character of an institution's theory of human nature is currently nicely expressed in progressive psychiatric establishments. The theories originally developed to deal with inmates are there being applied more and more to the staff as well, so that low-level staff must do its penance in group psychotherapy and high-level staff in individual psychoanalysis. There is even some movement to bring in consulting sociological therapists for the institution as a whole.

56. See the useful paper by Albert Biderman, 'Social-Psychological Needs and "Involuntary" Behavior as Illustrated by Compliance in Interrogation', *Sociometry*, XXIII (1960), pp. 120–47.

A theory of human nature is of course only one aspect of the interpretative scheme offered by a total institution. A further area covered by institutional perspectives is work. Since on the outside work is ordinarily done for pay, profit, or prestige, the withdrawal of these motives means a withdrawal of certain interpretations of action and calls for new interpretations. In mental hospitals there are what are officially known as 'industrial therapy' and 'work therapy'; patients are put to tasks, typically mean ones, such as raking leaves, waiting on table, working in the laundry, and washing floors. Although the nature of these tasks derives from the working needs of the establishment, the claim presented to the patient is that these tasks will help him to relearn to live in society and that his capacity and willingness to handle them will be taken as diagnostic evidence of improvement.[57] The patient may himself perceive work in this light. A similar process of redefining the meaning of work is found in religious institutions, as the comments of a Poor Clare suggest:

This is another of the marvels of living in obedience. No one is ever doing anything more important than you are, if you are obeying. A broom, a pen, a needle are all the same to God. The obedience of the hand that plies them and the love in the heart of the nun who holds them are what make an eternal difference to God, to the nuns, and to all the world.[58]

People in the world are forced to obey manmade laws and workaday restrictions. Contemplative nuns freely elect to obey a monastic Rule inspired by God. The girl pounding her typewriter may be pounding for nothing but dollars' sake and wishing she could stop. The Poor Clare sweeping the monastery cloisters is doing it for God's sake and

57. It would be quite wrong to view these 'therapies' too cynically. Work such as that in a laundry or shoe-repair shop has its own rhythm and is managed often by individuals more closely connected with their trade than with the hospital; hence, very often, time spent at these tasks is much more pleasant than time spent on a dark, silent ward. Further, the notion of putting patients to 'useful' work seems so captivating a possibility in our society, that operations such as shoe-repair shops or mattress-making shops may come to be maintained, at least for a time, at an actual cost to the institution.

58. Sister Mary Francis, P.C., *A Right to be Merry* (New York: Sheed and Ward, 1956), p. 108.

prefers sweeping, at that particular hour, to any other occupation in the world.[59]

Although heavily institutionalized motives such as profit or economy may be obsessively pursued in commercial establishments,[60] these motives, and the implied frames of reference, may nevertheless function to restrain other types of interpretation. When the usual rationales of the wider society cannot be invoked, however, the field becomes dangerously open to all kinds of interpretative flights and excesses and, in consequence, to new kinds of tyranny.

I would like to add a final point about institutional perspectives. The management of inmates is typically rationalized in terms of the ideal aims or functions of the establishment, which entail humane technical services. Professionals are usually hired to perform these services, if only to save management the necessity of sending the inmates out of the institution for servicing, it being unwise 'for the monks to go abroad, for this is not at all healthful for their souls'.[61] Professionals joining the establishment on this basis are likely to become dissatisfied, feeling that they cannot here properly practise their calling and are being used as 'captives' to add professional sanction to the privilege system. This seems to be a classic cry.[62] In many mental hospitals there is a record of disgruntled psychiatrists asserting they are leaving so that they can do psychotherapy. Often a special psychiatric service, such as group psychotherapy, psychodrama, or art therapy, is introduced with great support from higher hospital management; then slowly interest is transferred elsewhere, and the pro-

59. ibid., p. 99. The application of an alternate meaning to poverty is of course a basic strategy in the religious life. Ideals of Spartan simplicity have also been used by radical political and military groups; currently, beatniks impute a special meaning to a show of poverty.

60. A good representation of this interpretative spread and thickness is given in Bernard Malamud's novel about management problems in a small grocery store: *The Assistant* (New York: New American Library, 1958).

61. *The Holy Rule of Saint Benedict*, Ch. 66.

62. For example, Harvey Powelson and Reinhard B. Bendix, 'Psychiatry in Prison', *Psychiatry*, XIV (1951), pp. 73–86, and Waldo W. Burchard, 'Role Conflicts of Military Chaplains', *American Sociological Review*, XIX (1954), pp. 528–35.

fessional in charge finds that gradually his job has been changed into a species of public relations work – his therapy given only token support except when visitors come to the institution and higher management is concerned to show how modern and complete the facilities are.

Professionals, of course, are not the only staff grouping in a somewhat difficult relation to the official goals of the establishment. Those members of staff who are in continuous contact with inmates may feel that they, too, are being set a contradictory task, having to coerce inmates into obedience while at the same time giving the impression that humane standards are being maintained and the rational goals of the institution realized.

INSTITUTIONAL CEREMONIES

I HAVE described total institutions from the point of view of inmates and, briefly, from the point of view of staff. Each point of
view has as a crucial element an image of the other grouping. Although there is this image-of-the-other, it is seldom of the kind
that leads to sympathetic identification – except perhaps on the
part of those inmates, previously described, who take a trusty
role and seriously 'identify with the aggressor'. When unusual
intimacies and relationships do occur across the staff-inmate line,
we know that involvement cycles may follow and all kinds of
awkward reverberations are likely to occur,[63] with a sub-
version of authority and social distance that again gives one the
impression of an incest taboo operating within total institutions.

In addition to illicit or questionable 'personal' ties that cross
the staff-inmate line, a second irregular type of contact between
staff and inmate occurs. Staff, unlike inmates, hold some aspects
of their life separate from the institution – even though these may
be located on or near the grounds. At the same time it is understood that inmates' work time is of little value to inmates
themselves and is subject to the discretion of staff. Under these
circumstances role segregation seems difficult to maintain, and
inmates find themselves performing menial personal services for
staff – such as gardening, house-painting, house-cleaning, and
baby sitting. Because these services are not part of the official
frame of reference of the institution, the staff are forced to give
some consideration to their servants and are unable to maintain
the usual distance from them. The ordinary restrictions of institutional life make inmates usually quite happy to break through

63. See E. Goffman, *The Presentation of Self in Everyday Life* (New York:
Anchor Books, 1959), pp. 200–204; McCorkle and Korn, op. cit., pp. 93–4.
The leading study here is Alfred H. Stanton and Morris S. Schwartz, 'The
Management of a Type of Institutional Participation in Mental Illness',
Psychiatry, XII (1949), pp. 12–26.

staff-inmate alignments in this manner. Lawrence provides a military example:

The Sergeant Major set an example of misuse, when he led the last fatigue man in the rank to his wife's house, and had him black the grate and mind the children, while she shopped. 'Gave me a slab of jam-tart, she did,' boasted Garner, lightly forgiving the crying infant because of the belly-full he'd won.[64]

In addition to these incidental ways of crossing the line, every total institution seems to develop a set of institutionalized practices – whether spontaneously or by imitation – through which staff and inmates come close enough together to get a somewhat favourable image of the other and to identify sympathetically with the other's situation. These practices express unity, solidarity, and joint commitment to the institution rather than differences between the two levels.

In form these institutionalized get-togethers are characterized by a release from the formalities and the task orientation that govern inmate-staff contacts and by a softening of the usual chain of command. Often participation is relatively voluntary. Given the usual roles, these activities represent 'role releases';[65] of course, given the pervasive effect of inmate-staff distance, any alteration in the direction of expressing solidarity automatically represents a role release. It is possible to speculate on the many functions of these comings together, but the explanations seem far less impressive than the singular way in which these practices keep cropping up in every kind of total institution and in what would seem to be the poorest possible soil. One is led to feel that there must be very good reasons for these practices, even if they seem difficult to find.

One of the most common forms of institutional ceremony is

64. Lawrence, op. cit., p. 40. For a concentration-camp version, see Kogon, op. cit., pp. 84–6. As a qualification it should be added that in some total institutions, notably ships, these personal services may be legitimated as part of the proper duties of one of the ratings; the same is true of the role of batman in the British Army. But in these exceptions the staff may have little life that is not official.

65. This term was suggested by Everett C. Hughes and is employed in an unpublished paper, 'Social Control and Institutional Catharsis', by Joseph Gusfield.

the house organ – typically a weekly newspaper or a monthly magazine. Usually all the contributors are recruited from within inmate ranks, resulting in a kind of mock hierarchy, while supervision and censorship are provided by a member of the staff who is relatively congenial to the inmates yet reliably loyal to his fellow officials. The printed content is such as to draw a circle around the institution and to give the accent of public reality to the world within.

Two kinds of material that appear in the house organ may be mentioned. First, there is 'local news'. This includes reports about recent institutional ceremonies, as well as reference to 'personal' events, such as birthdays, promotions, trips, and deaths, occurring to members of the institution, especially high-placed or well-known members of the staff. This content is of a congratulatory or condolence-offering character, presumably expressing for the whole institution its sympathetic concern for the lives of the individual members. Here is an interesting aspect of role segregation: since the institutionally relevant roles of a member (e.g., doctor) tend to set him off against whole categories of other members (e.g., attendants and patients), these roles cannot be used as a vehicle for expressing institutional solidarity; instead, use tends to be made of non-relevant roles, especially those such as parent and spouse that are imaginable, if not possible, for all categories.

Second, there is material that can reflect an editorial view. This includes: news from the outside world bearing on the social and legal status of inmates and ex-inmates, accompanied by appropriate comment; original essays, short stories, and poetry; editorials. The writing is done by inmates but expresses the official view of the functions of the institution, the staff's theory of human nature, an idealized version of inmate-staff relationships, and the stance an ideal convert ought to take – in short, it presents the institutional line.

The house organ, however, survives in the delicacy of a nice balance. The staff allows itself to be interviewed, written about, and read about by inmates, thus coming under some slight control of the writers and readers; at the same time, inmates are given an opportunity to show that they are high enough on the human scale to handle the official language and the official line with educated competence.[66] Contributors, on the other hand, guarantee to follow the official ideology, presenting it for inmates by inmates. Interestingly enough, inmates who make this compact with the staff often do not cease to affirm the counter-mores. They introduce whatever open criticism of the institution the censors will permit; they add to this by means of oblique or veiled writing, or pointed cartoons; and, among their cronies, they may take a cynical view of their contribution, claiming that they write because it provides a 'soft' job setting or a good means of earning release recommendations.

Although house organs have been customary for some time, it is only recently that a somewhat similar form of role release has appeared in total institutions; I refer here to the several forms of 'self-government' and 'group therapy'. Typically, the inmates speak the lines and a congenial member of the staff performs the supervision. Again, a kind of compact between inmates and staff is found. The inmates are given the privilege of spending some time in a relatively 'unstructured' or equalitarian milieu, and even the right to voice complaints. In return they are expected to become less loyal to the counter-mores and more receptive to the ideal-for-self that the staff defines for them.

Inmate use of the official staff language and staff philosophy in discussing or publishing gripes is a mixed blessing for the staff. Inmates can manipulate the staff's own rationalization of the institution and through this threaten the social distance between the two groupings. Hence in mental hospitals we find the engaging phenomenon of the staff using stereotyped psychiatric terminology in talking to each other or to patients but chiding patients for being 'intellectualistic' and for avoiding the issues when they use this language, too. Perhaps the distinctive thing about this group-therapy form of institutional role release is that academically oriented professionals are interested in it, so that there already is more literature on this aspect of total institutions than on most other aspects combined.

A somewhat different type of institutional ceremony is found in the annual party (sometimes held more than once a year) at

66. The scholarly legal petitions, written by inmates, which circulate in many prisons and mental hospitals, seem to serve the same function.

which staff and inmates 'mix' through standard forms of sociability such as eating together, party games, or dancing. At such times staff and inmates will have the licence to 'take liberties' across the caste line, and social reachings may be expressed through sexual ones.[67] In some cases this liberty may be extended to the point of ritual role reversal, during which staff wait table for inmates and perform other menial services for them.[68]

Often linked with the annual party in total institutions is the Christmas celebration. Once a year inmates will decorate the establishment with easily removable decorations partly supplied by the staff, in this way banishing from the living quarters what an extra-special meal will then banish from the table. Small gifts and indulgences will be distributed among the inmates; some work duties will be cancelled; visitor time may be increased and restrictions on leave-taking decreased. In general, the rigours of institutional life for the inmates will be relaxed for a day. A British prison version may be cited:

The authorities did their best to cheer us. On Christmas morning we sat down to a breakfast of cornflakes, sausages, bacon, beans, fried bread, margarine and bread and marmalade. At midday we were given roast pork, Christmas pudding and coffee, and at supper, mince pies and coffee, instead of the nightly mug of cocoa.

The halls were decorated with paper streamers, balloons and bells, and each had its Christmas tree. There were extra cinema shows in the gymnasium. Two of the officers each presented me with a cigar. I was allowed to send and receive some greetings telegrams, and for the first time since I had been in prison, I had enough cigarettes to smoke.[69]

67. Of course, the 'office party' found in establishments not of the total kind have similar dynamics, and were the first no doubt to give rise to comment. See, for example, Gusfield, op. cit. The best reports on these events are still to be found in fiction. See, for example, Nigel Balchin's description of a factory party in *Private Interests* (Boston: Houghton-Mifflin, 1953), pp. 47–71; Angus Wilson's description of a hotel staff-guest party in his short story 'Saturnalia' in *The Wrong Set* (New York: William Morrow, 1950), pp. 68–89; and J. Kerkhoff's version of the annual party in a mental hospital, op. cit., pp. 224–5.

68. See Max Gluckman, *Custom and Conflict in Africa* (Glencoe, Ill.: The Free Press, 1955), ch. v, 'The Licence in Ritual', pp. 109–36.

69. Heckstall-Smith, op. cit., p. 199. See also McCreery in Hassler, op. cit., p. 157. For holiday licence in a mental hospital, see Kerkhoff, op. cit.,

In America, at Easter, the Fourth of July, Hallowe'en, and Thanksgiving, a watered-down version of the Christmas celebration may occur.

An interesting institutional ceremony, often connected with the annual party and the Christmas celebration, is the institutional theatrical.[70] Typically the players are inmates and the directors of the production are staff, but sometimes 'mixed' casts are found. The writers are usually members of the institution, whether staff or inmate, and hence the production can be full of local references, imparting through the private use of this public form a special sense of the reality of events internal to the institution. Very frequently the offering will consist of satirical skits that lampoon well-known members of the institution, especially high-placed staff members.[71] If, as is frequent, the inmate community is one-sexed, then some of the players are likely to perform in the costume and burlesqued role of members of the other sex. Limits of licence are often tested, the humour being a little more broad than some members of the staff would like to see tolerated. Melville, in commenting on the relaxation of discipline during and immediately after a theatrical on board ship, has the following to say:

And here White Jacket must moralize a bit. The unwonted spectacle of the row of gun-room officers mingling with *the people* in applauding a mere seaman like Jack Chase filled me at the time with the most pleasurable emotions. It is a sweet thing, thought I, to see these officers confess a human brotherhood with us, after all; a sweet thing to mark their cordial appreciation of the many merits of my matchless Jack. Ah! they are noble fellows all round, and I do not know but I have wronged them sometimes in my thoughts.[72]

---

pp. 185, 256. The same on a man-of-war is presented by Melville, op. cit., pp. 95–6.

70. See, for example, the prison version in Norman, op, cit., pp. 69–70

71. For an example of prisoners lampooning guards and the prison governor, see Dendrickson and Thomas, op. cit., pp. 110–11.

72. Melville, op. cit., p. 101. (Italics in the original.) Melville then proceeds to comment bitterly that soon after this role release the officers seemed to have a capacity to 'ship their quarter-deck faces', reverting fully to their usual strictness. See also Kerkhoff, op. cit., p. 229, and Heckstall-Smith, op. cit., pp. 195–9.

In addition to satirical sketches, there may be dramatic presentations recounting the bad historical past of similar total institutions, as a contrast to the presumably better present.[73] The audience for the production will pointedly contain both inmates and staff, although often ecologically segregated, and in some cases outsiders, too, may be permitted to come.

The fact that the institutional theatrical is sometimes presented before an outside audience no doubt provides inmates and staff with a contrasting background against which to sense their unity. Other kinds of institutional ceremony fulfil this function, too, often more directly. Increasingly there is the practice of the annual open house, during which the relatives of members, or even the public at large, may be invited to inspect the premises. They can then see for themselves that high humane standards are being maintained. At such times staff and inmates tend to be on visibly good terms with one another, the usual price for which is some tempering of ordinary stringencies.

Open house is a possibility and a likely success because it occurs in the context of an 'institutional display'. Sometimes this display or front is directed to an internal audience, most likely high staff members, as an ex-mental patient illustrates:

Breakfast over, some of the patients dressed and left the ward, reappearing shortly afterwards armed with mops and brushes with which they began, in a queer mechanical way, to clean the floors; like robots that had just been wound up. This sudden activity surprised me. The probationers rushed about bringing bright new rugs to spread on the polished boards. As if by magic, one or two lockers made a belated appearance and the flowers of mid-summer blossomed unexpectedly around. The ward was unrecognizable, so different did it seem. I wondered if the doctors ever saw it in its usual bareness, and was equally

73. Neither the 'before' nor the 'after' need have much relation to the facts, since each version is meant to clarify a situation, not to measure it, and in any case the 'past' may be slyly presented because of its similarity to the present. I have seen mental patients from good wards give a well-advertised, public stage performance of conditions which presumably used to prevail in backward mental hospitals. Victorian costumes were used. The audience consisted of psychiatrically enlightened well-wishers from the environing city. A few buildings away from where the audience sat, equally bad conditions could be observed in the flesh. In some cases, the performers knew their roles well because they had played them.

surprised when, after their visit, all this glory departed as swiftly as it had appeared.[74]

In the main, institutional display seems to be addressed to visitors. Sometimes the focus of concern is the visit to a particular inmate by a particular outsider. Often outsiders have not been initiated into hospital ways and, as suggested earlier, can make embarrassing demands. Here the inmate himself may play an important role in the institution's presentation. A physician-student of mental hospitals provides an example:

> The situation can be clarified by asking what happened when such a patient received a visitor. First the visitor was announced by telephone from the central office of the hospital. Then the patient concerned was taken out of restraint, bathed, and dressed. When ready for display the patient was taken to a 'visiting room' from which the ward could not be seen. If too intelligent to be trusted the patient was never left alone with the visitor. In spite of such precaution, however, suspicions were sometimes aroused, and it then became the duty of all the ward attendants to keep the situation under control.[75]

The visiting room in some total institutions is important here. Both décor and conduct in these places are typically much closer to outside standards than are those that prevail in the inmate's actual living quarters. The view of inmates that outsiders get thus helps to decrease the pressure these outsiders might otherwise bring to bear on the institution. It is a melancholy human fact that after a time all three parties – inmate, visitor, and staff – realize that the visiting room presents a dressed-up view, realize that the other parties realize this, too, and yet all tacitly agree to continue the fiction.

Institutional display may also be directed to visitors in general, giving them an 'appropriate' image of the establishment – this image being calculated to allay their vague dread about involuntary establishments. In the guise of being shown all, the visitors are of course likely to be shown only the more prepossessing, co-operative inmates and the more prepossessing parts of the establishment.[76] In large mental hospitals, modern treatment such as

74. Johnson and Dodds, op. cit., p. 92.

75. J. M. Grimes, M.D., *When Minds Go Wrong* (Chicago: published by the author, 1951), p. 81.

76. For a prison example, see Cantine and Rainer, op. cit., p. 62.

psychodrama or dance therapy may come to play a special role in this regard, as already suggested, with the therapist and his crew of regular patients developing the kind of capacity to perform before strangers that comes from constant experience. Furthermore, a small group of pet inmates may for years handle the task of escorting visitors around the institution's Potemkin village. Visitors can easily take the loyalty and social skills of these receptionists as a sample of the character of the entire inmate group. The right of staff to limit, inspect, and censor outgoing mail, and the frequent rule against writing anything negative about the institution, help to maintain the visitors' view of the establishment – and also alienate inmates from those on the outside to whom they cannot write frankly. Often the physical remoteness of the establishment from the homes of the inmates' kin functions not only to conceal 'conditions' on the inside but also to transform a family visit into something of a festive excursion, for which it will be feasible for the staff to make ample preparation.

It is possible, of course, for a visitor to be an official one, part of the institutional connexion between the highest staff officer and an agency responsible for controlling a whole class of institutions; then we can expect the preparation of a display to be especially elaborate. An example from British prison life (in the writer's prison lingo) may be cited:

Every now and again this nick like all other nicks in the country, would get a visit from the commissioner. Now this is a very big day in the life of screws and the governors, the day before he is due to arrive they start haveing a big clean up, all the floors are scrubed and the brasses are polished, also the recesses are give a good clean out. The exersize yard is swept and the flower beds are weeded and we are told to make sure our peters are clean and tiedy.

At last the great day is here. The Commissioner usualy wears a black over coat and black Antoney Edden hat even in the summer., he also quite often carrys an umbreler. I don't realy know why they make such a fuss of him as all he does is come and have lunch with the governor have a little look around the nick get in his big car and drive off again. Some times he comes round just as we are being fed, and may pick on some one and say. 'What's the food like? any complaints?'

You look at the governor and the chief in turn (for they are his constant companions while he is in the nick) you then answer. 'No complaints; sir.'[77]

Whatever such visits do for everyday standards, they do seem to serve as a reminder to everyone in the establishment that the institution is not completely a world of its own but bears some connexion, bureaucratic and subordinated, to structures in the wider world. Institutional display, whatever its audience, can also convey to inmates that they are connected with what is the best institution of its kind. Inmates seem surprisingly ready to believe this of their institution. Through such a belief, of course, they can feel they have a status in the wider world, even though through the very condition that exiles them from it.

The development of institutional display teaches us something in general about the symbolization process. First, the displayed part of the institution is likely to be the new, up-to-date part of the institution, which will change as new practices or equipment are added. Thus, when a new ward building is commissioned for use in a mental hospital, the staff of the previously 'new' building may relax in the knowledge that their role as model staff persons and official greeters has been passed along to someone else. Second, display certainly need not be connected with frankly ceremonial aspects of the institution, such as flower beds and starched curtains, but often stresses utilitarian objects such as the latest kitchen equipment, or an elaborate surgical suite; in fact the display function of such equipment may be part of the reason for acquiring it. Finally, each item of display will necessarily have substantive implications; although these can hardly equal the impression the item creates as display, they can none the less be significant. The display of photographs in the lobbies of total establishments, showing the cycle of activities the ideal inmate goes through with the ideal staff, often has extremely little to do with the facts of institutional life, but at least a few inmates spent a pleasant morning posing for the pictures. The inmate-painted mural that prisons, mental hospitals, and other establishments pridefully display in a conspicuous place is not evidence that inmates as a whole were encouraged in art work, or felt

77. Norman, op. cit., p. 103.

creatively inspired in the setting, but it does provide evidence that at least one inmate was allowed to throw himself into his work.[78] The food served on inspection and open-house days can provide at least a day's respite from the usual fare.[79] The favourable view of the establishment conveyed in the house organ and the theatricals carries at least some validity in terms of the round of life of the small fraction of inmates who participate in fabricating these ceremonies. And a prize admission building containing several comfortable admission wards can provide visitors with an impression that is correct for an appreciable fraction of the inmate population.

It might be added that the dynamics of appearance involve more than simple contrast between display and reality. In many total institutions punishments are meted out that are not legitimated by the rulings. These penalties are typically administered in a closed cell or some other place away from the attention of most of the inmates and most of the staff. Although these actions may not be frequent, they do tend to occur in a structured way, as a known or hinted consequence of certain types of transgression. These events are to the daily round in the institution what the daily round is to the display put on for outsiders, and all three aspects of reality – that which is concealed from inmates, that which is revealed to inmates, and that which is shown to visitors – must be considered together, three closely connected and differently functioning parts of a whole.

I have suggested that individual visits, open house, and inspections allow outsiders to see that everything is all right on the inside. Some other institutional practices offer the same opportunity. For example, there is an interesting arrangement between total institutions and stage performers who are amateurs or

78. An exemplary case of an inmate exploiting the public relations value of his hobby is the ornithological laboratory assembled by prisoner Robert Stroud at Leavenworth (see Gaddis, op. cit.). As one might expect, artist inmates have sometimes refused to cooperate, declining to accept liberty to paint in exchange for producing something that could be used by staff as evidence of the over-all character of the establishment. See Naeve, op. cit., pp. 51–5.

79. For example, Cantine and Rainer, op. cit., p. 61; Dendrickson and Thomas, op. cit., p. 70.

ex-professionals. The institution provides a stage and guarantees an appreciative audience; the performers contribute a free show. There can be such a compelling need of each for the services of the other that the relationship may pass beyond the matter of personal taste and become almost symbiotic.[80] In any case, while the members of the institution are watching the performers, the performers can see that staff-inmate relations are sufficiently harmonious for staff and patients to assemble together for what looks like a voluntary evening of unregimented recreation.

Institutional ceremonies that occur through such media as the house organ, group meetings, open house, and charitable performances presumably fulfil latent social functions; some of these seem particularly clear in another kind of institutional ceremony, intermural sports. The inside team tends to be a group of all-stars chosen by intramural contest among all inmates. By competing well with outsiders, the all-stars take roles that palpably fall outside the stereotype of what an inmate is – since team sport requires such qualities as intelligence, skill, perseverance, cooperativeness, and even honour – and these roles are taken right in the teeth of outsiders and staff observers. In addition, the outsider team, and any supporters it manages to bring into the grounds, are forced to see that there are natural places on the inside where natural things go on. In exchange for being allowed to

80. We appreciate how needful total institutions are of entertainment charity, but we tend to be less aware of how desperately non-professional entertainers need audiences for whom to be charitable. For example, the mental hospital I studied apparently had the only stage in the vicinity large enough for all the members of a particular dancing school to perform on at once. Some of the parents of the students did not particularly like coming onto the hospital grounds, but if the school was to have any ensemble numbers, the hospital stage had to be used. In addition, fee-paying parents expected their child to appear in the annual school show, regardless of how much training the child had had, or even in fact whether she was old enough to absorb training. Some numbers in the show, then, required an extremely indulgent audience. Patients can supply this, since most patients in the audience are marched to the auditorium under the discipline of an attendant; once there, they will watch anything under the same discipline, since infraction of rules may lead to cancellation of the privilege of leaving the ward on such occasions. The same kind of desperate bond ties the hospital audience to a group of mild office workers who belong to a bell-ringing choir.

demonstrate these things about themselves, inmates through their intermural team convey some things about the institution. In pursuing what is defined as an uncoercible endeavour, the inmate team demonstrates to outsiders and observing inmates that the staff, in this setting at least, are not tyrannical, and that a team of inmates is ready to take on the role of representing the whole institution and allowed to do so. By vocal support of the home team, both staff and inmates show a mutual and similar involvement in the institutional entity.[81] Incidentally, staff may not only coach these inmate teams but also participate on them occasionally, opening themselves up for the period of the game to the remarkable forgetfulness of social differences that can be generated in sports. Where intermural sports are not held, intramural competition may be substituted, with visitors coming in from the outside as a kind of symbolic team to watch, referee, and present the prizes.[82]

Sunday services and Sunday amusements are sometimes set in opposition to each other; in total institutions this can partly be understood in terms of an unnecessary duplication of function. Like sports events and charity performances, a religious service is a time when the unity of staff and inmates can be demonstrated by showing that in certain non-relevant roles both are members of the same audience vis-à-vis the same outside performer.

In all instances of unified ceremonial life that I have mentioned, staff are likely to play more than a supervisory role. Often a high-ranking officer attends as a symbol of management and (it is hoped) of the whole establishment. He dresses well, is moved by the occasion, and gives smiles, speeches, and handshakes. He dedicates new buildings on the grounds, gives his blessing to new equipment, judges contests, and hands out awards. When acting in this capacity, his interaction with inmates will take a special benign form; inmates are likely to show embarrassment and respect, and he is likely to display an avuncular interest in them. One of the functions of inmates who are well known within the institution is to provide ranking members of staff with subjects

81. See, for example, the comments on prison sports by Behan, op. cit., pp. 327–9.
82. For a prison example, see Norman, op. cit., pp. 119–20.

whom they know enough about to use as reciprocals for the avuncular role. In our very large and benevolently oriented mental hospitals, executive officers may be required to spend a good portion of their time putting in an appearance at these ceremonial occasions, providing us with some of the last occasions in modern society in which to observe a lord-of-the-manor role. The gentry aspects of these ceremonies, incidentally, should not be taken lightly, since the model for some of them seems to derive from the 'annual fête' which joined the tenants, servants, and masters associated with a 'great house' in competitive flower shows, sports, and even dances with 'mixing' of some kind.[83]

Some final comments should be added about these institutional ceremonies. They tend to occur with well-spaced periodicity and to give rise to some social excitement. All the groupings in the establishment join in, regardless of rank or position – but are given a place that expresses their position. These ceremonial practices are well suited to a Durkheimian analysis: a society dangerously split into inmates and staff can through these ceremonies hold itself together. The content of these ceremonies supports this same kind of functionalist interpretation. For example, there is often a hint or a splash of rebellion in the role that inmates take in these ceremonies. Whether through a sly article, a satirical sketch, or overfamiliarity during a dance, the subordinate in some way profanes the superordinate. Here we can follow Max Gluckman's analysis and argue that the very toleration of this skittishness is a sign of the strength of the establishment state.

Hence to act the conflicts, whether directly or by inversion or in other symbolical forms, emphasizes the social cohesion within which the conflicts exist.[84]

To act out one's rebellion before the authorities at a time

83. For a recent statement, complete with a report of skits put on by servants in mockery of masters, see, M. Astor, 'Childhood at Cliveden', *Encounter*, XIII (September 1959), pp. 27–8. Fêtes involving a whole village and sets of local gentry are, of course, described in many English novels, for example, L. P. Hartley's *The Go-Between*. A good fictional treatment is Alan Sillitoe's *The Loneliness of the Long-Distance Runner*.

84. Gluckman, op. cit., p. 125. See also his *Rituals of Rebellion in South-East Africa*, The Frazer Lecture, 1952 (Manchester: Manchester University Press, 1954).

when this is legitimate is to exchange conspiracy for expression.

But a simple functionalist analysis of institutional rituals is not wholly convincing, except in the effect that apparently results occasionally from group therapy. In many cases it is a nice question whether these role releases create any staff-inmate solidarity at all. Staff typically complain to each other of their boredom with these ceremonies and their obligation to participate because of their own *noblesse oblige* or, worse still, because of that of their superiors. Inmates often participate because, wherever the ceremony is held, they will be more comfortable and less restricted there than where they otherwise would be. Further, inmates sometimes participate to gain the eye of staff and to earn an early release. A total institution perhaps needs collective ceremonies because it is something more than a formal organization; but its ceremonies are often pious and flat, perhaps because it is something less than a community.

Whatever a ceremony offers the members of a total institution, it offers something appreciable to students of these organizations. In temporarily modifying the usual relation between staff and inmate, ceremony demonstrates that the difference in character between the two groupings is not inevitable and unalterable. However flat (and however functional), ceremony does mark a putting aside and even a reversal of the usual social drama, and so reminds us that what was put aside has a dramaturgical, not a material character. Intransigence, collective teasing of staff, and personal involvements that cross the staff-inmate line all similarly suggest the social reality in a total institution is precarious. I think we should not be surprised by these weaknesses in the staging of grim social distance but rather wonder that more flaws do not appear.

Starting with aims, regulations, offices, and roles, establishments of any kind seem to end up by adding depth and colour to these arrangements. Duties and economic rewards are allocated, but so, at the same time, are character and being. In total establishments the self-defining aspects of office seem to be carried to an extreme. In becoming a member, one becomes thought of as possessing certain essential traits and qualities of character;

moreover, these traits will differ radically, depending on whether one has joined staff or inmates.

The role of staff and the role of inmate cover every aspect of life. But these fully rounded characterizations must be played by civilians already deeply trained in other roles and other possibilities of relationship. The more the institution encourages the assumption that staff and inmate are of profoundly different human types (as, for example, by rules prohibiting informal social intercourse across the staff-inmate line) and the more profound the drama of difference between staff and inmate, the more incompatible the show becomes with the civilian repertoire of the players, and the more vulnerable to it.

There are grounds, then, for claiming that one of the main accomplishments of total institutions is staging a difference between two constructed categories of persons – a difference in social quality and moral character, a difference in perceptions of self and other. Thus every social arrangement in a mental hospital seems to point to the profound difference between a staff doctor and a mental patient; in a prison, between an official and a convict; and in military units (especially élite ones), between officers and men. Here, surely, is a magnificent social achievement, even though the similarity of the players, to which institutional ceremonies attest, can be expected to create some staging problems and therefore some personal strain.

I would like to mention one symptom of these staging problems. In total institutions we characteristically obtain identity anecdotes. Inmates tell of times they were mistaken for staff members and carried off the misidentification for a while, or of times they mistook a staff member for an inmate; staff persons similarly recount times when they were mistaken for inmates. We find identity joking, when a member of one group briefly acts like a member of the other, or briefly treats a co-member as someone of the other category, for the avowed purpose of amusement. Annual skits satirizing staff are one source of this joking; uneventful moments of horseplay during the day are another. And we also find identity scandals, a dwelling on cases where a person started out as a member of the staff, was disgraced in some way, and became a member of the inmate group in the same (or same kind of) institution. I assume these identity concerns point to the difficulty of sustaining a drama of difference between persons who could in many cases reverse roles and play on the other side. (In fact, these persons do engage in playful role reversal.) It is not clear what problems these ceremonies solve, but it is clear what problems they point to.

QUALIFICATIONS AND
CONCLUSIONS

I

I HAVE considered total institutions in terms of a single basic articulation: inmates and staff. Having done this, I am in a position to ask what this view leaves out and what it distorts.

In a closer study of total institutions it would be important to ask about the typical differentiation of role that occurs *within* each of the two main groups,[85] and to ask about the institutional function of these more specialized positions. Some of these special roles have been mentioned in discussing special institutional tasks: someone on the staff will have to be the official representative of the institution in the councils of the wider society and will have to develop a non-institutional polish in order to do this effectively; someone on staff will have to deal with visitors and other connexions of the inmates; someone will have to offer professional services; and someone will have to spend time in relatively close contact with inmates. Someone may even have to provide a personal symbol of the institution for the inmates – a symbol on which they may project many different kinds of emotion.[86] A close treatment of total institutions should give systematic attention to these intra-category differences.

There are two aspects of intra-group role differentiation that I would like to consider here, both having to do with the dynamics of the lowest level of staff. One special characteristic of this group

85. A treatment of role differentiation among prisoners may be found in Sykes, *Society of Captives*, ch. v, 'Argot Roles', pp. 84–108, and his 'Men, Merchants, and Toughs: A Study of Reactions to Imprisonment', *Social Problems*, IV (1956), pp. 130–38. For staff-defined types among mental-hospital patients, see Otto von Mering and S. H. King, *Remotivating the Mental Patient* (New York: Russell Sage Foundation, 1957), especially pp. 27–47, 'A Social Classification of Patients'.

86. The dynamics of this process are outlined in Freud's well-known *Group Psychology and the Analysis of the Ego*. For one application, see Etzioni, op. cit., p. 123. There are other such targets of projection, for example, the team mascot, and perhaps they should all be considered together.

is that they are likely to be the long-term employees and hence the tradition carriers, while higher staff, and even inmates, may have a high rate of turnover.[87] In addition, it is this group that must personally present the demands of the institution to the inmates. They can come, then, to deflect the hate of inmates from higher staff persons and make it feasible, should an inmate break through to contact with a higher staff person, for this person to grant avuncular kindness and even dispensations.[88] These acts of clemency are possible simply because, like all uncles, higher staff do not have the immediate task of disciplining inmates, and their contacts with inmates are so few that this leniency does not disrupt general discipline. I think that inmates very generally obtain some sense of security from the feeling, however illusory, that although most staff persons are bad, the man at the top is really good – but perhaps merely hoodwinked by those under him. (An expression of this appears in popular stories and movies involving police: the bottom levels may be sadistic, prejudiced, or corrupt, but the man at the top of the organization is 'O.K.'.) This is a nice example of what Everett Hughes refers to as 'the moral division of labor', for here a difference in the task performed by the individual clearly entails a difference in the moral attributes imputed to him.

The second aspect of role differentiation among staff that I want to consider has to do with deference patterns. In civil society the interpersonal rituals that persons accord one another while in each other's immediate physical presence have a crucial component of official spontaneity. The giver is obliged to perform the ritual in an uncalculated, immediate, unthinking fashion if it is to be a valid expression of his presumed regard for the recipient, else how could these acts 'express' inward feelings? The giver can manage this because he learned the quite standardized deference rituals of his society so early in his life that by adult years they are second nature. Now since the deference the giver shows a recipient is supposed to be a direct and free expression,

87. See, for example, Belknap, op. cit., p. 110.

88. See, for example, Elliott Jaques, 'Social Systems as a Defence against Persecutory and Depressive Anxiety', in Melanie Klein, *et al.*, *New Directions in Psycho-Analysis* (London: Tavistock, 1955), p. 483.

the recipient can hardly demand proper deference should it not be forthcoming. Action can be coerced, but a coerced show of feeling is only a show. An affronted recipient can take action against the person who is insufficiently deferential but typically must disguise the specific reason for this corrective action. Only children, presumably, can be openly sanctioned by the recipient for showing improper deference; this is one sign that we hold children to be not-yet-persons.

It seems characteristic of every establishment, and especially of total institutions, that some forms of deference will be specific to it, with inmates as givers and staff as recipients. For this to occur, those who are to receive spontaneous expressions of regard must be the very ones to teach the forms and enforce them. It follows that in total institutions one crucial difference from civil life is that deference is placed on a formal footing, with specific demands being made and specific negative sanctions accorded for infractions; not only will acts be required, but also the outward show of inward feelings. Expressed attitudes such as insolence will be explicitly penalized.

Staff partially protect themselves from this altered relation to deference by some standard devices. First, to the degree that the inmates are defined as not-fully-adults, staff need not feel a loss of self-respect by coercing deference from their charges. Second, we sometimes find, especially in the military, the notion that it is the uniform, not the man, that is saluted (so that the man is not demanding deference for himself); linked with this we find the notion that 'it does not matter what you feel as long as you don't show it.' Third, the lowest level of staff can perform the training, leaving the higher levels free to receive personally uncoerced grants of deference. As Gregory Bateson suggests:

Essentially, the function of the middle member is to instruct and discipline the third member in the forms of behavior which he should adopt in his contacts with the first. The nurse teaches the child how to behave towards its parents, just as the N.C.O. teaches and disciplines the private in how he should behave towards officers.[89]

89. Gregory Bateson, in M. Mead and R. Métraux, eds., *The Study of Culture at a Distance* (Chicago: University of Chicago Press, 1953), p. 372.

I have commented on some intra-group differences. Just as neither the staff nor the inmate group is homogeneous, so a simple division between staff and inmate groups can sometimes conceal important facts. In some establishments the trusty or straw boss of inmate rank is not too far away in function and prerogatives from the lowest staff level, the guards; sometimes, in fact, the highest man in the lower stratum has more power and authority than the lowest man in the higher stratum.[90] Further, there are some establishments that oblige *all* members to share some basic deprivations, a kind of collective hardship ceremony that might be considered (in its effects) along with the annual Christmas party and other institutional ceremonies. Good examples are recorded in the literature on nunneries:

Every member of the community including the Superior General was housed here regardless of age, rank or function. Choir nuns, artists, doctors of medicine and the humanities, cooks, laundresses, shoemaker nuns and the peasant sisters who worked the truck gardens lived in those boxlike cells, each one identical in form and content, in arrangement of bed, table and chair and thrice-folded coverlets over each chair.[91]

St Clare has legislated that the abbess and vicaress are to conform to the common life in all things. So, how much more the others! St Clare's idea of the prerogatives of a superior was entirely novel in her century. A Poor Clare abbess boasts neither staff nor train. She wears no pectoral cross, but the same little wedding-ring ($2.50 net) as her daughters. Our abbess is currently resplendent in a large patch across the front of her habit. It was put there by her own hands, the same hands that quarter and de-worm apples with the best of them, the same hands that wield a dish towel like a professional.[92]

For some nunneries, then, the notion of a staff-inmate division is

90. See, for example, the discussion of the bosun's role in Richardson, op. cit., pp. 15–18. The regimental and battalion sergeant-major compared to the platoon lieutenant provides another example.

91. Hulme, op. cit., p. 20.

92. Francis, op. cit., pp. 179–80. The rule in Anglo-American military tradition that officers should undergo all the risks they set their men and be concerned for the food and comforts of their men before their own during battle provides a subtle variation on these hardship ceremonies; by showing *more* concern for their men than for themselves, officers can at the same time reinforce ties with their men and maintain distance.

not fruitful; one apparently finds, rather, a single collegial group, internally stratified in terms of a single finely graded rank order. Further, in total institutions such as boarding schools, it may be useful to add to the strata of teachers and students a third one, the housekeeping staff.

Total institutions vary considerably in the amount of role differentiation found within the staff and the inmate groupings, and in the clarity of the line between the two strata. There are other important differences that have been only incidentally mentioned; one of these I would like to consider further here.

Recruits enter total institutions in different spirits. At one extreme we find the quite involuntary entrance of those who are sentenced to prison, committed to a mental hospital, or pressed into the crew of a ship. It is perhaps in such circumstances that staff's version of the ideal inmate has least chance of taking hold. At the other extreme, we find religious institutions that deal only with those who feel they have gotten the call and, of these volunteers, take only those who seem to be the most suitable and the most serious in their intentions. (Presumably some officer training camps and some political training schools qualify here, too.) In such cases, conversion seems already to have taken place, and it only remains to show the neophyte along what lines he can best discipline himself. Midway between these two extremes we find institutions, like the Army in regard to conscripts, where inmates are required to serve but are given much opportunity to feel that this service is a justifiable one required in their own ultimate interests. Obviously, significant differences in tone will appear in total institutions, depending on whether recruitment is voluntary, semi-voluntary, or involuntary.

Along with the variable mode of recruitment there is another variable – the degree to which a self-regulating change in the inmate is explicitly striven for by staff. In custodial and work institutions, presumably, the inmate need only comply with action standards; the spirit and inward feeling with which he goes about his assignment would not seem to be an official concern. In brainwashing camps, religious establishments, and institutions for intensive psychotherapy, the inmate's private feelings are presumably at issue. Mere compliance with work rulings would not here seem to be enough, and the inmate's incorporation of staff standards is an active aim as well as an incidental consequence.

Another dimension of variation among total institutions is what might be called their permeability, that is, the degree to which the social standards maintained within the institution and the social standards maintained in the environing society have influenced each other, the consequence being to minimize differences. This issue, incidentally, gives us an opportunity to consider some of the dynamic relations between a total institution and the wider society that supports it or tolerates it.

In examining the admission procedures of total institutions, one tends to be struck by the impermeable aspects of the establishment, since the stripping and levelling processes which occur at this time directly cut across the various social distinctions with which the recruits enter. St Benedict's advice to the abbot tends to be followed:

Let him make no distinction of persons in the monastery. Let not one be loved more than another, unless he be found to excel in good works or in obedience. Let not one of noble birth be raised above him who was formerly a slave, unless some other reasonable cause intervene.[93]

As cited earlier, the military cadet finds that discussions 'of wealth and family background are taboo', and that, 'although the pay of the cadet is very low, he is not permitted to receive money from home.'[94] Even the age-grading system of the wider society may be stopped at the gates, as illustrated, in the extreme, in some religious institutions:

Gabrielle moved to the place that would ever be hers, third in the line of forty postulants. She was third oldest in the group because she had been third to register on that day less than a week ago when the Order had opened its doors to new entrants. From that moment, her chronological age had ceased and the only age she would henceforth have, her age in the religious life, had started.[95]

93. *The Holy Rule of Saint Benedict*, Ch. 2.

94. Dornbusch, op. cit., p. 317. A famous case of this kind of echelon levelling is found in the fagging system in British public schools.

95. Hulme, op. cit., pp. 22–3. The Benedictine view of dis-ageing may be found in *The Holy Rule of Saint Benedict*, Ch. 63.

(Milder examples of the same process can be seen in Air Forces and university science departments, where, during periods of national crisis, very young men may be tolerated in very high ranks.) And just as age dates may be suppressed, so, in some quite radical total institutions, the names of members may be changed upon entrance, the better (presumably) to symbolize a break with the past and an embracing of the life of the establishment.

Some impermeability in an establishment seems necessary if morale and stability are to be maintained. It is by suppressing external social distinctions that a total institution can build up an orientation to its own scheme of honour. Thus, the few mental patients of high socio-economic status in a state mental hospital can provide everyone with assurance that there is a distinctive mental-patient role, that the institution is not merely a disposal station for some oddments from the lower classes, and that the fate of the inmate is not one he suffers merely because of his general social background; the same can be said of the role of 'toffs' in British prisons and nuns of noble lineage in French convents. Further, if the institution has a militant mission, as do some religious, military, and political units, then a partial reversal on the inside of external status arrangements can act as a constant reminder of the difference and enmity between the institution and its environing society. It should be noted that in thus suppressing externally valid differences, the harshest total institution may be the most democratic; and, in fact, the inmate's assurance of being treated no worse than any other of his fellows can be a source of support as well as a deprivation.[96] But there are some limits to the value of impermeability for these institutions.

I have already described the role of representative that topmost members of staff may be obliged to perform. If they are to move with grace and effectiveness in the wider community, then it may be advantageous for them to be recruited from the same small social grouping as leaders of other social units in the wider society. Further, if staff persons are uniformly recruited from a stratum in the wider society that has a firmly legitimated higher ranking than the stratum from which inmates are uniformly

96. Here of course is a drawback to the medical management of mental hospitals that would tailor treatment specifically to individual diagnosis.

recruited, then the cleavage in the wider society will presumably lend support and stability to the rule of the staff. The military in Britain up to the First World War seem to have illustrated this, with all ranks speaking in 'common' accents and all officers speaking public school English derived from what was called 'a good education'. So, too, since the crafts, trades, and professions of those who become inmates are often required within the institution, staff will understandably allow and even encourage some role carry-over.[97]

The permeability of a total institution can have, then, a variable consequence for its internal workings and cohesion. This is nicely illustrated by the precarious position of the lowest staff level. If the institution is appreciably permeable to the wider community, then these staff members may have the same, or even lower, social origins as the inmates. Sharing the culture of the inmates' home world, they can serve as a natural communication channel between high staff and inmates (albeit a channel that is often blocked to upward communication). But, on the same ground, they will have difficulty maintaining social distance from their charges. As a student of prisons has recently argued, this may merely complicate the warder's role, further opening him up to inmate derision and to inmate expectation that he will be decent, reasonable, and corruptible.[98]

Whatever the utilities and disutilities of impermeability, and regardless of how radical and militant a total institution appears to be, there will always be some limits to its reshuffling tendencies and some use made of social distinctions already established in the environing society, if only so the institution can conduct necessary affairs with this society and be tolerated by it. There

97. This holds even in concentration camps. See, for example, Cohen, op. cit., p. 154. St Benedict (Ch. 57) sagely notes the danger of this practice: 'Should there be craftsmen in the monastery, let them exercise their crafts with all humility and reverence, if the Abbot so command. But if one of them grow proud because of the knowledge of his craft, in that he seem to confer some benefit on the monastery, let such a one be taken away from this craft and not practice it again, unless perchance, after he has humbled himself, the Abbot may bid him resume it.'

98. Sykes, *Corruption of Authority*. See also Cantine and Rainer, op. cit., pp. 96–7.

does not seem to be a total institution in Western society which provides batch living completely independent of sex; and ones like convents that appear to be impervious to socio-economic gradings in fact tend to apportion domestic roles to converts of rural peasant background, just as the inmate garbage crews in our prize integrated mental hospitals tend to be wholly Negro.[99] Similarly, in some British boarding schools it is found that boys of noble lineage may be allowed extra infractions of the house rules.[1]

One of the most interesting differences among total institutions is to be found in the social fate of their graduates. Typically, these become geographically dispersed; the difference is found in the degree to which structural ties are maintained in spite of this distance. At one end of the scale are the year's graduates of a particular Benedictine abbey, who not only keep in touch informally but find that for the rest of their lives their occupation and geographical location have been determined by their original membership. At the same end of the scale are ex-cons whose stays in prison orient them to the calling and to the nationwide underworld community that will comprise their lives thereafter. At the other end of the scale, we find enlisted men from the same barracks who melt into private life immediately upon demobilization and even refrain from congregating for regimental reunions. Here, too, are ex-mental patients who studiously avoid all persons and events that might connect them with the hospital. Midway between these extremes we find 'old-boy' systems in private schools and graduate universities, which function as optional communities for the distribution of life chances among sets of fellow graduates.

II

I have defined total institutions denotatively by listing them and then have tried to suggest some of their common characteristics.

99. It seems to be true that within any given establishment the topmost and bottom-most roles tend to be relatively permeable to wider community standards, while the impermeable tendencies seem to be focused in the middle ranges of the institution's hierarchy.

1. Orwell, op. cit., pp. 510, 525.

We now have a sizeable literature on these establishments and should be in a position to supplant mere suggestions with a solid framework bearing on the anatomy and functioning of this kind of social animal. Certainly the similarities obtrude so glaringly and persistently that we have a right to suspect that there are good functional reasons for these features being present and that it will be possible to fit these features together and grasp them by means of a functional explanation. When we have done this, I feel we will give less praise and blame to particular superintendents, commandants, wardens, and abbots, and tend more to understand the social problems and issues in total institutions by appealing to the underlying structural design common to them all.

THE MORAL CAREER
OF THE MENTAL PATIENT

'The Moral Career of the Mental Patient' is reprinted from *Psychiatry: Journal for the Study of Interpersonal Processes* Volume 22, Number 2, May 1959. Copyright 1959 by the William Alanson White Psychiatric Foundation, Inc.

TRADITIONALLY the term *career* has been reserved for those who expect to enjoy the rises laid out within a respectable profession. The term is coming to be used, however, in a broadened sense to refer to any social strand of any person's course through life. The perspective of natural history is taken: unique outcomes are neglected in favour of such changes over time as are basic and common to the members of a social category, although occurring independently to each of them. Such a career is not a thing that can be brilliant or disappointing; it can no more be a success than a failure. In this light, I want to consider the mental patient.

One value of the concept of career is its two-sidedness. One side is linked to internal matters held dearly and closely, such as image of self and felt identity; the other side concerns official position, jural relations, and style of life, and is part of a publicly accessible institutional complex. The concept of career, then, allows one to move back and forth between the personal and the public, between the self and its significant society, without having to rely overly for data upon what the person says he thinks he imagines himself to be.

This paper, then, is an exercise in the institutional approach to the study of self. The main concern will be with the *moral* aspects of career – that is, the regular sequence of changes that career entails in the person's self and in his framework of imagery for judging himself and others.[1]

The category 'mental patient' itself will be understood in one strictly sociological sense. In this perspective, the psychiatric view of a person becomes significant only in so far as this view itself alters his social fate – an alteration which seems to become

1. Material on moral career can be found in early social anthropological work on ceremonies of status transition, and in classic social psychological descriptions of those spectacular changes in one's view of self that can accompany participation in social movements and sects. Recently new kinds of relevant data have been suggested by psychiatric interest in the problem of 'identity' and sociological studies of work careers and 'adult socialization'.

fundamental in our society when, and only when, the person is put through the process of hospitalization.[2] I therefore exclude certain neighbouring categories: the undiscovered candidates who would be judged 'sick' by psychiatric standards but who never come to be viewed as such by themselves or others, although they may cause everyone a great deal of trouble;[3] the office patient whom a psychiatrist feels he can handle with drugs or shock on the outside; the mental client who engages in psychotherapeutic relationships. And I include anyone, however robust in temperament, who somehow gets caught up in the heavy machinery of mental-hospital servicing. In this way the effects of being treated as a mental patient can be kept quite distinct from the effects upon a person's life of traits a clinician would view as psychopathological.[4] Persons who become mental-hospital patients vary widely in the kind and degree of illness that a psychiatrist would impute to them, and in the attributes by which laymen would describe them. But once started on the way, they are confronted by some importantly similar circumstances and respond to these in some importantly

2. This point has recently been made by Elaine and John Cumming, *Closed Ranks* (Cambridge: Commonwealth Fund, Harvard University Press, 1957), pp. 101–2. 'Clinical experience supports the impression that many people define mental illness as "that condition for which a person is treated in a mental hospital." ... Mental illness, it seems, is a condition which afflicts people who must go to a mental institution, but until they go almost anything they do is normal.' Leila Deasy has pointed out to me the correspondence here with the situation in white-collar crime. Of those who are detected in this activity, only the ones who do not manage to avoid going to prison find themselves accorded the social role of the criminal.

3. Case records in mental hospitals are just now coming to be exploited to show the incredible amount of trouble a person may cause for himself and others before anyone begins to think about him psychiatrically, let alone take psychiatric action against him. See John A. Clausen and Marian Radke Yarrow, 'Paths to the Mental Hospital', *Journal of Social Issues*, XI (1955), pp. 25–32; August B. Hollingshead and Frederick C. Redlich, *Social Class and Mental Illness* (New York: Wiley, 1958), pp. 173–4.

4. An illustration of how this perspective may be taken to all forms of deviancy may be found in Edwin Lemert, *Social Pathology* (New York: McGraw-Hill, 1951), see especially pp. 74–6. A specific application to mental defectives may be found in Stewart E. Perry, 'Some Theoretic Problems of Mental Deficiency and Their Action Implications', *Psychiatry*, XVII (1954), pp. 45–73, see especially pp. 67–8.

similar ways. Since these similarities do not come from mental illness, they would seem to occur in spite of it. It is thus a tribute to the power of social forces that the uniform status of mental patient cannot only assure an aggregate of persons a common fate and eventually, because of this, a common character, but that this social reworking can be done upon what is perhaps the most obstinate diversity of human materials that can be brought together by society. Here there lacks only the frequent forming of a protective group life by ex-patients to illustrate in full the classic cycle of response by which deviant subgroupings are psychodynamically formed in society.

This general sociological perspective is heavily reinforced by one key finding of sociologically oriented students in mental-hospital research. As has been repeatedly shown in the study of non-literate societies, the awesomeness, distastefulness, and barbarity of a foreign culture can decrease to the degree that the student becomes familiar with the point of view to life that is taken by his subjects. Similarly, the student of mental hospitals can discover that the craziness or 'sick behaviour' claimed for the mental patient is by and large a product of the claimant's social distance from the situation that the patient is in, and is not primarily a product of mental illness. Whatever the refinements of the various patients' psychiatric diagnoses, and whatever the special ways in which social life on the 'inside' is unique, the researcher can find that he is participating in a community not significantly different from any other he has studied. Of course, while restricting himself to the off-ward grounds community of paroled patients, he may feel, as some patients do, that life in the locked wards is bizarre; and while on a locked admissions or convalescent ward, he may feel that chronic 'back' wards are socially crazy places. But he need only move his sphere of sympathetic participation to the 'worst' ward in the hospital, and this, too, can come into social focus as a place with a livable and continuously meaningful social world. This in no way denies that he will find a minority in any ward or patient group that continues to seem quite beyond the capacity to follow rules of social organization, or that the orderly fulfilment of normative expectations in patient society is partly made possible by strategic measures that have somehow come to be institutionalized in mental hospitals.

The career of the mental patient falls popularly and naturalistically into three main phases: the period prior to entering the hospital, which I shall call the prepatient phase; the period in the hospital, the inpatient phase; the period after discharge from the hospital, should this occur, namely, the ex-patient phase.[5] This paper will deal only with the first two phases.

5. This simple picture is complicated by the somewhat special experience of roughly a third of ex-patients – namely, readmission to the hospital, this being the recidivist or 'repatient' phase.

THE PREPATIENT PHASE

A RELATIVELY small group of prepatients come into the mental hospital willingly, because of their own idea of what will be good for them, or because of wholehearted agreement with the relevant members of their family. Presumably these recruits have found themselves acting in a way which is evidence to them that they are losing their minds or losing control of themselves. This view of oneself would seem to be one of the most pervasively threatening things that can happen to the self in our society, especially since it is likely to occur at a time when the person is in any case sufficiently troubled to exhibit the kind of symptom which he himself can see. As Sullivan described it,

What we discover in the self-system of a person undergoing schizophrenic change or schizophrenic processes, is then, in its simplest form, an extremely fear-marked puzzlement, consisting of the use of rather generalized and anything but exquisitely refined referential processes in an attempt to cope with what is essentially a failure at being human – a failure at being anything that one could respect as worth being.[6]

Coupled with the person's disintegrative re-evaluation of himself will be the new, almost equally pervasive circumstance of attempting to conceal from others what he takes to be the new fundamental facts about himself, and attempting to discover whether others, too, have discovered them.[7] Here I want to stress that perception of losing one's mind is based on culturally derived and socially engrained stereotypes as to the significance of symptoms such as hearing voices, losing temporal and spatial orientation, and sensing that one is being followed, and that

6. Harry Stack Sullivan, *Clinical Studies in Psychiatry*, edited by Helen Swick Perry, Mary Ladd Gawel, and Martha Gibbon (New York: Norton, 1956), pp. 184–5.

7. This moral experience can be contrasted with that of a person learning to become a marihuana addict, whose discovery that he can be 'high' and still 'op' effectively without being detected apparently leads to a new level of use. See Howard S. Becker, 'Marihuana Use and Social Control', *Social Problems*, III (1955), pp. 35–44; see especially pp. 40–41.

many of the most spectacular and convincing of these symptoms in some instances psychiatrically signify merely a temporary emotional upset in a stressful situation, however terrifying to the person at the time. Similarly, the anxiety consequent upon this perception of oneself, and the strategies devised to reduce this anxiety, are not a product of abnormal psychology, but would be exhibited by any person socialized into our culture who came to conceive of himself as someone losing his mind. Interestingly, subcultures in American society apparently differ in the amount of ready imagery and encouragement they supply for such self-views, leading to differential rates of *self*-referral; the capacity to take this disintegrative view of oneself without psychiatric prompting seems to be one of the questionable cultural privileges of the upper classes.[8]

For the person who has come to see himself – with whatever justification – as mentally unbalanced, entrance to the mental hospital can sometimes bring relief, perhaps in part because of the sudden transformation in the structure of his basic social situation; instead of being to himself a questionable person trying to maintain a role as a full one, he can become an officially questioned person known to himself to be not so questionable as that. In other cases, hospitalization can make matters worse for the willing patient, confirming by the objective situation what has theretofore been a matter of the private experience of self.

Once the willing prepatient enters the hospital, he may go through the same routine of experiences as do those who enter unwillingly. In any case, it is the latter that I mainly want to consider, since in America at present these are by far the more numerous kind.[9] Their approach to the institution takes one of three classic forms: they come because they have been implored by their family or threatened with the abrogation of family ties

8. See Hollingshead and Redlich, op. cit., p. 187, Table 6, where relative frequency is given of self-referral by social-class grouping.

9. The distinction employed here between willing and unwilling patients cuts across the legal one of voluntary and committed, since some persons who are glad to come to the mental hospital may be legally committed, and of those who come only because of strong familial pressure, some may sign themselves in as voluntary patients.

unless they go 'willingly'; they come by force under police escort; they come under misapprehension purposely induced by others, this last restricted mainly to youthful prepatients.

The prepatient's career may be seen in terms of an extrusory model; he starts out with relationships and rights, and ends up, at the beginning of his hospital stay, with hardly any of either. The moral aspects of this career, then, typically begin with the experience of abandonment, disloyalty, and embitterment. This is the case even though to others it may be obvious that he was in need of treatment, and even though in the hospital he may soon come to agree.

The case histories of most mental patients document offences against some arrangement for face-to-face living – a domestic establishment, a work place, a semi-public organization such as a church or store, a public region such as a street or park. Often there is also a record of some *complainant*, some figure who takes that action against the offender which eventually leads to his hospitalization. This may not be the person who makes the first move, but it is the person who makes what turns out to be the first effective move. Here is the *social* beginning of the patient's career, regardless of where one might locate the psychological beginning of his mental illness.

The kinds of offences which lead to hospitalization are felt to differ in nature from those which lead to other extrusory consequences – to imprisonment, divorce, loss of job, disownment, regional exile, non-institutional psychiatric treatment, and so forth. But little seems known about these differentiating factors; and when one studies actual commitments, alternate outcomes frequently appear to have been possible. It seems true, moreover, that for every offence that leads to an effective complaint, there are many psychiatrically similar ones that never do. No action is taken; or action is taken which leads to other extrusory outcomes; or ineffective action is taken, leading to the mere pacifying or putting off of the person who complains. Thus, as Clausen and Yarrow have nicely shown, even offenders who are eventually hospitalized are likely to have had a long series of ineffective actions taken against them.[10]

10. Clausen and Yarrow, op. cit.

Separating those offences which could have been used as grounds for hospitalizing the offender from those that are so used, one finds a vast number of what students of occupation call career contingencies.[11] Some of these contingencies in the mental patient's career have been suggested, if not explored, such as socio-economic status, visibility of the offence, proximity to a mental hospital, amount of treatment facilities available, community regard for the type of treatment given in available hospitals, and so on.[12] For information about other contingencies one must rely on atrocity tales: a psychotic man is tolerated by his wife until she finds herself a boy friend, or by his adult children until they move from a house to an apartment; an alcoholic is sent to a mental hospital because the jail is full, and a drug addict because he declines to avail himself of psychiatric treatment on the outside; a rebellious adolescent daughter can no longer be managed at home because she now threatens to have an open affair with an unsuitable companion; and so on. Correspondingly there is an equally important set of contingencies causing the person to by-pass this fate. And should the person enter the hospital, still another set of contingencies will help determine when he is to obtain a discharge – such as the desire of his family for his return, the availability of a 'manageable' job, and so on. The society's official view is that inmates of mental hospitals are there primarily because they are suffering from mental illness. However, in the degree that the 'mentally ill' outside hospitals numerically approach or surpass those inside hospitals, one could say that mental patients distinctively suffer not from mental illness, but from contingencies.

Career contingencies occur in conjunction with a second feature of the prepatient's career – the circuit of agents – and

11. An explicit application of this notion to the field of mental health may be found in Edwin Lemert, 'Legal Commitment and Social Control', *Sociology and Social Research*, XXX (1946), pp. 370–78.

12. For example, Jerome K. Meyers and Leslie Sehaffer, 'Social Stratification and Psychiatric Practice: A Study of an Outpatient Clinic', *American Sociological Review*, XIX (1954), pp. 307–10; Lemert, op. cit., pp. 402–3; *Patients in Mental Institutions, 1941* (Washington, D.C.: Department of Commerce, Bureau of the Census, 1941), p. 2.

agencies – that participate fatefully in his passage from civilian to patient status.[13] Here is an instance of that increasingly important class of social system whose elements are agents and agencies which are brought into systemic connexion through having to take up and send on the same persons. Some of these agent roles will be cited now, with the understanding that in any concrete circuit a role may be filled more than once, and that the same person may fill more than one of them.

First is the *next-of-relation* – the person whom the prepatient sees as the most available of those upon whom he should be able to depend most in times of trouble, in this instance the last to doubt his sanity and the first to have done everything to save him from the fate which, it transpires, he has been approaching. The patient's next-of-relation is usually his next of kin; the special term is introduced because he need not be. Second is the *complainant*, the person who retrospectively appears to have started the person on his way to the hospital. Third are the *mediators* – the sequence of agents and agencies to which the prepatient is referred and through which he is relayed and processed on his way to the hospital. Here are included police, clergy, general medical practitioners, office psychiatrists, personnel in public clinics, lawyers, social service workers, schoolteachers, and so on. One of these agents will have the legal mandate to sanction commitment and will exercise it, and so those agents who precede him in the process will be involved in something whose outcome is not yet settled. When the mediators retire from the scene, the prepatient has become an inpatient, and the significant agent has become the hospital administrator.

While the complainant usually takes action in a lay capacity as a citizen, an employer, a neighbour, or a kinsman, mediators tend to be specialists and differ from those they serve in significant ways. They have experience in handling trouble, and some professional distance from what they handle. Except in the case of policemen, and perhaps some clergy, they tend to be more psychiatrically oriented than the lay public, and will

13. For one circuit of agents and its bearing on career contingencies, see Oswald Hall, 'The Stages of a Medical Career', *American Journal of Sociology*, LIII (1948), pp. 327–36.

see the need for treatment at times when the public does not.[14]

An interesting feature of these roles is the functional effects of their interdigitation. For example, the feelings of the patient will be influenced by whether or not the person who fills the role of complainant also has the role of next-of-relation – an embarrassing combination more prevalent, apparently, in the higher classes than in the lower.[15] Some of these emergent effects will be considered now.[16]

In the prepatient's progress from home to the hospital he may participate as a third person in what he may come to experience as a kind of alienative coalition. His next-of-relation presses him into coming to 'talk things over' with a medical practitioner, an office psychiatrist, or some other counsellor. Disinclination on his part may be met by threatening him with desertion, disownment, or other legal action, or by stressing the joint and exploratory nature of the interview. But typically the next-of-relation will have set the interview up, in the sense of selecting the professional, arranging for time, telling the professional something about the case, and so on. This move effectively tends to establish the next-of-relation as the responsible person to whom pertinent findings can be divulged, while effectively establishing the other as the patient. The prepatient often goes to the interview with the understanding that he is going as an equal of someone who is so bound together with him that a third person could not come between them in fundamental matters; this, after all, is one way in which close relationships are defined in our society. Upon arrival at the office the prepatient suddenly finds that he and his next-of-relation have not been accorded the same roles, and apparently that a prior understanding between the professional

14. See Cumming and Cumming, op. cit., p. 92.

15. Hollingshead and Redlich, op. cit., p. 187.

16. For an analysis of some of these circuit implications for the in-patient, see Leila Deasy and Olive W. Quinn, 'The Wife of the Mental Patient and the Hospital Psychiatrist', *Journal of Social Issues*, XI (1955), pp. 49–60. An interesting illustration of this kind of analysis may also be found in Alan G. Gowman, 'Blindness and the Role of the Companion'. *Social Problems*, IV (1956), pp. 68–75. A general statement may be found in Robert Merton, 'The Role Set: Problems in Sociological Theory', *British Journal of Sociology*, VIII (1957), pp. 106–20.

and the next-of-relation has been put in operation against him. In the extreme but common case, the professional first sees the prepatient alone, in the role of examiner and diagnostician, and then sees the next-of-relation alone, in the role of adviser, while carefully avoiding talking things over seriously with them both together.[17] And even in those non-consultative cases where public officials must forcibly extract a person from a family that wants to tolerate him, the next-of-relation is likely to be induced to 'go along' with the official action, so that even here the prepatient may feel that an alienative coalition has been formed against him.

The moral experience of being third man in such a coalition is likely to embitter the prepatient, especially since his troubles have already probably led to some estrangement from his next-of-relation. After he enters the hospital, continued visits by his next-of-relation can give the patient the 'insight' that his own best interests were being served. But the initial visits may temporarily strengthen his feeling of abandonment; he is likely to beg his visitor to get him out or at least to get him more privileges and to sympathize with the monstrousness of his plight – to which the visitor ordinarily can respond only by trying to maintain a hopeful note, by not 'hearing' the requests, or by assuring the patient that the medical authorities know about these things and are doing what is medically best. The visitor then nonchalantly goes back into a world that the patient has learned is incredibly thick with freedom and privileges, causing the patient to feel that his next-of-relation is merely adding a pious gloss to a clear case of traitorous desertion.

The depth to which the patient may feel betrayed by his next-of-relation seems to be increased by the fact that another witnesses his betrayal – a factor which is apparently significant in many three-party situations. An offended person may well act forbearantly and accommodatively towards an offender when the two are alone, choosing peace ahead of justice. The presence of a witness, however, seems to add something to the implications of the offence. For then it is beyond the power of the offended and

17. I have one case record of a man who claims he thought *he* was taking his wife to see the psychiatrist, not realizing until too late that his wife had made the arrangements.

offender to forget about, erase, or suppress what has happened; the offence has become a public social fact.[18] When the witness is a mental health commission, as is sometimes the case, the witnessed betrayal can verge on a 'degradation ceremony'.[19] In such circumstances, the offended patient may feel that some kind of extensive reparative action is required before witnesses, if his honour and social weight are to be restored.

Two other aspects of sensed betrayal should be mentioned. First, those who suggest the possibility of another's entering a mental hospital are not likely to provide a realistic picture of how in fact it may strike him when he arrives. Often he is told that he will get required medical treatment and a rest, and may well be out in a few months or so. In some cases they may thus be concealing what they know, but I think, in general, they will be telling what they see as the truth. For here there is quite relevant difference between patients and mediating professionals; mediators, more so than the public at large, may conceive of mental hospitals as short-term medical establishments where required rest and attention can be voluntarily obtained, and not as places of coerced exile. When the prepatient finally arrives he is likely to learn quite quickly, quite differently. He then finds that the information given him about life in the hospital has had the effect of his having put up less resistance to entering than he now sees he would have put up had he known the facts. Whatever the intentions of those who participated in his transition from person to patient, he may sense they have in effect 'conned' him into his present predicament.

I am suggesting that the prepatient starts out with at least a portion of the rights, liberties, and satisfactions of the civilian and ends up on a psychiatric ward stripped of almost everything. The question here is how this stripping is managed. This is the second aspect of betrayal I want to consider.

As the prepatient may see it, the circuit of significant figures can function as a kind of betrayal funnel. Passage from person to

18. A paraphrase from Kurt Riezler, 'Comment on the Social Psychology of Shame', *American Journal of Sociology*, XLVIII (1943), p. 458.

19. See Harold Garfinkel, 'Conditions of Successful Degradation Ceremonies', *American Journal of Sociology*, LXI (1956), pp. 420–24.

patient may be effected through a series of linked stages, each
managed by a different agent. While each stage tends to bring a
sharp decrease in adult free status, each agent may try to maintain the fiction that no further decrease will occur. He may even
manage to turn the prepatient over to the next agent while sustaining this note. Further, through words, cues, and gestures, the
prepatient is implicitly asked by the current agent to join with
him in sustaining a running line of polite small talk that tactfully
avoids the administrative facts of the situation, becoming, with
each stage, progressively more at odds with these facts. The
spouse would rather not have to cry to get the prepatient to visit
a psychiatrist; psychiatrists would rather not have a scene when
the prepatient learns that he and his spouse are being seen
separately and in different ways; the police infrequently bring a
prepatient to the hospital in a strait-jacket, finding it much easier
all around to give him a cigarette, some kindly words, and freedom to relax in the back seat of the patrol car; and finally, the
admitting psychiatrist finds he can do his work better in the
relative quiet and luxury of the 'admission suite' where, as an
incidental consequence, the notion can survive that a mental
hospital is indeed a comforting place. If the prepatient heeds all
of these implied requests and is reasonably decent about the
whole thing, he can travel the whole circuit from home to hospital without forcing anyone to look directly at what is happening
or to deal with the raw emotion that his situation might well
cause him to express. His showing consideration for those who are
moving him towards the hospital allows them to show consideration for him, with the joint result that these interactions can be
sustained with some of the protective harmony characteristic of
ordinary face-to-face dealings. But should the new patient cast
his mind back over the sequence of steps leading to hospitalization, he may feel that everyone's current comfort was being busily
sustained while his long-range welfare was being undermined.
This realization may constitute a moral experience that further
separates him for the time from the people on the outside.[20]

20. Concentration-camp practices provide a good example of the function
of the betrayal funnel in inducing cooperation and reducing struggle and
fuss, although here the mediators could not be said to be acting in the best

I would now like to look at the circuit of career agents from the point of view of the agents themselves. Mediators in the person's transition from civil to patient status – as well as his keepers, once he is in the hospital – have an interest in establishing a responsible next-of-relation as the patient's deputy or guardian; should there be no obvious candidate for the role, someone may be sought out and pressed into it. Thus while a person is gradually being transformed into a patient, a next-of-relation is gradually being transformed into a guardian. With a guardian on the scene, the whole transition process can be kept tidy. He is likely to be familiar with the prepatient's civil involvements and business, and can tie up loose ends that might otherwise be left to entangle the hospital. Some of the prepatient's abrogated civil rights can be transferred to him, thus helping to sustain the legal fiction that while the prepatient does not actually have his rights he somehow actually has not lost them.

Inpatients commonly sense, at least for a time, that hospitalization is a massive unjust deprivation, and sometimes succeed in convincing a few persons on the outside that this is the case. It often turns out to be useful, then, for those identified with inflicting these deprivations, however justifiably, to be able to point to the cooperation and agreement of someone whose relationship to the patient places him above suspicion, firmly defining him as the person most likely to have the patient's personal interest at heart. If the guardian is satisfied with what is happening to the new inpatient, the world ought to be.[21]

interests of the inmates. Police picking up persons from their homes would sometimes joke good-naturedly and offer to wait while coffee was being served. Gas chambers were fitted out like delousing rooms, and victims taking off their clothes were told to note where they were leaving them. The sick, aged, weak, or insane who were selected for extermination were sometimes driven away in Red Cross ambulances to camps referred to by terms such as 'observation hospital', See David Boder, *I Did Not Interview the Dead* (Urbana: University of Illinois Press, 1949), p. 81; and Elie A. Cohen, *Human Behaviour in the Concentration Camp* (London: Jonathan Cape, 1954), pp. 32, 37, 107.

21. Interviews collected by the Clausen group at NIMH suggest that when a wife comes to be a guardian, the responsibility may disrupt previous distance from in-laws, leading either to a new supportive coalition with them or to a marked withdrawal from them.

Now it would seem that the greater the legitimate personal stake one party has in another, the better he can take the role of guardian to the other. But the structural arrangements in society which lead to the acknowledged merging of two persons' interests lead to additional consequences. For the person to whom the patient turns for help – for protection against such threats as involuntary commitment - is just the person to whom the mediators and hospital administrators logically turn for authorization. It is understandable, then, that some patients will come to sense, at least for a time, that the closeness of a relationship tells nothing of its trustworthiness.

There are still other functional effects emerging from this complement of roles. If and when the next-of-relation appeals to mediators for help in the trouble he is having with the prepatient, hospitalization may not, in fact, be in his mind. He may not even perceive the prepatient as mentally sick, or, if he does, he may not consistently hold to this view.[22] It is the circuit of mediators, with their greater psychiatric sophistication and their belief in the medical character of mental hospitals, that will often define the situation for the next-of-relation, assuring him that hospitalization is a possible solution and a good one, that it involves no betrayal, but is rather a medical action taken in the best interests of the prepatient. Here the next-of-relation may learn that doing his duty to the prepatient may cause the prepatient to distrust and even hate him for the time. But the fact that this course of action may have had to be pointed out and prescribed by professionals, and be defined by them as a moral duty, relieves the next-of-relation of some of the guilt he may feel.[23] It is a poignant fact

22. For an analysis of these non-psychiatric kinds of perception, see Marian Radke Yarrow, Charlotte Green Schwartz, Harriet S. Murphy, and Leila Deasy, 'The Psychological Meaning of Mental Illness in the Family', *Journal of Social Issues*, XI (1955), pp. 12–24; Charlotte Green Schwartz, 'Perspectives on Deviance – Wives' Definitions of their Husbands' Mental Illness', *Psychiatry*, XX (1957), pp. 275–91.

23. This guilt-carrying function is found, of course, in other role complexes. Thus, when a middle-class couple engages in the process of legal separation or divorce, each of their lawyers usually takes the position that his job is to acquaint his client with all of the potential claims and rights, pressing his client into demanding these, in spite of any nicety of feelings about the rights and honourableness of the ex-partner. The client, in all good

that an adult son or daughter may be pressed into the role of mediator, so that the hostility that might otherwise be directed against the spouse is passed on to the child.[24]

Once the prepatient is in the hospital, the same guilt-carrying function may become a significant part of the staff's job in regard to the next-of-relation.[25] These reasons for feeling that he himself has not betrayed the patient, even though the patient may then think so, can later provide the next-of-relation with a defensible line to take when visiting the patient in the hospital and a basis for hoping that the relationship can be re-established after its hospital moratorium. And of course this position, when sensed by the patient, can provide him with excuses for the next-of-relation, when and if he comes to look for them.[26]

Thus while the next-of-relation can perform important functions for the mediators and hospital administrators, they in turn can perform important functions for him. One finds, then, an emergent unintended exchange or reciprocation of functions, these functions themselves being often unintended.

The final point I want to consider about the prepatient's moral career is its peculiarly retroactive character. Until a person actually arrives at the hospital there usually seems no way of knowing for sure that he is destined to do so, given the determinative role of career contingencies. And until the point of hospitalization is reached, he or others may not conceive of him as a person who is becoming a mental patient. However, since he will be held against his will in the hospital, his next-of-relation and the hospital staff will be in great need of a rationale for the hardships they are sponsoring. The medical elements of the staff

---

faith, can then say to self and to the ex-partner that the demands are being made only because the lawyer insists it is best to do so.

24. Recorded in the Clausen data.

25. This point is made by Cumming and Cumming, op. cit., p. 129.

26. There is an interesting contrast here with the moral career of the tuberculosis patient. I am told by Julius Roth that tuberculous patients are likely to come to the hospital willingly, agreeing with their next-of-relation about treatment. Later in their hospital career, when they learn how long they yet have to stay and how depriving and irrational some of the hospital rulings are, they may seek to leave, be advised against this by the staff and by relatives, and only then begin to feel betrayed.

will also need evidence that they are still in the trade they were trained for. These problems are eased, no doubt unintentionally, by the case-history construction that is placed on the patient's past life, this having the effect of demonstrating that all along he had been becoming sick, that he finally became very sick, and that if he had not been hospitalized much worse things would have happened to him – all of which, of course, may be true. Incidentally, if the patient wants to make sense out of his stay in the hospital, and, as already suggested, keep alive the possibility of once again conceiving of his next-of-relation as a decent, well-meaning person, then he, too, will have reason to believe some of this psychiatric work-up of his past.

Here is a very ticklish point for the sociology of careers. An important aspect of every career is the view the person constructs when he looks backward over his progress; in a sense, however, the whole of the prepatient career derives from this reconstruction. The fact of having had a prepatient career, starting with an effective complaint, becomes an important part of the mental patient's orientation, but this part can begin to be played only after hospitalization proves that what he had been having, but no longer has, is a career as a prepatient.

THE INPATIENT PHASE

THE last step in the prepatient's career can involve his realization – justified or not – that he has been deserted by society and turned out of relationships by those closest to him. Interestingly enough, the patient, especially a first admission, may manage to keep himself from coming to the end of this trail, even though in fact he is now in a locked mental-hospital ward. On entering the hospital, he may very strongly feel the desire not to be known to anyone as a person who could possibly be reduced to these present circumstances, or as a person who conducted himself in the way he did prior to commitment. Consequently, he may avoid talking to anyone, may stay by himself when possible, and may even be 'out of contact' or 'manic' so as to avoid ratifying any interaction that presses a politely reciprocal role upon him and opens him up to what he has become in the eyes of others. When the next-of-relation makes an effort to visit, he may be rejected by mutism, or by the patient's refusal to enter the visiting room, these strategies sometimes suggesting that the patient still clings to a remnant of relatedness to those who made up his past, and is protecting this remnant from the final destructiveness of dealing with the new people that they have become.[27]

Usually the patient comes to give up this taxing effort at anonymity, at not-hereness, and begins to present himself for conventional social interaction to the hospital community. Thereafter he withdraws only in special ways – by always using his nickname, by signing his contribution to the patient weekly with his initial only, or by using the innocuous 'cover' address tactfully provided by some hospitals; or he withdraws only at

27. The inmate's initial strategy of holding himself aloof from ratifying contact may partly account for the relative lack of group formation among inmates in public mental hospitals, a connexion that has been suggested to me by William R. Smith. The desire to avoid personal bonds that would give licence to the asking of biographical questions could also be a factor. In mental hospitals, of course, as in prisoner camps, the staff may consciously break up incipient group formation in order to avoid collective rebellious action and other ward disturbances.

special times, when, say, a flock of nursing students makes a passing tour of the ward, or when, paroled to the hospital grounds, he suddenly sees he is about to cross the path of a civilian he happens to know from home. Sometimes this making of oneself available is called 'settling down' by the attendants. It marks a new stand openly taken and supported by the patient, and resembles the 'coming-out' process that occurs in other groupings.[28]

Once the prepatient begins to settle down, the main outlines of his fate tend to follow those of a whole class of segregated establishments – jails, concentration camps, monasteries, work camps, and so on – in which the inmate spends the whole round of life on the grounds, and marches through his regimented day in the immediate company of a group of persons of his own institutional status.

Like the neophyte in many of these total institutions, the new inpatient finds himself cleanly stripped of many of his accustomed affirmations, satisfactions, and defences, and is subjected to a rather full set of mortifying experiences: restriction of free movement, communal living, diffuse authority of a whole echelon of people, and so on. Here one begins to learn about the limited extent to which a conception of oneself can be sustained when the usual setting of supports for it are suddenly removed.

While undergoing these humbling moral experiences, the inpatient learns to orient himself in terms of the 'ward system'.[29]

28. A comparable coming out occurs in the homosexual world, when a person finally comes frankly to present himself to a 'gay' gathering not as a tourist but as someone who is 'available'. See Evelyn Hooker, 'A Preliminary Analysis of Group Behavior of Homosexuals', *Journal of Psychology*, XLII (1956), pp. 217–25; see especially p. 221. A good fictionalized treatment may be found in James Baldwin's *Giovanni's Room* (New York: Dial, 1956), pp. 41–57. A familiar instance of the coming-out process is no doubt to be found among prepubertal children at the moment one of these actors sidles *back* into a room that had been left in an angered huff and injured *amour propre*. The phrase itself presumably derives from a *rite-de-passage* ceremony once arranged by upper-class mothers for their daughters. Interestingly enough, in large mental hospitals the patient sometimes symbolizes a complete coming out by his first active participation in the hospital-wide patient dance.

29. A good description of the ward system may be found in Ivan Belknap, *Human Problems of a State Mental Hospital* (New York: McGraw-Hill, 1956), Ch. ix, especially p. 164.

In public mental hospitals this usually consists of a series of graded living arrangements built around wards, administrative units called services, and parole statuses. The 'worst' level often involves nothing but wooden benches to sit on, some quite indifferent food, and a small piece of room to sleep in. The 'best' level may involve a room of one's own, ground and town privileges, contacts with staff that are relatively undamaging, and what is seen as good food and ample recreational facilities. For disobeying the pervasive house rules, the inmate will receive stringent punishments expressed in terms of loss of privileges; for obedience he will eventually be allowed to reacquire some of the minor satisfactions he took for granted on the outside.

The institutionalization of these radically different levels of living throws light on the implications for self of social settings. And this in turn affirms that the self arises not merely out of its possessor's interactions with significant others, but also out of the arrangements that are evolved in an organization for its members.

There are some settings that the person easily discounts as an expression or extension of him. When a tourist goes slumming, he may take pleasure in the situation not because it is a reflection of him but because it so assuredly is not. There are other settings, such as living-rooms, which the person manages on his own and employs to influence in a favourable direction other persons' views of him. And there are still other settings, such as a work place, which express the employee's occupational status, but over which he has no final control, this being exerted, however tactfully, by his employer. Mental hospitals provide an extreme instance of this latter possibility. And this is due not merely to their uniquely degraded living levels, but also to the unique way in which significance for self is made explicit to the patient, piercingly, persistently, and thoroughly. Once lodged on a given ward, the patient is firmly instructed that the restrictions and deprivations he encounters are not due to such blind forces as tradition or economy – and hence dissociable from self – but are intentional parts of his treatment, part of his need at the time, and therefore an expression of the state that his self has fallen to. Having every reason to initiate requests for better conditions, he

THE INPATIENT PHASE 139

is told that when the staff feel he is 'able to manage' or will be 'comfortable with' a higher ward level, then appropriate action will be taken. In short, assignment to a given ward is presented not as a reward or punishment, but as an expression of his general level of social functioning, his status as a person. Given the fact that the worst ward levels provide a round of life that inpatients with organic brain damage can easily manage, and that these quite limited human beings are present to prove it, one can appreciate some of the mirroring effects of the hospital.[30]

The ward system, then, is an extreme instance of how the physical facts of an establishment can be explicitly employed to frame the conception a person takes of himself. In addition, the official psychiatric mandate of mental hospitals gives rise to even more direct, even more blatant, attacks upon the inmate's view of himself. The more 'medical' and the more progressive a mental hospital is – the more it attempts to be therapeutic and not merely custodial – the more he may be confronted by high-ranking staff arguing that his past has been a failure, that the cause of this has been within himself, that his attitude to life is wrong, and that if he wants to be a person he will have to change his way of dealing with people and his conceptions of himself. Often the moral value of these verbal assaults will be brought home to him by requiring him to practise taking this psychiatric view of himself in arranged confessional periods, whether in private sessions or group psychotherapy.

Now a general point may be made about the moral career of inpatients which has bearing on many moral careers. Given the stage that any person has reached in a career, one typically finds that he constructs an image of his life course – past, present, and future – which selects, abstracts, and distorts in such a way as to provide him with a view of himself that he can usefully expound in current situations. Quite generally, the person's line concerning self defensively brings him into appropriate alignment with the

30. Here is one way in which mental hospitals can be worse than concentration camps and prisons as places in which to 'do' time; in the latter, self-insulation from the symbolic implications of the settings may be easier. In fact, self-insulation from hospital settings may be so difficult that patients have to employ devices for this which staff interpret as psychotic symptoms.

basic values of his society, and so may be called an apologia. If
the person can manage to present a view of his current situation
which shows the operation of favourable personal qualities in the
past and a favourable destiny awaiting him, it may be called a
success story. If the facts of a person's past and present are
extremely dismal, then about the best he can do is to show that
he is not responsible for what has become of him, and the term
sad tale is appropriate. Interestingly enough, the more the person's past forces him out of apparent alignment with central
moral values, the more often he seems compelled to tell his sad
tale in any company in which he finds himself. Perhaps he partly
responds to the need he feels in others of not having their sense of
proper life courses affronted. In any case, it is among convicts,
'winos', and prostitutes that one seems to obtain sad tales the
most readily.[31] It is the vicissitudes of the mental patient's sad
tale that I want to consider now.

In the mental hospital, the setting and the house rules press
home to the patient that he is, after all, a mental case who has
suffered some kind of social collapse on the outside, having

31. In regard to convicts, see Anthony Heckstall-Smith, *Eighteen Months*
(London: Allan Wingate, 1954), pp. 52–3. For 'winos' see the discussion in
Howard G. Bain, 'A Sociological Analysis of the Chicago Skid-Row Life-
way' (Unpublished M.A. thesis, Department of Sociology, University of
Chicago, September 1950), especially 'The Rationale of the Skid-Row
Drinking Group', pp. 141–6. Bain's neglected thesis is a useful source of
material on moral careers.

Apparently one of the occupational hazards of prostitution is that clients
and other professional contacts sometimes persist in expressing sympathy
by asking for a defensible dramatic explanation for the fall from grace. In
having to bother to have a sad tale ready, perhaps the prostitute is more
to be pitied than damned. Good examples of prostitute sad tales may be
found in Henry Mayhew, *London Labour and the London Poor*, Vol. IV,
Those That Will Not Work (London: Charles Griffin and Co., 1862), pp.
210–72. For a contemporary source, see *Women of the Streets*, edited by
C. H. Rolph (London: Secker and Warburg, 1955), especially p. 6: 'Almost
always, however, after a few comments on the police, the girl would begin
to explain how it was that she was in the life, usually in terms of self-
justification. . . .' Lately, of course, the psychological expert has helped out
the profession in the construction of wholly remarkable sad tales. See, for
example, Harold Greenwald, *The Call Girl* (New York: Ballantine Books,
1958).

failed in some over-all way, and that here he is of little social weight, being hardly capable of acting like a full-fledged person at all. These humiliations are likely to be most keenly felt by middle-class patients, since their previous condition of life little immunizes them against such affronts, but all patients feel some downgrading. Just as any normal member of his outside sub-culture would do, the patient often responds to this situation by attempting to assert a sad tale proving that he is not 'sick', that the 'little trouble' he did get into was really somebody else's fault, that his past life-course had some honour and rectitude, and that the hospital is therefore unjust in forcing the status of mental patient upon him. This self-respecting tendency is heavily institutionalized within the patient society where opening social contacts typically involve the participants' volunteering informa-tion about their current ward location and length of stay so far, but not the reasons for their stay – such interaction being con-ducted in the manner of small talk on the outside.[32] With greater familiarity, each patient usually volunteers relatively acceptable reasons for his hospitalization, at the same time accepting without open immediate question the lines offered by other patients. Such stories as the following are given and overtly accepted.

I was going to night school to get a M.A. degree, and holding down a job in addition, and the load got too much for me.

The others here are sick mentally but I'm suffering from a bad nervous system and that is what is giving me these phobias.

I got here by mistake because of a diabetes diagnosis, and I'll leave in a couple of days. [The patient had been in seven weeks.]

I failed as a child, and later with my wife I reached out for dependency.

My trouble is that I can't work. That's what I'm in for. I had two jobs with a good home and all the money I wanted.[33]

32. A similar self-protecting rule has been observed in prisons. Thus Alfred Hassler, *Diary of a Self-Made Convict* (Chicago: Regnery, 1954), p. 76, in describing a conversation with a fellow prisoner: 'He didn't say much about why he was sentenced, and I didn't ask him, that being the accepted behavior in prison.' A novelistic version for the mental hospital may be found in J. Kerkhoff, *How Thin the Veil: A Newspaperman's Story of His Own Mental Crack-up and Recovery* (New York: Greenberg, 1952), p. 27.

33. From the writer's field notes of informal interaction with patients, transcribed as nearly verbatim as he was able.

The patient sometimes reinforces these stories by an optimistic definition of his occupational status. A man who managed to obtain an audition as a radio announcer styles himself a radio announcer, another who worked for some months as a copy boy and was then given a job as a reporter on a large trade journal, but fired after three weeks, defines himself as a reporter.

A whole social role in the patient community may be constructed on the basis of these reciprocally sustained fictions. For these face-to-face niceties tend to be qualified by behind-the-back gossip that comes only a degree closer to the 'objective' facts. Here, of course, one can see a classic social function of informal networks of equals: they serve as one another's audience for self-supporting tales – tales that are somewhat more solid than pure fantasy and somewhat thinner than the facts.

But the patient's apologia is called forth in a unique setting, for few settings could be so destructive of self-stories except, of course, those stories already constructed along psychiatric lines. And this destructiveness rests on more than the official sheet of paper which attests that the patient is of unsound mind, a danger to himself and others – an attestation, incidentally, which seems to cut deeply into the patient's pride, and into the possibility of his having any.

Certainly the degrading conditions of the hospital setting belie many of the self-stories that are presented by patients, and the very fact of being in the mental hospital is evidence against these tales. And of course there is not always sufficient patient solidarity to prevent patient discrediting patient, just as there is not always a sufficient number of 'professionalized' attendants to prevent attendant discrediting patient. As one patient informant repeatedly suggested to a fellow patient:

If you're so smart, how come you got your ass in here?

The mental-hospital setting, however, is more treacherous still. Staff have much to gain through discreditings of the patient's story – whatever the felt reason for such discreditings. If the custodial faction in the hospital is to succeed in managing his daily round without complaint or trouble from him, then it will prove useful to be able to point out to him that the claims about himself upon which he rationalizes his demands are false, that he is not what he is claiming to be, and that in fact he is a failure as a person. If the psychiatric faction is to impress upon him its views about his personal make-up, then they must be able to show in detail how their version of his past and their version of his character hold up much better than his own.[34] If both the custodial and psychiatric factions are to get him to cooperate in the various psychiatric treatments, then it will prove useful to disabuse him of his view of their purposes, and cause him to appreciate that they know what they are doing, and are doing what is best for him. In brief, the difficulties caused by a patient are closely tied to his version of what has been happening to him, and if cooperation is to be secured, it helps if this version is discredited. The patient must 'insightfully' come to take, or affect to take, the hospital's view of himself.

The staff also have ideal means – in addition to the mirroring effect of the setting – for denying the inmate's rationalizations. Current psychiatric doctrine defines mental disorder as something that can have its roots in the patient's earliest years, show its signs throughout the course of his life, and invade almost every sector of his current activity. No segment of his past or present need be defined, then, as beyond the jurisdiction and mandate of psychiatric assessment. Mental hospitals bureaucratically institutionalize this extremely wide mandate by formally basing their treatment of the patient upon his diagnosis and hence upon the psychiatric view of his past.

The case record is an important expression of this mandate. This dossier is apparently not regularly used, however, to record occasions when the patient showed capacity to cope honourably

---

34. The process of examining a person psychiatrically and then altering or reducing his status in consequence is known in hospital and prison parlance as bugging, the assumption being that once you come to the attention of the testers you either will automatically be labelled crazy or the process of testing itself will make you crazy. Thus psychiatric staff are sometimes seen not as discovering whether you are sick, but as making you sick; and 'Don't bug me, man' can mean, 'Don't pester me to the point where I'll get upset.' Sheldon Messinger has suggested to me that this meaning of bugging is related to the other colloquial meaning, of wiring a room with a secret microphone to collect information usable for discrediting the speaker.

and effectively with difficult life situations. Nor is the case record typically used to provide a rough average or sampling of his past conduct. One of its purposes is to show the ways in which the patient is 'sick' and the reasons why it was right to commit him and is right currently to keep him committed; and this is done by extracting from his whole life course a list of those incidents that have or might have had 'symptomatic' significance.[35] The misadventures of his parents or siblings that might suggest a 'taint' may be cited. Early acts in which the patient appeared to have shown bad judgement or emotional disturbance will be recorded. Occasions when he acted in a way which the layman would consider immoral, sexually perverted, weak-willed, childish, ill-considered, impulsive, and crazy may be described. Misbehaviours which someone saw as the last straw, as cause for immediate action, are likely to be reported in detail. In addition, the record will describe his state on arrival at the hospital – and this is not likely to be a time of tranquillity and ease for him. The record may also report the false line taken by the patient in answering embarrassing questions, showing him as someone who makes claims that are obviously contrary to the facts:

Claims she lives with oldest daughter or with sisters only when sick and in need of care; otherwise with husband, he himself says not for twelve years.

Contrary to the reports from the personnel, he says he no longer bangs on the floor or cries in the morning.

... conceals fact that she had her organs removed, claims she is still menstruating.

35. While many kinds of organization maintain records of their members, in almost all of these some socially significant attributes can only be included indirectly, being officially irrelevant. But since mental hospitals have a legitimate claim to deal with the 'whole' person, they need officially recognize no limits to what they consider relevant, a sociologically interesting licence. It is an odd historical fact that persons concerned with promoting civil liberties in other areas of life tend to favour giving the psychiatrist complete discretionary power over the patient. Apparently it is felt that the more power possessed by medically qualified administrators and therapists, the better the interests of the patients will be served. Patients, to my knowledge, have not been polled on this matter.

At first she denied having had premarital sexual experience, but when asked about Jim she said she had forgotten about it 'cause it had been unpleasant.[36]

Where contrary facts are not known by the recorder, their presence is often left scrupulously an open question:

The patient denied any heterosexual experiences nor could one trick her into admitting that she had ever been pregnant or into any kind of sexual indulgence, denying masturbation as well.

Even with considerable pressure she was unwilling to engage in any projection of paranoid mechanisms.

No psychotic content could be elicited at this time.[37]

And if in no more factual way, discrediting statements often appear in descriptions given of the patient's general social manner in the hospital:

When interviewed, he was bland, apparently self-assured, and sprinkles high-sounding generalizations freely throughout his verbal productions.

Armed with a rather neat appearance and natty little Hitlerian mustache this 45 year old man who has spent the last five or more years of his life in the hospital, is making a very successful hospital adjustment living within the role of a rather gay liver and jim-dandy type of fellow who is not only quite superior to his fellow patients in intellectual respects but who is also quite a man with women. His speech is sprayed with many multi-syllabled words which he generally uses in good context, but if he talks long enough on any subject it soon becomes apparent that he is so completely lost in this verbal diarrhea as to make what he says almost completely worthless.[38]

The events recorded in the case history are, then, just the sort that a layman would consider scandalous, defamatory, and discrediting. I think it is fair to say that all levels of mental-hospital staff fail, in general, to deal with this material with the moral neutrality claimed for medical statements and psychiatric diagnosis, but instead participate, by intonation and gesture if by no other means, in the lay reaction to these acts. This will occur

36. Verbatim transcriptions of hospital case-record material.
37. Verbatim transcriptions of hospital case-record material.
38. Verbatim transcriptions of hospital case-record material.

in staff-patient encounters as well as in staff encounters at which no patient is present.

In some mental hospitals, access to the case record is technically restricted to medical and higher nursing levels, but even here informal access or relayed information is often available to lower staff levels.[39] In addition, ward personnel are felt to have a right to know those aspects of the patient's past conduct which, embedded in the reputation he develops, purportedly make it possible to manage him with greater benefit to himself and less risk to others. Further, all staff levels typically have access to the nursing notes kept on the ward, which chart the daily course of each patient's disease, and hence his conduct, providing for the near present the sort of information the case record supplies for his past.

I think that most of the information gathered in case records is quite true, although it might seem also to be true that almost anyone's life course could yield up enough denigrating facts to provide grounds for the record's justification of commitment. In any case, I am not concerned here with questioning the desirability of maintaining case records, or the motives of staff in keeping them. The point is that, these facts about him being true, the patient is certainly not relieved from the normal cultural pressure to conceal them, and is perhaps all the more threatened by knowing that they are neatly available, and that he has no control over who gets to learn them.[40] A manly looking youth

39. However, some mental hospitals do have a 'hot file' of selected records which can be taken out only by special permission. These may be records of patients who work as administration-office messengers and might otherwise snatch glances at their own files; of inmates who had élite status in the environing community; and of inmates who may take legal action against the hospital and hence have a special reason to manoeuvre access to their records. Some hospitals even have a 'hot-hot file', kept in the superintendent's office. In addition, the patient's professional title, especially if it is a medical one, is sometimes purposely omitted from his file card. All of these exceptions to the general rule for handling information show, of course, the institution's realization of some of the implications of keeping mental-hospital records. For a further example, see Harold Taxel, 'Authority Structure in a Mental Hospital Ward' (Unpublished M.A. thesis, Department of Sociology, University of Chicago, 1953), pp. 11–12.

40. This is the problem of 'information control' that many groups suffer from in varying degrees. See Goffman, 'Discrepant Roles', in *The Presenta-*

who responds to military induction by running away from the barracks and hiding himself in a hotel-room clothes closet, to be found there, crying, by his mother; a woman who travels from Utah to Washington to warn the President of impending doom; a man who disrobes before three young girls; a boy who locks his sister out of the house, striking out two of her teeth when she tries to come back in through the window – each of these persons has done something he will have very obvious reason to conceal from others, and very good reason to tell lies about.

The formal and informal patterns of communication linking staff members tend to amplify the disclosive work done by the case record. A discreditable act that the patient performs during one part of the day's routine in one part of the hospital community is likely to be reported back to those who supervise other areas of his life where he implicitly takes the stand that he is not the sort of person who could act that way.

Of significance here, as in some other social establishments, is the increasingly common practice of all-level staff conferences, where staff air their views of patients and develop collective agreement concerning the line that the patient is trying to take and the line that should be taken to him. A patient who develops a 'personal' relation with an attendant, or manages to make an attendant anxious by eloquent and persistent accusations of

---

tion of Self in Everyday Life (New York: Anchor Books, 1959), Ch. iv, pp. 141–166. A suggestion of this problem in relation to case records in prisons is given by James Peck in his story, 'The Ship that Never Hit Port', in *Prison Etiquette*, edited by Holley Cantine and Dachine Rainer (Bearsville, N.Y.: Retort Press, 1950), p. 66: 'The hacks of course hold all the aces in dealing with any prisoner because they can always write him up for inevitable punishment. Every infraction of the rules is noted in the prisoner's jacket, a folder which records all the details of the man's life before and during imprisonment. There are general reports written by the work detail screw, the cell block screw, or some other screw who may have overheard a conversation. Tales pumped from stool pigeons are also included.

'Any letter which interests the authorities goes into the jacket. The mail censor may make a photostatic copy of a prisoner's entire letter, or merely copy a passage. Or he may pass the letter on to the warden. Often an inmate called out by the warden or parole officer is confronted with something he wrote so long ago he had forgot all about it. It might be about his personal life or his political views – a fragment of thought that the prison authorities felt was dangerous and filed for later use.'

malpractice, can be put back into his place by means of the staff meeting, where the attendant is given warning or assurance that the patient is 'sick'. Since the differential image of himself that a person usually meets from those of various levels around him comes here to be unified behind the scenes into a common approach, the patient may find himself faced with a kind of collusion against him – albeit one sincerely thought to be for his own ultimate welfare.

In addition, the formal transfer of the patient from one ward or service to another is likely to be accompanied by an informal description of his characteristics, this being felt to facilitate the work of the employee who is newly responsible for him.

Finally, at the most informal of levels, the lunch-time and coffee-break small talk of staff often turns upon the latest doings of the patient, the gossip level of any social establishment being here intensified by the assumption that everything about him is in some way the proper business of the hospital employee. Theoretically there seems to be no reason why such gossip should not build up the subject instead of tear him down, unless one claims that talk about those not present will always tend to be critical in order to maintain the integrity and prestige of the circle in which the talking occurs. And so, even when the impulse of the speakers seems kindly and generous, the implication of their talk is typically that the patient is not a complete person. For example, a conscientious group therapist, sympathetic with patients, once admitted to his coffee companions:

I've had about three group disrupters, one man in particular – a lawyer [*sotto voce*] James Wilson – very bright – who just made things miserable for me, but I would always tell him to get on the stage and do something. Well, I was getting desperate and then I bumped into his therapist, who said that right now behind the man's bluff and front he needed the group very much and that it probably meant more to him than anything else he was getting out of the hospital – he just needed the support. Well, that made me feel altogether different about him. He's out now.

In general, then, mental hospitals systematically provide for circulation about each patient the kind of information that the patient is likely to try to hide. And in various degrees of detail this information is used daily to puncture his claims. At the admission and diagnostic conferences, he will be asked questions to which he must give wrong answers in order to maintain his self-respect, and then the true answer may be shot back at him. An attendant whom he tells a version of his past and his reason for being in the hospital may smile disbelievingly, or say, 'That's not the way I heard it,' in line with the practical psychiatry of bringing the patient down to reality. When he accosts a physician or nurse on the ward and presents his claims for more privileges or for discharge, this may be countered by a question which he cannot answer truthfully without calling up a time in his past when he acted disgracefully. When he gives his view of his situation during group psychotherapy, the therapist, taking the role of interrogator, may attempt to disabuse him of his face-saving interpretations and encourage an interpretation suggesting that it is he himself who is to blame and who must change. When he claims to staff or fellow patients that he is well and has never been really sick, someone may give him graphic details of how, only one month ago, he was prancing around like a girl, or claiming that he was God, or declining to talk or eat, or putting gum in his hair.

Each time the staff deflates the patient's claims, his sense of what a person ought to be and the rules of peer-group social intercourse press him to reconstruct his stories; and each time he does this, the custodial and psychiatric interests of the staff may lead them to discredit these tales again.

Behind these verbally instigated ups and downs of the self is an institutional base that rocks just as precariously. Contrary to popular opinion, the 'ward system' ensures a great amount of internal social mobility in mental hospitals, especially during the inmate's first year. During that time he is likely to have altered his service once, his ward three or four times, and his parole status several times; and he is likely to have experienced moves in bad as well as good directions. Each of these moves involves a very drastic alteration in level of living and in available materials out of which to build a self-confirming round of activities, an alteration equivalent in scope, say, to a move up or down a class in the wider class system. Moreover, fellow inmates with whom he has partially identified himself will similarly be moving, but in different directions and at different rates, thus reflecting feelings of social change to the person even when he does not experience them directly.

As previously implied, the doctrines of psychiatry can reinforce the social fluctuations of the ward system. Thus there is a current psychiatric view that the ward system is a kind of social hothouse in which patients start as social infants and end up, within the year, on convalescent wards as resocialized adults. This view adds considerably to the weight and pride that staff can attach to their work, and necessitates a certain amount of blindness, especially at higher staff levels, to other ways of viewing the ward system, such as a method for disciplining unruly persons through punishment and reward. In any case, this resocialization perspective tends to overstress the extent to which those on the worst wards are incapable of socialized conduct and the extent to which those on the best wards are ready and willing to play the social game. Because the ward system is something more than a resocialization chamber, inmates find many reasons for 'messing up' or getting into trouble, and many occasions, then, for demotion to less privileged ward positions. These demotions may be officially interpreted as psychiatric relapses or moral backsliding, thus protecting the resocialization view of the hospital; these interpretations, by implication, translate a mere infraction of rules and consequent demotion into a fundamental expression of the status of the culprit's self. Correspondingly, promotions, which may come about because of ward population pressure, the need for a 'working patient', or for other psychiatrically irrelevant reasons, may be built up into something claimed to be profoundly expressive of the patient's whole self. The patient himself may be expected by staff to make a personal effort to 'get well', in something less than a year, and hence may be constantly reminded to think in terms of the self's success and failure.[41]

In such contexts inmates can discover that deflations in moral status are not so bad as they had imagined. After all, infractions

41. For this and other suggestions, I am indebted to Charlotte Green Schwartz.

which lead to these demotions cannot be accompanied by legal sanctions or by reduction to the status of mental patient, since these conditions already prevail. Further, no past or current delict seems to be horrendous enough in itself to excommunicate a patient from the patient community, and hence failures at right living lose some of their stigmatizing meaning.[42] And finally, in accepting the hospital's version of his fall from grace, the patient can set himself up in the business of 'straightening up', and make claims of sympathy, privileges, and indulgence from the staff in order to foster this.

Learning to live under conditions of imminent exposure and wide fluctuation in regard, with little control over the granting or withholding of this regard, is an important step in the socialization of the patient, a step that tells something important about what it is like to be an inmate in a mental hospital. Having one's past mistakes and present progress under constant moral review seems to make for a special adaptation consisting of a less than moral attitude to ego ideals. One's shortcomings and successes become too central and fluctuating an issue in life to allow the usual commitment of concern for other persons' views of them. It is not very practicable to try to sustain solid claims about oneself. The inmate tends to learn that degradations and reconstructions of the self need not be given too much weight, at the same time learning that staff and inmates are ready to view an inflation or deflation of a self with some indifference. He learns that a defensible picture of self can be seen as something outside oneself that can be constructed, lost, and rebuilt, all with great speed and some equanimity. He learns about the viability of taking up a standpoint – and hence a self – that is outside the one which the hospital can give and take away from him.

The setting, then, seems to engender a kind of cosmopolitan sophistication, a kind of civic apathy. In this unserious yet oddly exaggerated moral context, building up a self or having it destroyed becomes something of a shameless game, and learning to view this process as a game seems to make for some demoralization, the game being such a fundamental one. In the hospital, then, the inmate can learn that the self is not a fortress, but rather

42. See 'The Underlife of a Public Institution', this book, p.264 fn. 67.

a small open city; he can become weary of having to show
pleasure when held by troops of his own, and weary of having to
show displeasure when held by the enemy. Once he learns what it
is like to be defined by society as not having a viable self, this
threatening definition – the threat that helps attach people
to the self society accords them – is weakened. The patient
seems to gain a new plateau when he learns that he can
survive while acting in a way that society sees as destructive of
him.

A few illustrations of this moral loosening and moral fatigue
might be given. In state mental hospitals currently a kind of
'marriage moratorium' appears to be accepted by patients and
more or less condoned by staff. Some informal peer-group
pressure may be brought against a patient who 'plays around'
with more than one hospital partner at a time, but little negative
sanction seems to be attached to taking up, in a temporarily
steady way, with a member of the opposite sex, even though both
partners are known to be married, to have children, and even to
be regularly visited by these outsiders. In short, there is licence in
mental hospitals to begin courting all over again, with the understanding, however, that nothing very permanent or serious can
come of this. Like shipboard or vacation romances, these entan-
glements attest to the way in which the hospital is cut off from the
outside community, becoming a world of its own, operated for
the benefit of its own citizens. And certainly this moratorium is
an expression of the alienation and hostility that patients feel for
those on the outside to whom they were closely related. But, in
addition, one has evidence of the loosening effects of living in a
world within a world, under conditions which make it difficult to
give full seriousness to either of them.

The second illustration concerns the ward system. On the worst
ward level, discreditings seem to occur the most frequently, in
part because of lack of facilities, in part through the mockery and
sarcasm that seem to be the occupational norm of social control
for the attendants and nurses who administer these places. At the
same time, the paucity of equipment and rights means that not
much self can be built up. The patient finds himself constantly
toppled, therefore, but with very little distance to fall. A kind of

jaunty gallows humour seems to develop in some of these wards, with considerable freedom to stand up to the staff and return insult for insult. While these patients can be punished, they cannot, for example, be easily slighted, for they are accorded as a matter of course few of the niceties that people must enjoy before they can suffer subtle abuse. Like prostitutes in connexion with sex, inmates on these wards have very little reputation or rights to lose and can therefore take certain liberties. As the person moves up the ward system, he can manage more and more to avoid incidents which discredit his claim to be a human being, and acquire more and more of the varied ingredients of self-respect; yet when eventually he does get toppled – and he does – there is a much further distance to fall. For instance, the privileged patient lives in a world wider than the ward, containing recreation workers who, on request, can dole out cake, cards, table-tennis balls, tickets to the movies, and writing materials. But in the absence of the social control of payment which is typically exerted by a recipient on the outside, the patient runs the risk that even a warm-hearted functionary may, on occasion, tell him to wait until she has finished an informal chat, or teasingly ask why he wants what he has asked for, or respond with a dead pause and a cold look of appraisal.

Moving up and down the ward system means, then, not only a shift in self-constructive equipment, a shift in reflected status, but also a change in the calculus of risks. Appreciation of risks to his self-conception is part of everyone's moral experience, but an appreciation that a given risk level is itself merely a social arrangement is a rarer kind of experience, and one that seems to help to disenchant the person who undergoes it.

A third instance of moral loosening has to do with the conditions that are often associated with the release of the inpatient. Often he leaves under the supervision and jurisdiction of his next-of-relation or of a specially selected and specially watchful employer. If he misbehaves while under their auspices, they can quickly obtain his readmission. He therefore finds himself under the special power of persons who ordinarily would not have this kind of power over him, and about whom, moreover, he may have had prior cause to feel quite bitter. In order to get out of the

hospital, however, he may conceal his displeasure in this arrangement, and, at least until safely off the hospital rolls, act out a
willingness to accept this kind of custody. These discharge procedures, then, provide a built-in lesson in overtly taking a role
without the usual covert commitments, and seem further to
separate the person from the worlds that others take seriously.

The moral career of a person of a given social category involves
a standard sequence of changes in his way of conceiving of selves,
including, importantly, his own. These half-buried lines of
development can be followed by studying his moral experiences–
that is, happenings which mark a turning point in the way in
which the person views the world – although the particularities of
this view may be difficult to establish. And note can be taken of
overt tacks or strategies – that is, stands that he effectively takes
before specifiable others, whatever the hidden and variable
nature of his inward attachment to these presentations. By taking
note of moral experiences and overt personal stands, one can
obtain a relatively objective tracing of relatively subjective
matters.

Each moral career, and behind this, each self, occurs within the
confines of an institutional system, whether a social establishment such as a mental hospital or a complex of personal and
professional relationships. The self, then, can be seen as something that resides in the arrangements prevailing in a social
system for its members. The self in this sense is not a property of
the person to whom it is attributed, but dwells rather in the
pattern of social control that is exerted in connexion with the
person by himself and those around him. This special kind of
institutional arrangement does not so much support the self as
constitute it.

In this paper, two of these institutional arrangements have
been considered, by pointing to what happens to the person when
these rulings are weakened. The first concerns the felt loyalty of
his next-of-relation. The prepatient's self is described as a function
of the way in which three roles are related, arising and declining
in the kinds of affiliation that occur between the next-of-relation
and the mediators. The second concerns the protection required

by the person for the version of himself which he presents to others, and the way in which the withdrawal of this protection can form a systematic, if unintended, aspect of the working of an establishment. I want to stress that these are only two kinds of institutional rulings from which a self emerges for the participant; others, not considered in this paper, are equally important.

In the usual cycle of adult socialization one expects to find alienation and mortification followed by a new set of beliefs about the world and a new way of conceiving of selves. In the case of the mental-hospital patient, this rebirth does sometimes occur, taking the form of a strong belief in the psychiatric perspective, or, briefly at least, a devotion to the social cause of better treatment for mental patients. The moral career of the mental patient has unique interest, however; it can illustrate the possibility that in casting off the raiments of the old self – or in having this cover torn away – the person need not seek a new robe and a new audience before which to cower. Instead he can learn, at least for a time, to practise before all groups the amoral arts of shamelessness.

THE UNDERLIFE
OF A PUBLIC INSTITUTION

A STUDY OF WAYS OF MAKING OUT
IN A MENTAL HOSPITAL

A shorter version of this paper was presented at the annual meeting of the American Sociological Society, Washington, D.C., August 1957.

PART ONE: INTRODUCTION

ACTION AND BEING

I

THE bonds that tie the individual to social entities of different sorts themselves exhibit common properties. Whether the entity is an ideology, a nation, a trade, a family, a person, or just a conversation, the individual's involvement in it will have the same general features. He will find himself with obligations: some will be cold, entailing alternatives forgone, work to be done, service rendered, time put in, or money paid; some will be warm, requiring him to feel belongingness, identification, and emotional attachment. Involvement in a social entity, then, entails both a *commitment* and an *attachment*.

One cannot think clearly about the claims of commitment or of attachment that a social entity makes on its participants without thinking of the limits felt proper on these claims. An army requires a soldier to be brave but establishes a limit past which his bravery will be above and beyond the call of duty; furthermore, he may have a right to compassionate leave when his father dies or his wife gives birth to a baby. Similarly, a wife can assume that her husband will publicly stand by her side to form a visible social unit, yet each weekday she must give him up to the world of work; and he may exert the occasional right to spend an evening alone in a bar, play cards with the boys, or engage in some other bargain of liberty.

Here, in the social bond and the restrictions on it, is the classic double theme of sociology. In Western society the formal agreement or contract is a symbol of this dual theme, celebrating with one stroke of the pen the bond that ties and the acknowledged limits to what is tied by it.

But something must be added to this double theme. As Durkheim taught us, behind each contract there are non-contractual assumptions about the character of the participants.[1] In agreeing

1. Emile Durkheim, *Professional Ethics and Civic Morals*, trans. Cornelia Brookfield (London: Routledge & Kegan Paul, 1957), pp. 171–220.

about what they owe and do not owe each other, the parties tacitly agree about the general validity of contractual rights and obligations, the various conditions for invalidation, and the legitimacy of types of sanction against breaking one's contract; the contracting parties also tacitly agree as to their legal competency, their good faith, and the limits to which trustworthy contractees ought to be trusted. In agreeing to give up certain things and hold back others, the individual tacitly agrees that he is the kind of person who has these sorts of things to give up and hold back, and that he is the kind of person who considers it legitimate to enter into a contract regarding these matters. In short, to enter into a contract is to assume that one is a person of a given character and being. A niggling narrow contract that carefully circumscribes the duties and rights of an individual can therefore rest upon a very broad set of assumptions concerning his character.

If there are such self-defining implications for oneself and the other in a formal contract – a bond that is, after all, established to be as free as possible from the personal whims and character of the participants – then there are even more implications for self-definition underlying other, less restricted kinds of ties. In bonds such as those of friendship and kinship, where it is sometimes said that anything can be asked that is not explicitly excluded, an important implication of being a good friend or a loyal brother is that one *is* the sort of person who can be a good friend or loyal brother. In failing to support one's wife and four children, one becomes the sort of person who can fail in this way.

If every bond implies a broad conception of the person tied by it, we should go on to ask how the individual handles this defining of himself.

There are some extreme possibilities. He can openly default his obligations, separate himself from what he has been tied to, and brazen out the redefining looks that people give him. He can reject the bond's implication for his conception of himself but prevent this alienation from being apparent in any of his actions. He can privately embrace the self-implications of his involvement, being to himself what the others who are involved feel he ought to be.

In actual practice the individual often abjures all of these extremes. He holds himself off from fully embracing all the self-implications of his affiliation, allowing some of this disaffection to be seen, even while fulfilling his major obligations.

It is this theme of expressed distance, and some patterns of behaviour upon which it bears, that I want to explore here. I propose to discuss mainly one type of social entity, 'instrumental formal organizations', relying largely on case-history material from a mental hospital as one instance of one class of these.

II

An 'instrumental formal organization' may be defined as a system of purposely coordinated activities designed to produce some over-all explicit ends. The intended product may be material artifacts, services, decisions, or information, and may be distributed among the participants in a great variety of ways. I will be mainly concerned with those formal organizations that are lodged within the confines of a single building or complex of adjacent buildings, referring to such a walled-in unit, for convenience, as a social establishment, institution, or organization.

Some qualifications might be suggested to my traditional approach. Formal organizations may have a multiplicity of conflicting official goals, each with its own special adherents, and some doubt as to which faction is to be the spokesman for the organization. Further, while a goal like cost reduction or asepsis can be objectively applied as a detailed standard for many of the minor activities occurring within some organizations, other establishments, such as some clubs and community recreation centres, do not have the kind of goals that provide a clear-cut standard against which to examine details of life within the establishment. In still other formal organizations the official goal may be of small importance, the main issue being the conservation or survival of the organization itself. Finally, physical boundaries such as walls may in the last analysis be an incidental feature of organizations, not an analytical one.[2]

Walled-in organizations have a characteristic they share with

2. Amitai Etzioni has suggested this argument in personal conversation.

few other social entities: part of the individual's obligation is to be *visibly* engaged at appropriate times in the activity of the organization, which entails a mobilization of attention and muscular effort, a bending of oneself to the activity at hand. This obligatory engrossment in the activity of the organization tends to be taken as a symbol both of one's commitment and one's attachment, and, behind this, of one's acceptance of the implications of participation for a definition of one's nature. Any study, then, of how individuals adapt to being identified and defined is likely to focus on how they deal with exhibiting engrossment in organizational activities.

III

An instrumental formal organization survives by being able to call forth usable contributions of activity from its members; stipulated means must be employed, stipulated ends must be achieved. However, as Chester Barnard has suggested, an organization, acting through its management, must recognize limits upon the degree to which a member can be relied upon to contribute suitable activity.[3] The human vessel is defined as notoriously weak; compromises must be made, consideration must be shown, protective measures must be taken. The particular way in which these limitations to the use of participants are formulated in a given culture would seem to be a very important characteristic of it.[4]

Our Anglo-American imagery for delineating these limits appears to be something like the following, as expressed from the point of view taken here, which identifies an organization with its managers.

First, the participant is granted certain 'standards of welfare' while he is engaged in the activity of the organization, these being above the minimum required to keep the human organism going. Standards here pertain to: levels of comfort, health, and safety;

3. Chester Barnard, *The Functions of the Executive* (Cambridge: Harvard University Press, 1947), Ch. xi, 'The Economy of Incentives'.

4. For economic institutions this has recently been summarized by Talcott Parsons and Neil J. Smelser, *Economy and Society* (Glencoe, Ill.: The Free Press, 1956), Ch. iii, 'The Institutional Structure of the Economy'. A detailed treatment regarding industrial organizations may be found in Reinhard Bendix, *Work and Authority in Industry* (New York: Wiley, 1956).

limits on the kind and amount of effort required; consideration for the member's participation in other organizations that have a legitimate claim upon him; rights regarding retirement and vacations; expression of grievances and even legal review; and, at least at the level of public pronouncements, a right to dignity, self-expression, and opportunities for creativity.[5] These standards of welfare clearly acknowledge that a human being is something more than just a member of the particular organization.

Second, the imagery of our society suggests that the member of an organization may voluntarily cooperate because of 'joint values' through which the interests of the organization and the individual member coalesce, intrinsically as well as strategically. In some cases it is presumably the individual who identifies himself with the organization's goals and fate, as when someone takes personal pride in his school or place of work. In other cases the organization appears to become involved in the personal fate of a particular member, as when a hospital staff becomes genuinely excited over a patient's recovery. In most organizations some of both kinds of joint value serve to motivate the member.

Third, it is sometimes recognized that 'incentives' may have to be provided, these being rewards or side payments that frankly appeal to the individual in his capacity as someone whose ultimate interests are not those of the organization.[6] Some of these incentives are externally relevant, being rewards that the recipient can carry off the premises and use at his own discretion without implicating other members of the organization; money payments, training, and certification are the three principal instances. Some incentives are internally relevant, being perquisites that require the organization's own stage setting for their realization; important here are increases in rank and improvement in one's

5. Bendix, op. cit., 'Managerial Conceptions of "The Worker"', pp. 288–97.

6. Our way of thinking easily distinguishes between organizational goals and payments to employees, when in fact these may coincide. It is possible to define the goal of the organization as the allocation of privately consumable rewards to its employees, the janitor's pay having the same status as an organizational goal as the stockholder's profits. See R. M. Cyert and J. G. March, 'A Behavioral Theory of Organizational Objectives', in Mason Haire, ed., *Modern Organization Theory* (New York: Wiley, 1959), p. 80.

allotment of institutional conveniences. Many incentives carry both types of relevance, as in the case of occupational titles such as 'executive'.

Finally, it is perceived that participants may be induced to cooperate by threats of punishment and penalty if they do not. These 'negative sanctions' can involve an eventful decrease in usual rewards or in usual levels of welfare, but something other than mere reduction in reward seems to be involved. The notion that punishment can be an effective means of calling forth desired activity is one that requires assumptions about the nature of human nature different from those needed to account for the motivating effect of incentives. Fear of penalization seems adequate to prevent the individual from performing certain acts, or from failing to perform them; but positive rewards seem necessary if long-range, sustained, personal effort is to be obtained.

In our society, then, as presumably in some others, a formal instrumental organization does not merely use the activity of its members. The organization also delineates what are considered to be officially appropriate standards of welfare, joint values, incentives, and penalties. These conceptions expand a mere participation contract into a definition of the participant's nature or social being. These implicit images form an important element of the values which every organization sustains, regardless of the degree of its efficiency or impersonality.[7] Built right into the social arrangements of an organization, then, is a thoroughly embracing conception of the member – and not merely a conception of him *qua* member, but behind this a conception of him *qua* human being.[8]

We can readily see these organizational conceptions of man in those radical political movements and evangelical religious groups that stress Spartan standards of welfare and joint values that are at once intense and pervasive. Here the member is expec-

7. For a consideration of the value tasks of economic organizations, see Philip Selznick, *Leadership in Administration* (Evanston, Ill: Row, Peterson & Co., 1957).

8. For a case study see Alvin Gouldner, *Wildcat Strike* (London: Routledge & Kegan Paul, 1955), especially 'The Indulgency Pattern', pp. 18–22, where he outlines workers' moral expectations of the organization which are not an official part of the work contract.

ted to place himself at the disposal of the current needs of the organization. In telling him what he should do and why he should want to do this, the organization presumably tells him all that he may be. There will be many ways of backsliding, and even where backsliding does not occur frequently, concern that it may happen may be great, clearly pointing to the question of identity and self-definition.[9]

But we should not overlook that when an institution officially offers external incentives and openly admits to having a limited claim on the loyalty, the time, and the spirit of the participant, then the participant who accepts this – whatever he does with his reward and wherever he suggests his heart really lies – is tacitly accepting a view of what will motivate him, and hence a view of his identity. That he may feel that these assumptions about him are perfectly natural and acceptable tells us why, as students, we are generally unaware of them, not that they do not exist. A hotel that respectfully keeps its nose out of almost all of a guest's business and a brainwashing camp that feels the guest ought to have no private business for noses to be kept out of are similar in one regard: both have a general view of the guest that is important to him and with which he is expected to agree.

Extreme situations do, however, provide instruction for us, not so much in regard to the grander forms of loyalty and treachery as in regard to the small acts of living. It is perhaps only when we begin to study the memoirs of meticulous idealists, such as jailed conscientious objectors or politicized prisoners of war, with their problems of conscience in deciding how far to 'cooperate' with the authorities, that we begin to see the self-defining implications of even the minor give-and-take in organizations. For example, to move one's body in response to a polite request, let alone a command, is partly to grant the legitimacy of the other's line of action. To accept privileges like yard exercise or art materials while in jail is to accept in part the captor's view as to what one's desires and needs are, placing one in a position of having to show a little gratitude and cooperativeness (if only in taking what is being given) and through this some acknowledgement of the right of the

9. This is nicely portrayed in Isaac Rosenfeld's story, 'The Party', *The Kenyon Review*, Autumn 1947, pp. 572–607.

captor to make assumptions about oneself.[10] The issue of collaboration with the enemy is thus raised. Even a kind warden's polite request to show one's paintings to visitors may have to be rejected, lest this degree of cooperativeness seems to underwrite the legitimacy of the jailer's position and, incidentally, the legitimacy of his conception of oneself.[11] Similarly, although it is apparent that a political prisoner who dies silently in the face of physical torture may disprove his captors' conception of what will motivate him and hence disprove their conception of his human nature, there are important less apparent things to learn from the P.O.W.'s position. For example, under subtle interrogation a sophisticated prisoner may come to feel that even silence in response to questions can give information away, making him a collaborator in spite of himself, the situation thereby having self-defining power that he cannot wriggle out of merely by being staunch and true.[12]

Moralistic prisoners are of course not the only persons of high conscience whose stand leads us to become aware of the self-defining implications of minor aspects of participation in an organization. Another crucial group are those schooled and militant non-workers who extract an existence from a city like New York without paying for it with money. As they wend their way through the city, they construe each scene in terms of its possibilities for free food, free warmth, and free sleeping, thereby forcing us to see that ordinary people in these situations are expected to be caught up in other concerns, being of a character to possess such concerns. To learn of the implicit assumptions about proper use of a city's institutions is to learn about the character and concerns imputed to its citizens and held to be legitimate for them. Following a recent handbook in this area,[13] we are led to

10. For example, see Lowell Naeve, 'A Field of Broken Stones', in Holley Cantine and Dachine Rainer, eds., *Prison Etiquette* (Bearsville, N.Y.: Retort Press, 1950), pp. 28–44.

11. ibid., p. 35.

12. Albert Biderman, 'Social-Psychological Needs and "Involuntary" Behavior as Illustrated by Compliance in Interrogation', *Sociometry*, XXIII (1960), pp. 120–47, especially pp. 126–8.

13. Edmund G. Love, *Subways Are for Sleeping* (New York: Harcourt Brace and Company, 1957).

see that Grand Central Station is really for people with destinations or with friends to meet, and not a place to live; that a subway car is for travel, a hotel lounge to meet people in, a library for reading, a fire escape for survival, a movie house for viewing movies, and that any stranger who uses these places for a bedroom does not have the motivational make-up approved in these places. When we are told of a man going to the Hospital for Special Surgery every afternoon for a whole winter month to call on a girl confined there whom he hardly knew, because the hospital was warm and he was cold,[14] we can appreciate that a hospital expects a range of motives of its visitors but, like any other social entity, can be made a convenience of, taken advantage of, used, in short, in a way that is out of character with what its participants were supposed to be. Similarly, when we learn that militantly professional pickpockets may engage in petty but dangerous shoplifting because they have too much self-respect to pay for what they want,[15] we can appreciate the self-implications of a routine purchase in the Five and Dime.

Today discrepancies between the official view of the participants of an organization and the participants' own view are particularly visible in industry, in the question of rightful incentives and the concept of the 'steady worker'. Management often assumes that employees will want to work continuously towards the accumulation of savings and seniority. Yet from what seems true of the social world of some lower-class urban workers and of many workers reared in settlements at the periphery of industrial society, the 'steady-worker' concept applied to them is inappropriate. A Paraguayan case may be cited:

The behavior of peasants in a wageworking context is instructive. The more overt and idealized attitude is that, in working for someone, you are doing him a personal favor; the wages received in return are presents or tokens of esteem. More covertly, working for wages is seen as a means of raising a little cash for some specific purpose. Labor is not seen as a commodity, impersonally bought and sold, nor is working for an employer viewed as a possible means of making a living. The

14. ibid., p. 12.
15. David Maurer, *Whiz Mob*, Publication No. 24 of the American Dialect Society, 1955, p. 142.

labor turnover on the few plantations and in the brick factory is rapid, because, usually, as soon as a worker saves the small amount of cash which was his goal, he quits. Foreign employers in Paraguay have decided, in some instances, to pay higher than prevailing wages in order to obtain the highest-quality labor and to have satisfied workers who would be more permanent. The consequence of the higher wage rate was the opposite; the labor turnover was accelerated. It was not understood that those who work for wages do so only occasionally in order to obtain a certain sum of money; the sooner that amount is reached, the sooner they quit.[16]

It is not just industrial organizations that find that some of their participants have unanticipated definitions of the situation. Prisons could serve as an example. When an ordinary inmate is locked in his cell, he may suffer the deprivation that management anticipates; but for an upper-middle-class Englishman, thrust among the lower oddments of British society, solitary confinement may have an unanticipated meaning:

For the first five weeks of my sentence, except for two hours' work in the morning and afternoon and the exercise periods, I was locked in my cell, fortunately alone. The majority of men dreaded the long hours they were locked up. But after a while I came to look forward to being alone as a blessed relief from being shouted at by the officers or listening to the endlessly foul language of the majority of the other prisoners. I spent the greater part of those hours of solitude, reading.[17]

A French civil servant in West Africa provides by implication a more extreme case:

Now imprisonment is not always understood in the same way among the peoples of French West Africa. In one place it seems an adventure that has nothing dishonourable about it; in another, on the contrary, it is equivalent to being condemned to death. There are some Africans who, if you put them in prison, will become a sort of domestic servant, and end by regarding themselves as members of your family. But if you imprison a Fulani he will die.[18]

16. E. R. and H. S. Service, *Tobatí: Paraguayan Town* (Chicago: University of Chicago Press, 1954), p. 126.

17. Anthony Heckstall-Smith, *Eighteen Months* (London: Allan Wingate, 1954), p. 34.

18. Robert Delavignette, *Freedom and Authority in French West Africa* (London: International African Institute, Oxford University Press, 1950),

I do not mean in this discussion to point only to the explicit verbal ideology of organizational management concerning the human nature of its members, although this is certainly a significant element in the situation.[19] I mean to refer also to the *action* taken by management in so far as this expresses a conception of the persons acted upon.[20] Here prisons again provide a clear example. Ideologically, prison officials can, and sometimes do, take the stand that the prisoner should accept, if not embrace, the fact of being in prison, since prisons (at least the 'modern' type) are supposed to provide a way for the prisoner to pay his penalty to society, cultivate respect for the law, contemplate his sins, learn a legitimate trade, and in some cases obtain needed psychotherapy. But in terms of action, prison management largely focuses on the question of 'security', that is, the prevention of disorder and escape. An important aspect of prison management's definition of the character of inmates is that if you give inmates the slightest chance, they will try to escape their legal term. It may be added that the desire of inmates to escape, and their usual willingness to suppress this desire due to the likelihood of being caught and penalized, expresses (through sentiment and action, not words) an agreement with the view that management takes of them. A very great amount of conflict and hostility between management and inmates is therefore consistent with agreement concerning some aspects of the latter's nature.

In summary, then, I suggest that we look at participation in an organization from a special point of view. What the participant is expected to do, and what he actually does, will not be the real concern. I am interested in the fact that expected activity in the organization implies a conception of the actor and that an

---

p. 86. In short, stone walls do not necessarily a prison make, a theme treated under that chapter heading in Evelyn Waugh's *Decline and Fall*.

19. See Bendix, op. cit.

20. On assumptions covering economic motivation, see, for example, Donald Roy, 'Work Satisfaction and Social Reward in Quota Achievement: An Analysis of Piecework Incentive', *American Sociological Review*, XVIII (1953), pp. 507–14, and William F. Whyte *et al.*, *Money and Motivation* (New York: Harper, 1955), especially p. 2 ff., where Whyte discusses the managerial conceptions of the worker's human nature implied in piecework arrangements.

organization can therefore be viewed as a place for generating assumptions about identity. In crossing the threshold of the establishment, the individual takes on the obligation to be alive to the situation, to be properly oriented and aligned in it. In participating in an activity in the establishment, he takes on the obligation to involve himself at the moment in the activity. Through this orientation and engagement of attention and effort, he visibly establishes his attitude to the establishment and to its implied conceptions of himself. To engage in a particular activity in the prescribed spirit is to accept being a particular kind of person who dwells in a particular kind of world.

Now if any social establishment can be seen as a place where implications about self systematically arise, we can go on to see it as a place where these implications are systematically dealt with by the participant. To forgo prescribed activities, or to engage in them in unprescribed ways or for unprescribed purposes, is to withdraw from the official self and the world officially available to it. To prescribe activity is to prescribe a world; to dodge a prescription can be to dodge an identity.

I cite two examples. Musicians in the orchestra pit of a Broadway musical show are supposed to come to work on time, properly dressed, properly rehearsed, and properly alive to the business at hand. When they take their place in the 'gutter' they are supposed to give themselves up, in an attentive, decorous fashion, to playing their music or waiting for their cues. As musicians, they are expected to discipline themselves for containment in a musical world. This is the being that the pit and its music work generates for them.

Once the musical score of the particular show is learned, however, they find themselves with nothing to do and are, moreover, half hidden from those who expect them to be merely and fully musicians at work. In consequence, pit musicians, although physically immobilized, tend to wander from their work, surreptitiously exhibiting both a self and a world quite removed from the auditorium. By being careful about being seen, they may engage in writing letters or composing music, re-reading the classics, doing crossword puzzles, sending each other notes, playing chess with a set slid along the floor, or engaging in horseplay with water pistols. Obviously, when a musician with an earplug pocket radio suddenly startles theatre-goers in the front row by exclaiming, 'Snider hit a homer!'[21] he is not active in a capacity and a world that has been programmed for him – as audience complaints to the management attest.

A second example comes from life in a German prisoner-of-war camp.[22] An inmate meeting and passing an officer without causing the officer to correct the prisoner's manner appears to be an inmate properly contained in the prison and properly accepting of his imprisonment. But we know that in some cases such an inmate might be concealing under his coat a couple of bed boards to be used as roof timbers of an escape tunnel. An inmate thus equipped could stand before a prison officer and not be the person the officer was seeing, nor be in the world that the camp was supposed to impose upon him. The inmate is fixed in the camp, but his capacities have migrated. Moreover, since an overcoat *can* conceal clear evidence of this migration, and since a personal front involving clothing accompanies our participation in every organization, we must appreciate that *any* figure cut by *any* person *may* conceal evidence of spiritual leave-taking.

Every organization, then, involves a discipline of activity, but our interest here is that at some level every organization also involves a discipline of being – an obligation to be of a given character and to dwell in a given world. And my object here is to examine a special kind of absenteeism, a defaulting not from prescribed activity but from prescribed being.

PRIMARY AND SECONDARY ADJUSTMENTS

I

A concept can now be introduced. When an individual co-operatively contributes required activity to an organization and under required conditions – in our society with the support of

21. Albert M. Ottenheimer, 'Life in the Gutter', *The New Yorker*, 15 August, 1959.

22. P. R. Reid, *Escape from Colditz* (New York: Berkley Publishing Corp., 1956), p. 18.

institutionalized standards of welfare, with the drive supplied through incentives and joint values, and with the promptings of designated penalties – he is transformed into a cooperator; he becomes the 'normal', 'programmed', or built-in member. He gives and gets in an appropriate spirit what has been systematically planned for, whether this entails much or little of himself. In short, he finds that he is officially asked to be no more and no less than he is prepared to be, and is obliged to dwell in a world that is in fact congenial to him. I shall speak in these circumstances of the individual having a *primary adjustment* to the organization and overlook the fact that it would be just as reasonable to speak of the organization having a primary adjustment to him.

I have constructed this clumsy term in order to get to a second one, namely, *secondary adjustments*, defining these as any habitual arrangement by which a member of an organization employs unauthorized means, or obtains unauthorized ends, or both, thus getting around the organization's assumptions as to what he should do and get and hence what he should be. Secondary adjustments represent ways in which the individual stands apart from the role and the self that were taken for granted for him by the institution. For example, it is currently assumed in America that prisoners are persons who should have library facilities, the minds of prisoners being something that can and ought to be allowed to profit from reading. Given this legitimate library activity, we can anticipate Donald Clemmer's finding that prisoners often order books not for self-edification but to impress the parole board, give trouble to the librarian, or merely receive a parcel.[23]

There are sociological terms that refer to secondary adjustments, but these also refer to other things. The term 'informal' might be used, except that an organization can formally provide a time and place where members can be officially on their own, to create and enjoy recreational activity of their own choosing while exercising a behavioural style of locker-room informality: morning recess at school is an example. Informality here is part of primary adjustment. The term 'unofficial' might be used, except that this concept tends to pertain only to what would ordinarily

23. Donald Clemmer, *The Prison Community* (reissue; New York: Rinehart, 1958), p. 232.

be the official part of activity in the organization, and in any case the term 'unofficial' can properly be applied to those tacit understandings and uncodified activities through which the official aims of the organization can be furthered and the participants attain whatever primary adjustment is possible in the situation.[24]

I want to mention here some difficulties in using the concept of secondary adjustments. There are some secondary adjustments, such as a worker's practice of supplying his family's needs for the product he helps produce, that become so much an accepted part of the workings of an organization that they take on the character of 'perquisites', combining the qualities of being neither openly demanded nor openly questioned.[25] And some of these activities are not merely ones that are soon to be made legitimate but rather ones that must remain unofficial if they are to be effective. As Melville Dalton has shown, special capacities of a participant may have to be underwritten with rewards that no one else of his

24. In the classic Hawthorne study of informal or unofficial work groups, the main function of worker solidarity seems to have been to counter management's view of what workers ought to do and what they ought to be, in which case secondary adjustments and informal adjustments would refer to the same thing. However, later studies illustrated the fact that informal cliques at work might sustain activities perfectly compatible with, and even supportive of, the role established by management for workers. See Edward Gross, 'Characteristics of Cliques in Office Organizations', *Research Studies*, State College of Washington, XIX (1951), especially p. 135; 'Some Functional Consequences of Primary Controls in Formal Work Organizations', *American Sociological Review*, XVIII (1953), pp. 368–73. Obviously, a choice of 'substantive' rationality over 'formal' rationality – the selective pursuit of some official goals over other conflicting official goals – may be exhibited by management as well as by subordinates. See, for example, Charles Page, 'Bureaucracy's Other Face', *Social Forces*, XXV (1946), pp. 88–94; A. G. Frank, 'Goal Ambiguity and Conflicting Standards: An Approach to the Study of Organization', *Human Organization*, XVII (1959), pp. 8–13. See also the very remarkable study by Melville Dalton, *Men Who Manage* (New York: Wiley, 1959), for example, p. 222: '...informal action may work for many ends: to change and preserve the organization, to protect weak individuals, punish erring ones, reward others, to recruit new personnel, and to maintain dignity of the formal, as well as, of course, to carry on power struggles, and to work for ends we would all frown on.'

25. See, for example, the discussion by Paul Jacobs, 'Pottering about with the Fifth Amendment', *The Reporter*, 12 July 1956.

category receives. And what the courted participant may see as something he is getting away with – a secondary adjustment – may be deliberately allowed him by a conscientious official acting solely from a desire to see the over-all efficiency of the organization sustained.[26] Further, as previously suggested, there may be little agreement as to who are the spokesmen of the organization, and, where there is agreement, the spokesmen may be doubtful in their own minds as to where to draw the line between primary and secondary adjustments. For example, in many American colleges it would be considered a wrongheaded view of the nature of the student to curb too much the extracurricular 'social' part of college experience. This is in line with current views as to the necessity of having 'all-round' or 'well-rounded' students. But there is less consensus about exactly how the student's time is to be divided between academic and extracurricular work. Similarly, it is understandable and widely accepted that some female students will meet their future husbands at college and, once married, feel it more appropriate to drop out of school than to com-

26. Dalton, op. cit., especially Ch. vii, 'The Interlocking of Official and Unofficial Reward'. Dalton argues (pp. 198–9) that, in industry, corresponding to a wide range of unofficial rewards there is a very wide range of unofficial services that the executive must somehow call forth from his men if the organization is to function smoothly: 'Although informal reward ideally is given for effort and contribution beyond what is expected of a specific rank, it is also granted for many other purposes, often unexpected and formally taboo yet important for maintaining the organization and winning its ends. For example, it may be given (1) in lieu of a promotion or salary increase that could not be effected; (2) as a bonus for doing necessary but unpleasant or low-prestige things; (3) as an opiate to forget defeats in policy battles or status tiffs; (4) as a price for conciliating an irate colleague or making, in effect, a treaty with another department; (5) as a perquisite to key persons in clerical or staff groups to prevent slowdowns, and to bolster alertness against errors during critical periods; (6) as a frank supplement to a low but maximum salary; (7) for understanding and aid in the operation, and the defence, of the unofficial incentive system; (8) for great personal sacrifices. There are, of course, more subtle supports which may not be articulated but are intuitively recognized and rewarded where possible. These include: ability to maintain morale in the group or department; skill in picking and holding good subordinates; habitual tacit understanding of what superiors and colleagues expect but would not in some cases want to phrase, even unofficially; and expertness in saving the face of superiors and maintaining the dignity of the organization under adverse conditions.'

plete work for a degree. But college deans show varying degrees of concern when a female student switches her major each year upon playing out the field of men that the courses made accessible. Similarly, the managers of a commercial office may be clear about feeling it permissible for clerks and secretaries to select one another for personal relationships – provided that not too much working time is wasted in this way – and just as clearly disapprove of trainees who stay only long enough to check through the courting possibilities before going on to a fresh office and a new pasture. But management may be much more vague as to where between these two extremes the line is to be drawn separating the legitimate incidental use of an establishment as a convenience from illegitimately making a convenience of an institution.

Another problem associated with the distinction between primary and secondary adjustments is that these two modes of adaptation do not exhaust the possibilities; to get a rounded picture we may have to introduce another possibility. In whatever direction management presses the participants, it is possible for the participants to show more commitment and attachment to the entity than has been asked for or, sometimes, than is desired by management. A parishioner may try to live too much in and for the church; a housewife can keep her domain too clean; a junior officer can insist on going down with the ship. I do not think we have a major social problem here, except perhaps for those inmates of jails, mental hospitals, barracks, colleges, and parental homes who decline to use their discharge; analytically, however, we must see that just as there will always be persons who are felt not to embrace sufficiently a social entity to which they belong, so we will always find at least a few who may embarrass an organization by embracing it too warmly.

Finally, as we shall see later, the official doctrine according to which an institution is run may be so little honoured in practice, and a semi-official perspective may be so firmly and fully established, that we must analyse secondary adjustments relative to this authorized-but-not-quite-official system.

II

It should be quite plain that primary and secondary adjustments
are matters of social definition and that an adaptation or incentive that is legitimated at one period in a given society may not be
legitimated at a different time in its history or in another society.
An American convict who manages to spend a night with his wife
inside or outside the prison is attaining something of a high in
secondary adjustment;[27] a prisoner in a Mexican jail apparently
counts such an arrangement as part of the minimal standards of
welfare, a primary adjustment in the situation. In American in-
ternment camps, access to a prostitute is not conceived of as a
need to be honoured within the establishment; some German
concentration camps, on the other hand, did have this wider view
of the essential and characteristic needs of men.[28] In the nine-
teenth century, the American Navy recognized the drinking
character of its men and served daily grog; today this would be
counted a secondary adjustment. On the other hand, Melville
tells us that in the Navy then recreational games (like checkers) at
off-time were considered a special privilege;[29] today off-hour
games on board ship are considered an obvious natural right. In
British industry today, an eight-hour day, with an hour off for
lunch and ten minutes off for morning coffee or tea, attests to
current conceptions of the person who works. In the 1830s some
British spinning factories operated on the assumption that workers did not have a nature that needed fresh air or water to drink,
and workers were fined if caught in sly actions calculated to
obtain such pleasures during the working day.[30] At that time in
Britain, some managers apparently conceived of their employees on a purely stress basis, to be worked as long and as hard
as was consistent with getting them roused for the next day's
labour.

27. See James Peck, in Cantine and Rainer, op. cit., p. 47.
28. Eugen Kogon, *The Theory and Practice of Hell* (New York: Berkley
Publishing Corp., n.d.), pp. 123–4.
29. Herman Melville, *White Jacket* (New York: Grove Press, n.d.), p.
346.
30. Bendix, op. cit., p. 39.

Physical punishment provides a good example of a practice that clearly implies beliefs concerning the self of the person punished, and a practice subject to greatly changing conceptions. In the sixth century, St Benedict, considering what should be done with those who made recitation mistakes in the oratory, ruled that boys should receive corporal punishment.[31] This conception of how to induce obedience in disobedient boys has remained remarkably constant in Western society. Only in the last few decades have American schools come to define boys as objects that should not be touched for corrective purposes by persons other than their parents. In the last half century, our Navy, too, has come to feel that seamen, as 'human beings' with certain minimum dignities, ought not to be subject to the lash as a form of punishment. Currently the prison punishment of solitary confinement is being seriously re-examined, the belief becoming more widespread that our natures are such that isolation is contrary to them and ought not to be inflicted.

Religious observances provide another interesting participation condition to consider. In our society there is no residential institution without Sabbath observances, the implication being that a man's nature requires time for prayer, no matter what he has done; we are felt to have an inalienable capacity as religious beings. In commerce and industry, this assumption underlies Sunday off and a few annual religious holidays. In some Latin American countries, however, work organizations must give much more weight than this to what is felt to be the religious nature of man. Those who employ Ecuadorian Indians, for example, may have to allow one third of the year as time off for the alcoholic celebration of various fiestas and personal-life events having a sacred character.[32]

Even within the same class of establishments in the same society at the same time there may be appreciable differences in the line that is to be drawn between primary and secondary adjustments. The term 'fringe benefits' seems to refer to means and ends that

31. *The Holy Rule of Saint Benedict*, Ch. 45.

32. See the useful discussion by Beate R. Salz, *The Human Element in Industrialization*, Memoir No. 85, *American Anthropologist*, LVII (1955) No. 6, Part 2, pp. 97–100.

persons in one building will take for granted as legitimately their due but that persons across the street will still be denied officially. And within the same establishment there are marked changes with time. For example, in Nazi Germany an officially tabooed inmate organization for policing a concentration camp eventually became officially accepted,[33] in somewhat the same way that in the United States secret union organizers in plants and factories eventually became officially recognized shop stewards. In any case, it should be apparent that within a given establishment what is a primary adjustment for one category of participant can be a secondary adjustment for another, as when army kitchen workers regularly manage to eat above their rank, or when a maid surreptitiously enjoys the household liquor, or when a baby-sitter uses her place of work as a place for a party.

In addition to noting these variations, we must appreciate that organizations have a tendency to adapt to secondary adjustments not only by increasing discipline but also by selectively legitimating these practices, hoping in this way to regain control and sovereignty even at the loss of some of the participant's obligations. Domestic establishments are not the only ones in which there is a regularization through marriage of previous living in sin. When we learn something about the role of secondary adjustments we will also learn something about the mixed consequences of attempting to legitimate them.

III

Although I have so far considered secondary adjustments only in relation to the formal organization in which the individual is participating, it should be clear that these adjustments can and do arise in connexion with the individual's bondage to other types of social entity. In this light we can consider drinking relative to the public standards of a 'dry' town,[34] underground movements relative to the state, sexual affairs relative to marital life, and the various rackets relative to the legal world of business and

33. Kogon, op. cit., p. 62.
34. See, for example, C. K. Warriner, 'The Nature and Functions of Official Morality', *American Journal of Sociology*, LXIV (1958), pp. 165–8.

property arrangements.[35] Similarly, entities other than walled organizations attempt to maintain control over participants by legitimating secondary adjustments into primary ones. A city administration example may be cited:

At this time of the summer, our [New York City] police force, assisted by operatives of the Fire Department and the Department of Water Supply, Gas, and Electricity, is customarily engaged in widespread local skirmishes with children who wrench fire hydrants open to create their own bathing fountains. It is a practice that has been on the increase over the years, and both punitive and preventive measures have proved, for the most part, ineffectual. As a result, the Police, Fire, and Water Departments are trying to popularize a benevolent compromise whereby they hope to placate the city's children without unduly jeopardizing its supply of water. Under this plan, any 'reputable group or individual' (applicants are thoroughly investigated by the police) may apply for a special hydrant spray cap, which resembles a standard cap except that it is orange and is perforated in some fifty places, allowing the hydrant water to spurt out like a shower, in an orderly, restrained, but, it is hoped, satisfactory fashion.[36]

But whatever the social entity relative to which we want to consider secondary adjustments, we are likely to have to refer to wider units, for we must consider both the actual place in which the secondary adjustment occurs and the 'drawing region' from which the participants come. With children who snitch cookies from their mother's kitchen jar and consume them in the cellar, these distinctions are neither apparent nor important, since the household is at once the organization involved, the region from which the practitioners are drawn, and, roughly, the place in which the practice occurs. But in other cases the organization itself is not the only relevant unit. Thus, children from a whole neighbourhood may gather in a vacant house to engage in activities forbidden in the households of the neighbourhood, and the swimming hole outside some small towns may provide a place of forbidden behaviour that draws youths from the whole town.

35. A well-known statement of this theme relative to political regimes is David Riesman's 'Some Observations on the Limits of Totalitarian Power', *The Antioch Review*, Summer, 1952, pp. 155–68.
36. *The New Yorker*, 27 August 1960, p. 20.

There is a section of the city, sometimes called the 'tenderloin', that draws some husbands from households in every section of the city; and some towns, such as Las Vegas and Atlantic City, themselves became tenderloin districts for the whole nation.

An interest in the actual place in which secondary adjustments are practised and in the drawing region from which practitioners come shifts the focus of attention from the individual and his act to collective matters. In terms of a formal organization as a social establishment, the corresponding shift would be from an individual's secondary adjustment to the full set of such adjustments that all the members of the organization severally and collectively sustain. These practices together comprise what can be called the *underlife* of the institution, being to a social establishment what an underworld is to a city.

Reverting once again to the social establishment, an important characteristic of primary adjustments is their contribution to institutional stability: the participant who adapts to the organization in this way is likely to keep on participating as long as the organization wants him to, and, if he leaves before this, to leave in a way that smooths the transition for his replacement. This aspect of primary adjustments leads us to distinguish two kinds of secondary adjustments: first, *disruptive* ones, where the realistic intentions of the participants are to abandon the organization or radically alter its structure, in either case leading to a rupture in the smooth operation of the organization; second, *contained* ones, which share with primary adjustments the characteristic of fitting into existing institutional structures without introducing pressure for radical change,[37] and which can, in fact, have the obvious function of deflecting efforts that might otherwise be disruptive. The settled and established parts of an organization's underlife

37. This defining characteristic of contained secondary adjustments has been noted by Richard Cloward. See Session Four of *New Perspectives for Research on Juvenile Delinquency*, eds. Helen L. Witmer and Ruth Kotinsky, U.S. Department of Health, Education and Welfare, Children's Bureau Publication No. 356 (1956), especially p. 89. See also his 'Social Control in the Prison', in Social Science Research Council Pamphlet No. 15, *Theoretical Studies in Social Organization of the Prison* (1960), pp. 20–48, especially p. 43 ff., where Cloward examines the 'conservative' character of élite inmate adjustment.

tend, therefore, to be composed primarily of contained, not disruptive, adjustments.

Disruptive secondary adjustments have been studied in the dramatic processes of unionization and infiltration of governments. Because disruptive secondary adjustments are by definition temporary things, as in the planning for a mutiny, the term 'adjustment' may not be quite suitable.

I shall restrict myself primarily to contained secondary adjustments and will often refer to them simply as 'practices'. Although the form taken by these practices will often be similar to that of disruptive secondary adjustments, the ends are typically different and there is a greater likelihood of only one or two persons being involved – a question of personal not conspiratorial gains. Contained secondary adjustments are given different folk titles, depending on the social entity relative to which they are practised. Our chief sources regarding these practices come from the study of human relations in industry and from students of prisoner society, the latter employing such terms as 'informal adjustments' or 'conways'.[38]

An individual's use of a secondary adjustment is inevitably a social-psychological matter, affording him gratifications he might not otherwise obtain. But precisely what an individual 'gets out of' a practice is perhaps not the sociologist's first concern. From a sociological point of view, the initial question to be asked of a secondary adjustment is not what this practice brings to the practitioner but rather the character of the social relations that its acquisition and maintenance require. This constitutes a structural as opposed to a consummatory or social-psychological point of view. Given the individual and one of his secondary adjustments, we can start with the abstract notion of the full set of others involved in the practice and go on from there systematically to consider the characteristics of this set: its size, the nature of the bond that holds members in it, and the type of sanctions that ensure maintenance of the system. Further, given the set associated with any individual's secondary adjustment, we can go on to ask

38. Clemmer, op. cit., pp. 159–60; Norman S. Hayner and Ellis Ash, 'The Prisoner Community as a Social Group', *American Sociological Review*, IV (1939), pp. 362–9.

about the proportion of persons of this kind in the institution, and, of these, the proportion who are involved in similar sets, thus getting a measure of one kind of 'saturation' that can occur regarding a given practice.

IV

We can begin to look at secondary adjustments – at the practices comprising the underlife of social establishments – by noting that they occur with different frequency and in different forms according to the location of the practitioner in the hierarchy of the organization. Persons at the bottom of large organizations typically operate in drab backgrounds, against which higher-placed members realize their internal incentives, enjoying the satisfaction of receiving visible indulgences that others do not. Low-placed members tend to have less commitment and emotional attachment to the organization than higher-placed members. They have jobs, not careers. In consequence they seem more likely to make wide use of secondary adjustments. Although people toward the top of organizations are likely to be appreciably motivated by joint values, their special duties as representatives of the organization are also likely to lead to travel, entertaining, and ceremonials – that special class of secondary adjustments recently publicized in descriptions of the 'expense account' round of life. Perhaps secondary adjustments are least found in the middle range of organizations. It is here, perhaps, that people most closely approach what the organization expects them to be, and it is from here that models of good conduct can be drawn for the edification and inspiration of those lower down.[39]

At the same time, of course, the character of primary adjustments will differ according to rank. Workers at the bottom may not be expected to throw themselves into the organization or 'take it home' with them, but high officers are likely to have these identificatory obligations. For example, an attendant in a state mental hospital who leaves work as soon as his shift is over may be acting in a way that has been legitimated for him, expressing the nature the organization accords him; if a head of a service gives this nine-to-five impression, however, he may be considered

39. Suggested by Paul Wallin.

dead wood by management – someone who is not living up to the standards of devotion expected of a real doctor. Similarly, an attendant who reads a magazine during working hours on the ward may be considered within his rights as long as no immediate duty calls him; a nurse who thus conducts herself is more likely to offend because this is 'unprofessional' conduct.

The undergrowth of secondary adjustments also differs in extent according to the type of establishment.

Presumably the shorter the period of continuous time that a given category of participant spends on the premises, the more possible it will be for management to maintain a programme of activity and motivation that these participants accept. Thus, in those establishments whose purpose is the sale of a minor standardized item such as cigarettes, customers will usually complete the purchase cycle without deviating very far from the role programmed for them – except, perhaps, in demanding or declining a moment's sociability. Establishments that oblige the participant to 'live in' will presumably be rich in underlife, for the more time that is programmed by the organization, the less likelihood of successfully programming it.

So also in those organizations where recruitment is involuntary, we can expect that, at least initially, the recruit will not be in harmony with the self-definitions officially available for persons like himself and will therefore orient himself to unlegitimized activities.

Finally, as previously suggested, establishments that do not provide appreciable external incentives, not having made their peace with what is seen as the Adam in man, are likely to find that some external incentives are unofficially developed.

All of the conditions that are likely to promote active underlife are present in one institution that is receiving considerable attention today: the mental hospital. In what follows I want to consider some of the main themes that occur in the secondary adjustments I recorded in a year's participant observation study of patient life in a public mental hospital of over 7,000 patients, hereafter called 'Central Hospital'.[40]

Institutions like mental hospitals are of the 'total' kind, in the

40. Acknowledgements are given in the Preface.

sense that the inmate lives all the aspects of his life on the premises in the close company of others who are similarly cut off from the wider world. These institutions tend to contain two broad and quite differently situated categories of participants, staff and inmates, and it is convenient to consider the secondary adjustments of the two categories separately.

Something could be said of staff secondary adjustments at Central Hospital. For example, staff occasionally made use of patients as baby-sitters,[41] gardeners, and general handymen.[42] Patients with town parole were sometimes sent on errands for physicians and nurses. Attendants expected to eat some hospital food even though this was forbidden, and those with kitchen jobs were known to 'liberate' food. The hospital garage was sometimes used as a source of repairs and parts for staff automobiles.[43] A night-shift attendant often maintained a day job and realistically expected to sleep during his shift, sometimes asking other attendants or even friendly patients to give him a warning signal in order to do this safely.[44] One or two rackets may have flourished,

41. Apparently wherever there are total institutions with staff families in residence there are inmate baby-sitters. See, for example, T. E. Lawrence's fine work on army and air force barracks life in Britain in the twenties, *The Mint* (London: Jonathan Cape, 1955), p. 40.

42. See the interesting material in Kogon (op. cit., pp. 84–6) on the private use that SS men made of inmate work in camp tailor shops, photographic departments, print shops, armament works, pottery and paint shops, etc., especially during the Christmas season. Dalton (op. cit., p. 199), analysing unofficial rewards in an American industrial plant, cites a case of *specialization* in this function: 'Ted Berger, officially foreman of Milo's carpenter shop, was *sub rosa* a custodian and defender of the supplementary reward system. Loyal beyond question, he was allowed great freedom from formal duties and expected, at least through the level of department heads, to function as a clearinghouse for the system. His own reward was both social and material, but his handling of the system unintentionally produced a social glue that bound together people from various levels and departments. Not required to operate machines, Berger spent a minimum of six hours daily making such things as baby beds, storm windows, garage windows, doll buggies, rocking horses, tables, meat boards, and rolling pins. These objects were custom built for various managers.'

43. For an example from industry, see Dalton, op. cit., p. 202.

44. Night-shift laxity is of course a standard phenomenon throughout American work organizations. See, for example, S. M. Lipset, M. A. Trow,

such as (one patient claimed) the diverting of the canteen funds of mute patients to items that attendants could distribute or personally consume.

I think these secondary adjustments on the part of Central Hospital employees should be considered minor. Much greater elaboration of staff underlife can be found in many other mental hospitals[45] as well as in establishments such as army installations. Furthermore, these practices in Central Hospital ought to be evaluated alongside the large number of instances of staff persons giving time and attention to inmate recreational activity during off-hours, thereby exhibiting more devotion to their job than was expected of them by management. I will therefore not consider many of the standard secondary adjustments practised by subordinates in work organizations, such as restriction of output,[46] 'make-work', 'government work',[47] collusive control of productivity reporting,[48] suggesting only that the meticulous and tender care that students like Donald Roy and Melville Dalton exert in reporting these techniques of adjustment is a model for students of other establishments.

In considering the secondary adjustments of mental patients in Central Hospital, I will cite, where possible, parallel practices

and J. S. Coleman, *Union Democracy* (Glencoe, Ill.: The Free Press, 1956), p. 139.

45. For example, the use of electroshock for disciplinary purposes. John Maurice Grimes, *Why Minds Go Wrong* (Chicago: published by the author, 1951), p. 100, cites the well-known 'soap-sock' as an effective attendant's instrument: it leaves no mark, is easily concealed, and never kills.

46. A leading paper here is Donald Roy's 'Quota Restriction and Goldbricking in a Machine Shop', *American Journal of Sociology*, LVII (1952), pp. 427–42. See also O. Collins, M. Dalton, and D. Roy, 'Restriction of Output and Social Cleavage in Industry', *Applied Anthropology* [now *Human Organization*], V (1946), pp. 1–14.

47. As footnoted by Edward Gross, *Work and Society* (New York: Crowell, 1958), p. 521: 'Sometimes also called "home work" and used to refer to doing personal jobs [*on company time*], such as repairing the leg on the dining-room table, mending home tools, making toys for one's children, and so on.'

48. For example, Donald Roy, 'Efficiency and "The Fix": Informal Intergroup Relations in a Piecework Machine Shop', *American Journal of Sociology*, LX (1954), pp. 255–66.

reported in other types of establishments and employ a thematic analysis of secondary adjustments that I think applies to all establishments. An informal combination of the case-history and comparative approach will therefore be involved, with more emphasis, in some cases, on comparisons than on the mental hospital studied.

From the point of view of psychiatric doctrine, apparently, there are no secondary adjustments possible for inmates: everything a patient is caused to do can be described as a part of his treatment or of custodial management; everything a patient does on his own can be defined as symptomatic of his disorder or of his convalescence. A criminal who 'cops a plea' and elects to serve his time in a mental hospital instead of a jail can thus be thought to be really, underneath it all, in search of therapy, just as a malingerer in the army who affects mental symptoms can be thought to be genuinely ill, even though not ill with the particular disorder he is affecting. Similarly, a patient who settles down in the hospital, making a good thing of it, may be felt not to be abusing a place of treatment but to be really still ill since he elects this adaptation.

In the main, state mental hospitals do not function on the basis of psychiatric doctrine, but in terms of a 'ward system'. Drastically reduced living conditions are allocated through punishments and rewards, expressed more or less in the language of penal institutions. This framework of actions and words is the one employed almost entirely by attendants and to a considerable degree by higher staff, especially in connexion with the day-to-day problems of running the hospital. The disciplinary frame of reference lays out a relatively full set of means and ends that patients can legitimately obtain, and against the background of this authoritative but not quite official system, a great number of patient activities *effectively* become illicit or not permissible. So emptied is the effectively authorized life given some patients on some wards that almost any move they make is likely to add an unplanned-for satisfaction.

PART TWO: HOSPITAL UNDERLIFE

SOURCES

I TURN now to consider the sources of materials that patients employ in their secondary adjustments.

I

The first thing to note is the prevalence of *make-do's*. In every social establishment participants use available artifacts in a manner and for an end not officially intended, thereby modifying the conditions of life programmed for these individuals. A physical reworking of the artifact may be involved, or merely an illegitimate context of use, in either case providing homely illustrations of the Robinson Crusoe theme. Obvious examples come from prisons, where, for example, a knife may be hammered from a spoon, drawing ink extracted from the pages of *Life* magazine,[49] exercise books used to write betting slips,[50] and cigarettes lit by a number of means – sparking an electric-light outlet,[51] a homemade tinderbox,[52] or a match split into quarters.[53] While this transformation process underlies many complex practices, it can be most clearly seen where the practitioner is not involved with others (except in learning and teaching the technique), he alone consuming what he just produced.

In Central Hospital many simple make-do's were tacitly tolerated. For example, inmates widely used free standing radiators to dry personal clothing that they had washed, on their own, in the bathroom sink, thus performing a private laundry cycle that was officially only the institution's concern. On hard-bench

49. Cantine and Rainer, op. cit., p. 42.

50. Frank Norman, *Bang to Rights* (London: Secker and Warburg, 1958), p. 90.

51. ibid., p. 92.

52. George Dendrickson and Frederick Thomas, *The Truth About Dartmoor* (London: Goliancz, 1954), p. 172.

53. ibid., pp. 172–3.

wards, patients sometimes carried around rolled-up newspapers to place between their necks and the wooden benches when lying down. Rolled-up coats and towels were used in the same way. Patients with experience in other imprisoning institutions employed an even more effective artifact in this context, a shoe.[54] In transferring from one ward to another, patients would sometimes carry their belongings in a pillow slip knotted at the top, a practice which is semi-official in some jails.[55] The few ageing patients fortunate enough to have a private sleeping room would sometimes leave a towel underneath their room washstand, transforming the stand into a reading desk and the towel into a rug to protect their feet from the cold floor. Older patients who were disinclined or unable to move around sometimes employed strategies to avoid the task of going to the toilet: on the ward, the hot steam radiator could be urinated on without leaving too many long-lasting signs; during twice-weekly shaving visits to the basement barber shop, the bin reserved for used towels was used for a urinal when the attendants were not looking. Backward patients of all ages sometimes carried around paper drinking cups to serve as portable spittoons and ashtrays, since attendants were sometimes more concerned about keeping their floors clean than they were in suppressing spitting or smoking.[56]

In total institutions make-do's tend to be focused in particular areas. One area is that of personal grooming – the fabrication of devices to facilitate presenting oneself to others in a seemly guise. For example, nuns are said to have placed a black apron behind a window pane to create a mirror – a mirror being a means of self-examination, correction, and approval ordinarily denied the

54. Compare the naval equivalent (Melville, op. cit., p. 189): '...the hard, unyielding, and ponderous man-of-war and Navy regulation tarpaulin hat which, when new, is stiff enough to sit upon, and indeed, in lieu of his thumb, sometimes serves the common sailor for a bench.'

55. For a British example, see Dendrickson and Thomas, op. cit., p. 66.

56. In Central Hospital many patients remained entirely mute, were incontinent, hallucinated, and practised other classic symptoms. However, very few patients, as far as I could see, had the temerity purposely and persistently to drop ashes on the linoleum floor, just as few declined to line up for food, take their shower, go to bed, or get up on time. Behind a ward show of frank psychosis was a basic ward routine that was quite fully adhered to.

sisterhood.[57] In Central Hospital, toilet paper was sometimes 'organized'; neatly torn, folded, and carried on one's person, it was apologetically used as Kleenex by some fastidious patients. So, too, during the hot summer months a few male patients cut and tailored their hospital-issue khaki pants into neat-appearing summer shorts.

II

The simple make-do's I have cited are characterized by the fact that to employ them one need have very little involvement in and orientation to the official world of the establishment. I consider now a set of practices that imply somewhat more aliveness to the legitimated world of the institution. Here the spirit of the legitimate activity may be maintained but is carried past the point to which it was meant to go; we have an extension and elaboration of existing sources of legitimate satisfactions, or the exploitation of a whole routine of official activity for private ends. I shall speak here of 'working' the system.

Perhaps the most elementary way of working the system in Central Hospital was exhibited by those patients on back wards who went on sick call or declined to comply with ward discipline in order, apparently, to trap the attendant or physician into taking notice of them and engaging them in social interaction, however disciplinarian.

Most hospital techniques for working the system did not seem to be closely connected with mental illness, however. An example of such techniques is the elaborate set of practices associated with food-getting. For example, in a large cafeteria where the 900 patients of a male chronic service[58] ate in shifts, some would

57. Kathryn Hulme, *The Nun's Story* (London: Muller, 1956), p. 33. Norman, op. cit., p. 87, states that during Christmas-Day relaxation of discipline at the British prison, Camp Hill, homosexuals made their faces up with white tooth powder and reddened their lips with dye obtained by wetting the covers of books.

58. Residentially speaking, American mental hospitals are typically organized officially by wards and services. A ward usually consists of sleeping quarters (which often can be locked off), a day room, a nurses' station with a view of the day room, various maintenance and administrative offices, a row of isolation cells, and sometimes a dining-room area. A service consists

bring their own condiments so as to season their own food to their own taste; sugar, salt, pepper, and catsup were brought in for this purpose in small bottles carried in jacket pockets. When coffee was served in paper cups, patients sometimes protected their hands by inserting their cup in a second paper cup. On days when bananas were made available, a few of the patients would spirit away a cup of milk from the jug meant for those who required milk on their diet, and would cut their bananas up in slices, put on some sugar, and expansively eat a 'proper' dessert. On days when the food was both liked and portable, for example when frankfurters or liver were served, some patients would wrap up their food in a paper napkin and then go back for 'seconds', taking the first serving back to the ward for a night snack. A few patients brought empty bottles on days when milk was served, taking some of this back to the ward, too. If more of a given item on the menu was desired, one device was to eat just that item, dump the remainder of one's serving in the slop pail, and return (when this was allowed) for a full course of seconds. A few of the paroled patients assigned to eat in this cafeteria would, for the evening meal in summer, put their cheese between two slices of bread, wrap up what had now become a sandwich, and eat in peace outside the patient canteen, buying a cup of coffee. Patients with town parole would sometimes top this off by buying pie and ice cream at the local drugstore. In a smaller dining-room in a different hospital service, patients who (rightly) feared that seconds would not be available for long would sometimes take their portion of meat from their plate, put it between two pieces of bread, leave this by their place, and immediately return to the line to get seconds. These farsighted patients would sometimes return to their places to find that a fellow inmate had made off with the first serving, cheating the cheaters at the cost of very little effort.

---

of a set of these wards filling one or more separate buildings, involving a common administration, and having some basis of patient homogeneity – age, sex, race, chronicity, etc. This homogeneity allows the service to evolve wards of differentiated character and function, roughly providing a ladder of privilege, up and down which any patient in the service can be shifted with minimum bureaucratic effort. The hospital as a whole tends to repeat through its services what, in miniature, each service does through its wards.

In order to work a system effectively, one must have an intimate knowledge of it;[59] it was easy to see this kind of knowledge put to work in the hospital. For example, it was widely known by parole patients that at the end of charitable shows at the theatre hall cigarettes or candy would probably be given out at the door, as the patient audience filed out. Bored by some of these shows, some patients would come a few minutes before closing time in order to file out with the others; still others would manage to get back into the line several times and make the whole occasion more than ordinarily worthwhile. Staff were of course aware of these practices, and late-comers to some of the hospital-wide patient dances were locked out, the assumption being that they timed their arrival so as to be able to eat and run. The Jewish Welfare women apparently served brunch after the weekly morning service and one patient claimed that 'by coming at the right time you can get the lunch and miss the service'. Another patient, alive to the little-known fact that the hospital had a team of seamstresses to keep clothes in repair, would take his own clothes there and get shirts and pants tailored to a good fit, showing his gratitude by a package or two of cigarettes or a small sum of money.

Timing was important in other means of working the hospital. For example, old magazines and pocket books donated through the Red Cross were delivered once a week by truck to the recreation building located on the hospital grounds, from the library of which these reading materials would be distributed to individual patients and to wards. A few avid readers knew the truck's exact routine and would await its coming in order to have first choice. A few patients who knew the timing of the underground food runs between one of the central kitchens and a chronic service would sometimes pause near ground-level points of the

59. Knowledge of a guard's routine figures in many fictional escape stories. Desperation and knowledge of routines are also linked in real experience as Kogon (op. cit., p. 180) illustrates in discussing the response of Buchenwald prisoners to reduction and withdrawal of rations: '...When an inmate had died in the tents, the fact was concealed and the dead man was dragged or carried by one or two men to the bread issue point, where the ration was issued to the "helpers". The body was then simply dumped anywhere in the roll-call area.'

tracks, hoping to snag a portion of food from the mobile vats.
Another example has to do with obtaining information. The
meals served in one of the large patient cafeterias were first served
to a ward-bound group of old men. Ambulatory patients who
wanted to know whether to go to the cafeteria or to buy sandwiches from the patients' canteen would regularly look through
the window of this ward at the right moment to learn what was
on the menu.

Another hospital example of working the system was scaven-
ging. A few patients made the rounds of the refuse dumps near their
service just prior to collection time. They poked through the top
layers of garbage collected in the large wooden storage boxes,
searching for food, magazines, newspapers, or other oddments
that were made meaningful to these collectors by short supply and
by the necessity of humbly asking an attendant or other official
for them, the means by which these materials could be obtained
in a legitimate way.[60] Saucers used by staff as ashtrays in the hallways of the administrative offices of some services were periodically searched for usable butts. Open communities of course have
scavengers, too, and it would seem that any large system for
collecting and then destroying used objects will provide a way for
someone to get by.[61]

The possibility of working the system was one that a few
patients excelled in exploiting, leading to individual feats that
could hardly be called customary secondary adjustments. On a
service with two convalescent wards, one locked and one open,
one patient claimed he arranged a transfer from the locked ward
to the open one because the cloth on the pool table in the open
ward was in superior condition; another patient claimed to have
arranged a transfer in the other direction because the locked ward
was 'more sociable', some of its members being forced to remain

60. Compare concentration-camp experience (Kogon, op. cit., p. 111):
' ...there were hundreds who time and again tried to ransack the garbage
pails in search of edible offal, who gathered and boiled bones.'

61. A significant part of the equipment that small-town boys use to build
their worlds out of comes from refuse depositories of various kinds. The
psychoanalytical version of these cloacal-like activities is interesting, but
perhaps occasionally suggests over much ethnographic distance from the
scavengers in question.

on it. Another patient, with town parole, would periodically get excused from his hospital job and be given carfare to ride into town to look for work; he claimed that once in town he would settle down for the afternoon in a movie.

I would like to add that patients with experience in other situations of deprivation, patients who were in some sense con-wise, often showed very rapidly that they knew how to work the system. For example, one inmate, with prior experience in Lexington, on his first morning in the hospital had rolled himself a supply of roll-your-owns, obtained polish and done two pairs of his shoes, uncovered which fellow inmate had a large cache of detective stories, organized himself a supply of coffee by means of instant coffee and the hot-water tap, and found himself a place in the group psychotherapy sessions, sitting up close and waiting quietly for a few minutes before beginning to build up what was to be an active role. It is understandable, then, why an attendant claimed that 'it takes no more than three days and you can tell if a man's off the street.'

The means of working the system that I have so far mentioned are ones that profit only the actor himself or the persons he is closely related to. Practices designed with corporate interests in mind are found in many total institutions,[62] but collective means of working the system seem not too common in mental hospitals. Collective secondary adjustments that were found in Central Hospital seemed to be sustained mostly by patients who were graduates of the jail-like institution within the institution – 'Prison Hall' – which housed those with the legal status of the criminally insane. For example, one ward of ex-imprisoned patients would send one of its members to the supply kitchen just before mealtime to bring the food back hot in a covered tray; otherwise

62. For example, Kogon, op. cit., p. 137: 'In every concentration camp where the political prisoners attained any degree of ascendancy, they turned the prisoner hospital, scene of fearful SS horrors that it was, into a rescue station for countless prisoners. Not only were patients actually cured wherever possible; healthy prisoners, in danger of being killed or shipped to a death camp, were smuggled on the sick list to put them beyond the clutches of the SS. In special cases, where there was no other way out, men in danger were nominally permitted to "die", living on under the names of prisoners who had actually died.'

the food would be cold from its slow underground passage.

In considering the process of 'working the system', one must inevitably consider the ways in which hospitalization itself was worked. For example, both the staff and inmates sometimes claimed that some patients came into the hospital to dodge family and work responsibilities,[63] or to obtain free some major medical and dental work, or to avoid a criminal charge.[64] I cannot speak for the validity of these claims. There were also cases of patients with town parole who claimed they used the hospital as a tank to sober up in after weekend drinking episodes, this function being apparently facilitated by the claimed value of tranquillizers as a treatment for acute hangovers. And there were other town parolees who could accept below-subsistence pay for part-time civilian work, ensuring their own competitive position on the basis of free hospital food and lodging.[65]

There were in addition some less traditional ways in which patients worked the hospital system. Every social establishment

63. In one service in the hospital there were a considerable number of male patients who entered at a time when jobs were scarce and, being somewhat cut off from the flow of events outside, still believed that the 'deal' they were getting on the inside was a good one. As one suggested upon receiving his free dessert, 'You don't get apple pie like this on the outside for twenty-five cents, you don't.' Here the apathy and quest for a safe berth, characteristic of the depression years, could still be studied, preserved in institutional amber.

64. For a lower-class male who already has the stigma of having been in a mental hospital and who is restricted to the kind of job in which length of work experience or seniority is of small significance, coming into a mental hospital where he knows the ropes and has friends among the attendants is no great deprivation. It was claimed that a few of these ex-patients carried a card attesting to their medical history; when picked up by police, on whatever charge, they produced their medical card, thereby influencing their disposition. Patients I knew, however, claimed that, except for a murder charge, hospitalization was in general a poor way to beat a rap: prisons provide determinate sentences, the possibility of earning a little money, and, increasingly, good TV facilities. I felt, however, that this line ought really to be considered as part of anti-staff morale, except in those hospitals, such as Central, which had a specially walled-in building for the 'criminally insane'.

65. In militant psychiatric doctrine, as suggested, these motives for exploiting hospitalization can be interpreted as symptomatic of a 'real' need for psychiatric treatment.

brings its participants into preferential face-to-face contact, or at least increases the probability of such contact, providing a basis of secondary adjustment in the mental hospital as in other institutions. One group of patients who exploited the social possibilities of the hospital were the ex-prisoners, the graduates of Prison Hall. These men were relatively young and tended to be of urban working-class background. Once graduated to the hospital proper, they acquired more than their share of the pleasant job assignments and the female patients felt to be attractive; most of the men who in another institution would be called 'campus wheels' came from their ranks. Another group were Negroes: some of these who so wished were able to some degree to cross the class and colour line, cliquing with and dating white patients,[66] and receiving from the psychiatric staff some of the middle-class professional conversation and treatment denied them outside the hospital. A third group were the homosexuals: incarcerated for their proclivities, they found a one-sexed dormitory life awaiting them, with concomitant sexual opportunities.

One of the interesting means by which a few patients worked the hospital system had to do with sociable association with outsiders. Concern for interaction with outsiders seemed to be related to the caste-like position of patients in the hospital and to myths associated with the stigma label of insanity. Although some patients claimed they could not feel comfortable with someone not a patient, other patients, exhibiting the opposite side of the same coin, felt that it was intrinsically healthier to associate with non-patients and, in addition, a recommendation of some kind. Also, outsiders were less likely to be as offensive as staff members about patient status; outsiders did not know how lowly the position of patient was. Finally, a few patients claimed to be very tired of talking about their incarceration and their case with fellow patients and looked to conversation with outsiders as a

66. I often heard old-line white attendants and old-line patients grumble about the occasional sight of a Negro male patient dating a white female. Opposed to this old-line group, and separated from it by some kind of social epoch, were the hospital administration, which had desegregated the admissions and geriatrics services and had begun desegregating the other services, and the leading cliques of patients, who were young and more concerned, apparently, to be 'hip' than to hold to a colour line.

means of forgetting about the culture of the patient.[67] Association
with outsiders could confirm a sense of not being a mental patient.
Understandably, therefore, on the grounds and in the recreation
building some 'passing' was effected, serving as an important
source of assurance that one was really indistinguishable from the
sane and that the sane themselves were really not very smart.

There were several strategic points in the hospital social system where association with outsiders was possible. Some of the
adolescent female children of the resident doctors participated as
social equals in the small circle of paroled male patients and student nurses who dominated the hospital tennis court.[68] During
and after games this group would lounge on the nearby grass, engage in horseplay, and in general maintain a non-hospital tone.
Similarly, on evenings when outside charitable organizations ran a
dance, bringing some young females with them, one or two male
patients affiliated themselves with these women, apparently obtaining from them a non-hospital response. So, too, on the admission ward where student nurses were spending their period of
psychiatric training, some young male patients regularly played
cards and other games with them, during which a dating, not a
nursing, ethos was maintained. And during the 'higher' therapies
such as psychodrama or group therapy, visiting professionals
would often sit in to observe the latest methods; these persons,
too, provided patients with a source of interaction with normals.
Finally, patients on the all-star hospital baseball team, when
playing against teams from the environing community, were able
to enjoy the special camaraderie that develops between opposing
teams in a game and that separates both teams off from the
spectators.

67. All of these themes may of course be traced in any stigmatized group,
Ironically, patients, in saying, 'We're just different from normal people,
that's all,' do not appreciate, just as other 'normal deviants' do not, that
there are few sentiments so stereotyped, predictable, and 'normal' in any
stigmatized grouping.

68. Socially speaking, no female patient 'made it' with this group.
Incidentally, children of resident doctors were the only non-patient category
I found that did not evince obvious caste distance from patients; why I do
not know.

III

Perhaps the most important way in which patients worked the system in Central Hospital was by obtaining a 'workable' assignment, that is, some special work, recreation, therapy, or ward assignment that alone could make available certain secondary adjustments – and often a whole set of them. This theme can be cited from an ex-prisoner's report on the British prison, Maidstone:

Three times a year in the Education Office, at the end of each term, we forwarded a report to the Prison Commissioners on the progress made in the various classes. We produced figures and more figures to show the numbers of prisoners who attended classes in this and that. We stated, for instance, that one of the most popular classes was a discussion group that debated 'Current Affairs'. We did not say why it was so popular, which was because the well-meaning woman who conducted the debate each week came supplied with tobacco for her students. The class was held in a haze of blue smoke, and while the teacher held forth upon 'Current Affairs' the students, consisting of the old lags, loafers and morons, sat back enjoying a free smoke! [69]

Assignments can be sought with these use-possibilities in mind, or these uses may develop after the assignment was obtained, then functioning as a reason for holding on to it. In either case, we have in 'working an assignment' one of the basic similarities among mental hospitals, prisons, and concentration camps. More than he does in connexion with simple make-do's, the inmate implies to the relevant officials that the assignment is being pursued for appropriate motives – especially where the assignment is voluntary and involves relatively intimate cooperation between staff and inmates, for here 'sincere effort' is often expected. In such cases, the inmate can appear to be actively embracing his assignment, and through this the institution's view of him, when in fact his special way of profiting from the assignment acts as a wedge between himself and the institution's heightened expectations regarding him. In fact, acceptance of an assignment that through some device could have been refused begins a courtship of good opinion between inmate and staff, and the development of

69. Heckstall-Smith, op. cit., p. 65.

a staff attitude to the inmate that is easier than the usual one for the inmate to compromise by manipulative activity.

The first general point to note I have already suggested, that if some product results from a work assignment the worker is likely to be in a position to avail himself informally of some of the fruit of his labour. In the hospital, those with kitchen assignments were in a position to obtain extra food;[70] those who worked in the laundry obtained a more frequent supply of clean clothes; those in the shoe-repair shop were rarely in want of good shoes. Similarly the patients who serviced the staff-patient tennis court were in a position to play frequently, and with fresh balls; a volunteer library assistant obtained new books first;[71] the ice-truck workers kept cool in the summer; the patients employed in the central clothing storehouse were able to dress well; patients who went to the canteen to fetch cigarettes, candy, or soft drinks for attend-

---

70. Compare a British mental-hospital case described in D. McI. Johnson and N. Dodds, eds., *The Plea for the Silent* (London: Christopher Johnson, 1957), pp. 17–18: 'Soon, I had teamed up with the two reasonably sane people in this ward of thirty or more. Firstly, the young lad mentioned earlier; the chef readily agreed to my helping in the kitchen, and my reward was two extra cups of tea each day.'

A concentration-camp illustration is provided by Kogon, op. cit., pp. 111–12: 'And outside the barbed-wire compound the pet dogs that most of the S S officers kept were fed on meat, milk, cereal, potatoes, eggs and claret; so fine a diet, indeed, that many a starving prisoner took advantage of every chance to work in the dog mess, hoping to garner some of the animals' food.'

A prison example is provided in Don Devault's description of McNeil Island, Cantine and Rainer, op. cit., p. 92: 'It helped the food situation a lot to be working on the orchard crew during the fruit-picking season. We had all the fruit we could eat there and brought in much to other inmates. It helped also to be on the repair crew later as we could go up to the chicken house to fix up the wiring and boil ourselves an egg at the same time, or go to the kitchen to repair the sink and get a hamburger fried by the cooks, when no one was looking or maybe an extra bottle of milk.'

Heckstall-Smith, an ex-inmate of the British prison Wormwood Scrubs, suggests, op. cit., p. 35: 'I spent most of my time planting cabbages and weeding the spring onion beds. As we never saw a fresh vegetable, in the first few days I ate so many spring onions I was afraid the gaps in the ranks would be spotted by the officers.'

71. Just as a person enamoured of movies may take a job as an usher, receiving thereby a compensation other than pay.

ants were often given some of what they had fetched.[72]

In addition to these direct uses of an assignment, there were also many incidental ones.[73] For example, some patients pressed for gym periods because in the basement gym they could sometimes manage to use the relatively soft gym mats for a daytime nap, one of the great passions of hospital life. Similarly, in the admission service a few patients looked forward to the twice-weekly shave, because if a barber's chair was free they could sometimes obtain a few minutes of comfortable chair rest. (Gym instructors and barbers correctly felt that they need only turn their backs and some patient would take advantage of the setting, making a convenience of it, this being a possibility and an issue throughout the hospital.) Men who worked in the hospital laundry could manage to shave in the basement bathroom alone and at their own pace – a great privilege in the hospital. An elderly patient who performed janitorial jobs in the staff residence hall was able to collect left-over food and drink from staff parties, and, during the quiet daytime period, enjoy the staff television set, one of the best in the hospital. Some patients claimed to me that they made an effort to be sent to the medical and surgical service because there, sometimes, one would be treated as a patient, which

72. It should be noted that while these various efforts seem enterprising, the private use of material and tools described by Dalton, op. cit., p. 199 ff., in an industrial and a merchandising establishment has a scale and splendour very difficult for inmates of total institutions to approach. For still more magnificent achievements we probably have to look to the great 'organizing' operation conducted by American military personnel in Paris at the end of the European phase of the Second World War.

73. The literature on total institutions provides some fine examples. Convicts sometimes favour farm and quarry work even in the winter because of the fresh air and exercise involved (Dendrickson and Thomas, op. cit., p. 60), correspondence courses in structural engineering as an aid to prison breaks (Thomas Gaddis, *Birdman of Alcatraz* [New York: New American Library, 1958], p. 31), or law courses in order to learn to present one's own brief, and art courses in order to steal the fresh fruit used as models (J.F.N. 1797, 'Corrective Training', *Encounter*, X [May 1958], p. 17). Kogon, op. cit., p. 83, suggests the following about concentration-camp work: 'In all the labor details, the concern of the prisoners was primarily directed toward two things: shelter and fire. This meant a great rush on certain desirable details during the winter season. Huge premiums were paid to corrupt Prisoner Foremen for jobs near a fire, even out in the open.'

treatment my own observations suggest occurred.[74] Interestingly
enough, some inmates even managed to find hidden values in
insulin shock therapy: patients receiving insulin shock were
allowed to lie in bed all morning in the insulin ward, a pleasure impossible in most other wards, and were treated quite like patients
by nurses there.

As might be expected, many assignments gave patients a chance
to make contact with members of the relevant sex, a secondary
adjustment that is exploited and partly legitimized by many
recreational and religious organizations in civil society. Similarly,
some assignments made it possible for two persons, cut off by the
internal residential segregation of the hospital, to consummate 'a
meet'.[75] For example, patients would come a little early to the
movies and the charity performances in the auditorium building,
engage in some cross-sex banter, and then attempt to arrange
seating in the auditorium, or, if not seating, then communication
channels, so as to carry on this activity during the performance.[76]
Leave-taking was also an occasion for these communications,
giving to the evening the air of a small-town social function. Meetings on hospital grounds of Alcoholics Anonymous seemed to

74. Illegitimate use of sick bay is of course a traditional theme in total
institutions. See, for example, Melville's naval version, op. cit., p. 313: 'But,
notwithstanding all this, notwithstanding the darkness and closeness of the
sick-bay, in which an alleged invalid must be content to shut himself up till
the surgeon pronounces him cured, many instances occur, especially in protracted bad weather, where pretended invalids will submit to this dismal
hospital durance in order to escape hard work and wet jackets.'

75. Norman, op. cit., p. 44, provides a British prison example (in his own
words): 'The sick parade is the biggest giggle you know, if there is twenty
men on the sick list may be one of them has got something wrong with them
maybe, most of the chaps on the sick parade either go because they don't
feel like going to work that morning or they arrange with someone they want
to see, who is in another hall to go sick as well. Which is one of the only
ways of being sure of making a meet, and keeping it. In some of the very big
nicks you can have a mate in one hall and you are in another and it is quite
possible that you may not see him or he you the whole time you are there,
even if you are both there for years. So you have to make these sort of
arrangements so that you can.'

76. Prison chapels, apparently, sometimes become a place for homosexuals to meet, thereby giving religion a bad name. See, for example, Dendrickson and Thomas, op. cit., pp. 117–18.

function in a similar way, providing a means by which patients, now friends, whose drinking escapades had gotten them locked up, could get together once every two weeks to exchange gossip and renew ties. Athletics was similarly used. During the inter-service volleyball tournament, it was not surprising to see a player rush over to the side lines whenever time was called in order to hold hands with his girl friend, who, in turn, having been let off her ward supposedly only to watch the game, had in fact come to hold hands.

One of the distinctive mental-hospital assignments worked for purposes of sociable contact with one's fellow patients and for purposes of 'making a meet' was therapy. In Central Hospital the chief forms of psychotherapy were group therapy, dance therapy, and psychodrama. All were conducted in a relatively indulgent atmosphere and tended to recruit the kinds of patients who were interested in contact with the opposite sex. Psycho-drama was especially workable because lights would be turned low during a performance; dance therapy was especially work-able because it often involved periods of ballroom dancing with a person of one's choice.

In the hospital one of the most general reasons for taking on an assignment was to get away from the ward and the level of super-visory control and physical discomfort there. The ward functioned as a kind of piston, causing patients to be desirous on their own of participating in all kinds of community undertakings and making it easy for these undertakings to appear successful.[77] Whether a staff person offered work, therapy, recreation, or even educational talks, a crowd could usually be guaranteed simply because the suggested activity, whatever it was, was likely to pro-vide a great improvement in life conditions. Thus, those who en-rolled in the art class had an opportunity to leave the ward and spend half a day in a cool, quiet basement, drawing under the

77. A similar situation exists in regard to prison cells. See, for example, Norman, op. cit., p. 32. For some heads-of-household, wife and children create the same piston effect, driving males outward to bowl, drink, fish, attend conferences, and pursue other activities that take place off the domes-tic premises. By looking only at these activities it would be difficult to ac-count for the pleasure found in them.

soft care of an upper-class woman doing her weekly stint of charity work; a large phonograph played classical music, and candy and tailor-made cigarettes were given out at each session. In general, then, the various hospital audiences were ones that freely marched into captivity.

While attendants, nurses, and often medical staff frankly presented ward tasks (such as pushing the polishing block) as the principal means for promotion to better living conditions, participation in any of the forms of psychotherapy did not tend to be defined in this *quid pro quo* manner by staff, so we can consider participation in these 'higher' therapies as a secondary adjustment if done for promotion. Rightly or not, many patients also felt that participation in these activities would be taken as a sign that they had been 'treated', and some felt that on leaving the hospital this participation could be presented as evidence to employees and kin that actual treatment had occurred. Patients also felt that willingness to participate in these therapies would bring the therapist over to their side in their efforts to improve their living conditions in the hospital or to get a discharge.[78] Thus, for example, one patient, already described as quick to work the hospital system, remarked to another patient who asked him how he planned to get out: 'Man, I'm going to attend everything.'

It was to be expected that members of staff at times felt unhappy with the unanticipated use that was made of their therapy. Thus, as a psychodramatist suggested to me:

When I see a patient comes merely to meet his girl or to socialize and not present problems and try to get better, I have a talk with him.

Similarly, group psychotherapists found it necessary to rail at their patients for bringing gripes about the institution to the meetings instead of their personal emotional problems.

In Central Hospital, one of the characteristic concerns in selecting assignments was the degree of contact they provided with higher staff levels. Given usual ward conditions, any patient who

78. A leading case here was the enthusiastic espousal of religion by prison inmates when chaplains were first introduced to American prisons. See H. E. Barnes and N. K. Teeters, *New Horizons in Criminology* (2nd ed., New York: Prentice-Hall, 1951), p. 732.

worked surrounded by higher staff members improved his lot, tending to be granted the softer conditions of staff life. (This has been a traditional factor in dividing field servants from household ones, and combat soldiers from those assigned to rear-area administrative jobs.) A patient who was a good typist was therefore in an excellent position to make out well during the working day, to the point of enjoying a kind of honorary treatment as a non-patient, the only price for which, as is usual in such cases, was to have to overhear the way the staff talked about patients out of their presence.

An instance of this kind of adaptation was to be found on the worst hospital wards, where a patient in relatively good contact and self-control might elect to remain on the ward and there obtain and easy monopoly of good jobs and the perquisites associated with them. For example, one patient, who managed to remain on a bad ward by refusing to talk to the psychiatrist, was given free use of the nursing station in the evening, including the little room behind the station where staff had soft leather chairs, a supply of magazines and books, a radio and TV, and flowers.

PLACES

I

Some of the elementary sources of material for secondary adjustments in Central Hospital have been considered. I turn now to the question of the setting, for if these activities of underlife are to occur, they must occur in some place or region.[79]

In Central Hospital, as in many total institutions, each inmate tended to find his world divided into three parts, the partitioning drawn similarly for those of the same privilege status.

First, there was space that was off-limits or out of bounds. Here mere presence was the form of conduct that was actively

79. The study of the social use of space has recently been restimulated by the work of animal ethologists such as H. Hediger and Konrad Lorenz. See, for example, the very interesting paper by Robert Sommer, 'Studies in Personal Space', *Sociometry*, XXII (1959), pp. 247–60, and H. F. Ellenberger, 'Zoological Garden and Mental Hospital', *Canadian Psychiatric Association Journal*, V (1960), pp. 136–49.

prohibited – unless, for example, the inmate was specifically 'with' an authorized agent or active in a relevant service role. For example, according to the rules posted in one of the male services, the grounds behind one of the female services were out of bounds, presumably as a chastity measure. For all patients but the few with town parole, anything beyond the institution walls was out of bounds. So, too, everything outside a locked ward was off-limits for its resident patients, and the ward itself was off-limits for patients not resident there. Many of the administrative buildings and administrative sections of buildings, doctors' offices, and, with some variations, ward nursing stations were out of bounds for patients. Similar arrangements have of course been reported in other studies of mental hospitals:

When the charge [attendant] is in his office, the office itself and a zone of about 6 square feet outside the office is off limits to all except the top group of ward helpers among the privileged patients. The other patients neither stand nor sit in this zone. Even the privileged patients may be sent away with abrupt authority if the charge or his attendants desire it. Obedience when this order occurs – usually in a parental form, such as 'run along now' – is instantaneous. The privileged patient is privileged precisely because he understands the meaning of this social space and other aspects of the attendant's position.[80]

Second, there was *surveillance space*, the area a patient needed no special excuse for being in, but where he would be subject to the usual authority and restrictions of the establishment. This area included most of the hospital for those patients with parole. Finally, there was space ruled by less than usual staff authority; it is the varieties of this third kind of space that I want to consider now.

The visible activity of a particular secondary adjustment may be actively forbidden in a mental hospital, as in other establishments. If the practice is to occur, it must be shielded from the eyes and ears of staff. This may involve merely turning away from a staff person's line of vision.[81] The inmate may smile derisively

80. Ivan Belknap, *Human Problems of a State Mental Hospital* (New York: McGraw-Hill, 1956), pp. 179–80.

81. An American prison example may be cited from Alfred Hassler's *Diary of a Self-Made Convict* (Chicago: Regnery, 1954), p. 123: 'A few minutes later the guard makes his "count", at which time each man is

by half-turning away, chew on food without signs of jaw motion when eating is forbidden, cup a lighted cigarette in the hand when smoking is not permitted, and use a hand to conceal cigarette chips during a ward poker game when the supervising nurse passes through the ward. These were concealment devices employed in Central Hospital. A further example is cited from another mental institution:

> My total rejection of psychiatry, which had, after coma, become a fanatical adulation, now passed into a third phase – one of constructive criticism. I became aware of the peripheral obtuseness and the administrative dogmatism of the hospital bureaucracy. My first impulse was to condemn; later, I perfected means of maneuvering freely within the clumsy structure of ward politics. To illustrate, my reading matter had been kept under surveillance for quite some time, and I had at last perfected a means of keeping *au courant* without unnecessarily alarming the nurses and attendants. I had smuggled several issues of *Hound and Horn* into my ward on the pretext that it was a field-and-stream magazine. I had read Hoch and Kalinowski's *Shock Therapy* (a top secret manual of arms at the hospital) quite openly, after I had put it into the dust jacket of Anna Balakian's *Literary Origins of Surrealism*.[82]

In addition, however, to these temporary means of avoiding hospital surveillance, inmates and staff tacitly cooperated to allow the emergence of bounded physical spaces in which ordinary levels of surveillance and restriction were markedly reduced, spaces where the inmate could openly engage in a range of tabooed activities with some degree of security. These places often also provided a marked reduction in usual patient population density, contributing to the peace and quiet characteristic of them. The staff did not know of the existence of these places, or knew but either stayed away or tacitly relinquished their authority when entering them. Licence, in short, had a geography. I shall call these regions *free places*. We may especially expect to find them when authority in an organization is lodged in a whole

---

supposed to be standing, fully dressed, at his door. Since the hack simply glances in at the window, however, it is a simple enough matter to slip one's shirt on and, by standing close to the door, give the desired impression.'

82. Carl Solomon, 'Report from the Asylum', in G. Feldman and M. Gartenberg, eds., *The Beat Generation and the Angry Young Men* (New York: Dell Publishing Co., 1959), pp. 177–8.

echelon of staff instead of in a set of pyramids of command. Free places are backstage to the usual performance of staff-inmate relationships.

Free places in Central Hospital were often employed as the scene for specifically tabooed activities: the patch of woods behind the hospital was occasionally used as a cover for drinking; the area behind the recreation building and the shade of a large tree near the centre of the hospital grounds were used as locations for poker games.

Sometimes, however, free places seemed to be employed for no purpose other than to obtain time away from the long arm of the staff and from the crowded, noisy wards. Thus, underneath some of the buildings there was an old line of cart tracks once used for moving food from central kitchens; on the banks of this underground trench patients had collected benches and chairs, and some patients sat out the day there, knowing that no attendant was likely to address them. The underground trench itself was used as a means of passing from one part of the grounds to another without having to meet staff on ordinary patient-staff terms. All of these places seemed pervaded by a feeling of relaxation and self-determination, in marked contrast to the sense of uneasiness prevailing on some wards. Here one could be one's own man.[83]

83. A fine example on board a frigate is provided by Melville, op. cit., pp. 305–7: 'Notwithstanding the domestic communism to which the seamen in a man-of-war are condemned, and the publicity in which actions the most diffident and retiring in their nature must be performed, there is yet an odd corner or two where you may sometimes steal away, and, for a few moments, almost be private.

'Chief among these places is the *chains*, to which I would sometimes hie during our pleasant homeward-bound glide over those pensive tropical latitudes. After hearing my fill of the wild yarns of our top, here would I recline – if not disturbed – serenely concocting information into wisdom.

'The chains designates the small platform outside of the hull, at the base of the large shrouds leading down from the three mast-heads to the bulwarks.... Here a naval officer might lounge away an hour after action, smoking a cigar to drive out of his whiskers the villainous smoke of the gunpowder....

'But though the quarter-galleries and the stern-gallery of a man-of-war are departed, yet the *chains* still linger; nor can there be imagined a more

As suggested earlier, free places vary according to the numbers of persons who make use of them, and according to drawing region, that is, residence of users. Some free places in Central Hospital drew their users from only one ward. An instance of this was the toilet and the hall leading to it in the chronic male wards. Here the floor was stone and the windows had no curtains. It was here patients were sent who wanted to smoke, and here it was understood attendants would exercise little surveillance.[84] Regardless of the smell in this section of the ward, some patients elected to spend part of the day there, reading, looking out of the window, or just sitting on the relatively comfortable toilet seats. In winter, the open-air porches of some wards came to have a similar status, some patients electing to be relatively cold in exchange for being relatively free of surveillance.

agreeable retreat. The huge blocks and lanyards forming the pedestals of the shrouds divide the chains into numerous little chapels, alcoves, niches, and altars, where you lazily lounge – outside of the ship, though on board. But there are plenty to divide a good thing with you in this man-of-war world. Often, when snugly seated in one of these little alcoves, gazing off to the horizon, and thinking of Cathay, I have been startled from my repose by some old quarter-gunner, who, having newly painted a parcel of match-tubs, wanted to set them to dry.

'At other times, one of the tattooing artists would crawl over the bulwarks, followed by his sitter; and then a bare arm or leg would be extended, and the disagreeable business of "*pricking*" commence, right under my eyes; or an irruption of tars, with ditty-bags or sea-reticules, and piles of old trowsers to mend, would break in upon my seclusion, and, forming a sewing circle, drive me off with their chatter.

'But once – it was a Sunday afternoon – I was pleasantly reclining in a particularly shady and secluded little niche between two lanyards, when I heard a low, supplicating voice. Peeping through the narrow space between the ropes, I perceived an aged seaman on his knees, his face turned seaward, with closed eyes, buried in prayer.'

84. Toilets serve a similar function in other institutions, too. Kogon, op. cit., p. 51, provides a concentration-camp illustration: 'When a camp had been fully established, a washroom and open privy might be installed between each two wings. This was where the prisoners secretly smoked when they had the chance, smoking in the barracks being strictly forbidden.'

A prison instance may be cited from Heckstall-Smith, op. cit., p. 28: 'In the mail bag shop, as in all prison workshops, there were lavatories where the men seemed to spend as much time as possible. They went to them for a surreptitious smoke or simply to sit so as to dodge work, for one seldom meets a man in prison who has the slightest interest in the work he is doing.'

Other free places drew their users from a whole psychiatric service made up of one or more buildings. The disused sub-basement of one building in a chronic male service had been informally taken over by the patients, who had brought in a few chairs and a ping-pong table. There some members of the service spent the day under no one's authority. When attendants came to use the ping-pong table, they did so almost as patients' equals; attendants not prepared to sustain this kind of fiction tended to stay away.

In addition to ward and service free places, there were free places that drew patients from the whole hospital community. The partly wooded field behind one of the main buildings, providing an excellent hilltop view of the neighbouring city, was one such place. (Families not connected with the hospital sometimes came to picnic here.) This area was important in the mythology of the hospital, being *the* place where nefarious sexual activity was said to occur. Another community free place, oddly, was the guardhouse at the main entrance to the hospital grounds. It was heated during the winter, gave a view of those entering and leaving the hospital grounds, was close to ordinary civilian streets, and was a usable destination point for walks. The guardhouse was under the jurisdiction of police guards, not attendants, who – apparently because they were somewhat isolated from other hospital staff – tended to rely on sociable interaction with patients; a relatively free atmosphere prevailed.

Perhaps the most important community free place was the area immediately around the small free-standing shop that served as the patients' canteen, which was run by the Association of the Blind and included a few patients on its staff. Here patients and a few attendants passed the time of day around a few outdoor benches, lounging, gossiping, commenting on the state of the hospital, drinking coffee and soft drinks, and eating sandwiches. In addition to being a free place, this area had the added function of the town pump, that is, an informal centre of information exchange.[85]

Another free place for some patients was the staff cafeteria, a

85. Melville, op. cit., pp. 363–4, provides a naval example: 'In men-of-war, the galley, or cookery, on the gun-deck is the grand centre of gossip and news among the sailors. Here crowds assemble to chat away the half-hour elapsing after every meal. The reason why this place and these hours

building where patients were officially allowed to go if they had ground parole (or responsible visitors) and the money to pay for the food.[86] While many patients felt in awe of this place, and were uncomfortable when there, others managed to make very full use of it, exploiting the tacit understanding that here a patient was to be treated like anyone else. A handful of patients came for coffee after each meal on the ward, washing away the taste of a meal under ward conditions, mixing with student nurses and residents, and generally using the place as a social centre – to such an extent that they were periodically banned from it.

It was evident that as patients progressed through the 'ward system' to increasing privileges they tended to get access to free places that drew from wider and wider regions.[87] Further, the status of space was tied into the ward system, so that what was off-limits for a disobedient patient could come eventually to be a free space for an obedient one.[88] It should be also stated that a ward

---

are selected rather than others is this: in the neighbourhood of the galley alone, and only after meals, is the man-of-war's man permitted to regale himself with a smoke.'

In American small towns, the front of certain business establishments may serve in this way for categories of citizens; a good description is provided by James West, *Plainville, U.S.A.* (New York: Columbia University Press, 1945), 'Loafing and Gossip Groups', pp. 99–107.

86. This ruling is a good example of the humane and liberal policy maintained in Central Hospital in regard to certain aspects of hospital life. A hospital report could be constructed entirely from such liberalisms, and journalists have in fact done so. In reviewing a preliminary report of my study, the then First Assistant Physician suggested that, while he did not dispute any particular statement, he could match the over-all result with equally true statements favourable to the hospital. And he could. The issue, however, is whether a liberal feature of hospital administration touches the lives of only a handful of patients during a handful of moments, or whether it pertains to a crucial and recurrent feature of the social system governing central aspects of the lives of the bulk of the patients.

87. In civil society, as previously suggested, a free place may be fed by individuals from a very broad area, as in the case of a city's parks. In London, up to the eighteenth century, that city fed harassed thieves into free places called 'sanctuaries', which sometimes gave freedom from arrest. See L. O. Pike, *History of Crime in England* (2 vols.; London: Smith, Elder & Co., 1876), Vol. II, pp. 252–4.

88. It may be added that some of the places that were off-limits for patients, such as the staff single-male living quarters, were, in fact, by virtue

itself could become a free place, at least for the members of the relevant service. Thus, a few of the wards on one of the chronic services, and a discharge or convalescent ward on a male admission service, were 'open' at the time of study. No staff or very few staff were assigned to these wards during the day, and hence these places were relatively free from surveillance. Since the admission service ward was also stocked with a pool table, magazines, TV, cards, books, and student nurses, an atmosphere of security, ease, and pleasure developed, likened by some patients to an army recreation hall.

Many types of assignment provided patients with free places, especially if work was done under the guidance of a specialist in the work instead of an attendant – for at such times the milieu of a work place tended to be maintained, and this marked a distinct freedom from authority and restraint as compared to ward life. This was so at the major scenes of industrial therapy, the laundry and the shoe shop. Obtaining a free place, then, was a principal way of working an assignment. For some patients the occupational therapy room in the admission service, where woodworking was done, provided a free place. The basement where dance therapy was given also served in this way, especially for the group of young patients, of wide and leading reputation among fellow patients and staff, who formed a kind of stage company for producing dramatic and dance presentations, and who enjoyed long hours of training and rehearsal under the guidance of the well-liked dance therapist. During mid-period breaks, and for a few moments after the dance sessions, patients would, for example, wander into the anteroom off the dance chamber and, with cokes obtained from the machine, and cigarettes, sometimes contributed by the therapist, congregate around a piano, dancing a little, making a pass at a jitterbug step, chatting, and having what on the outside would be called an informal break. Compared to the lives many of these favoured patients lived on the ward, these moments were incredibly soft, harmonious, and free from hospital pressure.

---

of such a ruling, places where staff could 'relax', free of that constraint upon their behaviour that the presence of patients invoked.

Although the provision of a free place was an incidental aspect of many assignments, it was apparently the main gain of some assignments. For example, off the insulin room adjoining the admission ward on one service was a small anteroom where nurses could lie down and where nourishment could be prepared for patients coming out of shock. The few patients who managed to get the job of helping in the insulin room could enjoy the quiet medical note sustained there and also some of the T L C that was given to those in shock; in the anteroom they could come out of the patient role, relax, smoke, polish their shoes, banter with the nurses, and make themselves coffee.

Free places in which tenure was not firmly established were to be found, some, paradoxically, in quite central parts of the buildings.[89] In one of the older buildings the main hallway onto which the administrative offices entered was large, high-ceilinged, and cool in summer; cutting into it at right angles was a hallway about twelve feet wide, leading, through a locked door, to wards. Benches lined both sides of this dark alcove, and there was a coke machine and phone booth. Throughout the main hallway and the alcove an administrative civil service atmosphere tended to prevail. Officially, patients were not supposed to 'hang around' this alcove and in some cases were even cautioned against passing through the hallway. However, a few patients, well-known to the staff and having some trusty-like duties, were allowed to sit in the alcove, and during hot summer afternoons they could be found there, sometimes pressing their claim to the point of playing cards, and in general getting away from the hospital although sitting in one of the centres of it.

The vicarious consumption of free places was one of the most poignant instances of make-do in the hospital. Patients in seclusion would sometimes spend time looking out the outside window, when this was within reach, or out of the Judas hole in the door,

89. It is an odd social fact that free places are often to be found in the immediate vicinity of officials, part of whose function is to exercise surveillance over broad physical regions. For example, winos in small towns sometimes congregate on the lawn of the county courthouse, enjoying there some rights of lounging assembly denied them in the main streets. See Irwin Deutscher, 'The Petty Offender: A Sociological Alien', *Journal of Criminal Law, Criminology and Police Science*, XLIV (1954), p. 595, fn.

vicariously following the activity on the grounds or in the ward. Some male patients in back wards would vie with each other for possession of a window sill; once obtained, the sill was used as a seat, the patient curling up in the window, looking outside through the bars, pressing the nose or his whole body up against the outside, and in this way somewhat removing himself from the ward and somewhat freeing himself from its territorial restrictions. Parole patients on the grounds would sometimes take the benches closest to the outside fence and spend time watching civilians walk and ride past the hospital, gaining thereby a minor sense of participation in the free world outside.

It may be suggested that the more unpalatable the environment in which the individual must live, the more easily will places qualify as free ones. Thus, in some of the worst wards, housing up to sixty patients, many 'regressed', the problem of reduced personnel on the evening (4:00 to 12:00 P.M.) shift was met by herding all the patients into the day room and blocking the entrance so that every patient on the ward could be placed under the surveillance of one pair of eyes. This time corresponded with the departure of medical staff; with dusk (in winter), which was very apparent because the wards were ill-lit; and, often, with the shutting of windows. At this time a pall fell on what was already a pall, and there was an intensification of negative affect, tension, and strife. A few patients, often ones willing to sweep down the floor, prepare the beds, and herd other patients to sleep, were allowed to stay outside of this pen and wander freely in the then-emptied hallways between the dormitory and the maintenance offices. At such times any place not in the day room took on a quiet tone, with a relatively unhostile staff definition of the situation prevailing. What was off-limits for the bulk of the patients became, through the same ruling, a free place for a select few.

II

The kind of free place considered until now is a categorical one: the patient who used the place had to appreciate that other patients, to whom he was not particularly related, would or could have access to it, too; exclusiveness and sense of ownership were not involved. In some cases, however, a group of patients added to their access to a free place the proprietary right to keep out all other patients, except when properly invited. We can speak here of group territories.[90]

Group territories seem very little developed in Central Hospital, appearing merely as extensions of rights regarding use of a particular space that are legitimately accorded patients. For example, one of the continued-treatment services had a glassed-in porch off one of the wards containing a pool table, a card table, TV, magazines, and other recreational equipment. Here attendants and well-established, long-term patients of the elder-statesman class mixed with sociable equality, talking over the news of the hospital and in general functioning as a sergeant-majors' mess. An attendant might bring in his dog to show to others present, occasionally arrange fishing dates with town-parole patients, and consult the racing form with the group at large, kidding and joking about bets that had been or were to be

90. A well-known example of territory was the division of Chicago into zones each controlled by a different gang. See, for example, John Landesco, *Organized Crime in Chicago*, Part III of The Illinois Crime Survey, 1929, p. 931: 'While the heavy casualties of the beer war did not lead to the extermination of gangsters, as many law-abiding citizens optimistically expected, they did induce the leading gangsters, for different reasons, to agree to peace terms which defined the territory within which each gang or syndicate might operate without competition and beyond which it should not encroach upon the territory of others.' A type of territory that has recently received attention is the delinquent's 'turf'.

The original concept of territory derives from ethology, especially ornithology; it refers to the area that an animal or pack of animals defends, usually against males of the same species. This area varies greatly in what it includes, with, at one extreme, only the nest or lair of the animal, and, at the other, the whole of the 'home range', that is, the area within which the animal limits his regular movements. Within the home range there will be specialized localities: nurseries, drinking places, bathing places, rubbing posts, and so forth. See W. H. Burt, 'Territoriality and Home Range Concepts as Applied to Mammals', *Journal of Mammology*, XXIV (1943), pp. 346–52; H. Hediger, *Studies of the Psychology and Behaviour of Captive Animals in Zoos and Circuses* (London: Butterworths Scientific Publications, 1955), pp. 16–18; C. R. Carpenter, 'Territoriality: A Review of Concepts and Problems', in A. Roe and G. G. Simpson, eds., *Behaviour and Evolution* (New Haven: Yale University Press, 1958), pp. 224–50. On the concept of territoriality I am indebted to Irven DeVore for help.

placed. The poker game that attendants and patients played here on weekends brought the attendants somewhat into the power of the patients, as did the fact that here an attendant felt secure enough to eat openly food brought him from the patient kitchen – a use of patient food that was forbidden. Attendants could sanction noisy patients but could hardly do so without the tacit approval of the other patients present. Here was a clear case of fraternization, providing an interesting contrast to the kind of relationship that the medical psychiatric staff proffered those patients in whom they developed an interest. And here attendants and patients made a joint effort to keep patients from other services out of the room and, especially, out of the poker game.

Just as assignments that brought patients into close contact with the work milieu of the staff could provide a free place for these patients, so a place of this kind, restricted to a small number of patients officially assigned to it, could become a territory for them.[91] For example, one of the offices in the recreation building was assigned to a few patients who actively participated in producing the weekly patient paper. Here they could enjoy not only the work conditions of any small business office staff but also the expectation that other patients would not intrude without good reason. During the many occasions when no specific duty was pressing, a member of this group could sit back in a comfortable office chair, put his or her feet up on the desk, and quietly leaf through a magazine, enjoying a coke, cigarette, or other treat supplied by the generous recreational

91. These arrangements have been cited in other mental-hospital reports, for example, Belknap, op. cit., p. 174: 'Both the toilet facilities and the clothes room and closets were forbidden territory except at authorized times to most patients. A selected group of patients, however, was allowed in the clothes room and, under certain circumstances, in the mop and broom room.'

Prisons of course are famous for such possibilities. A British example is provided by Heckstall-Smith, op. cit., p. 70: 'Up in the Education Office I had plenty of opportunities of talking frankly and openly with the prison officials. Our position there was somewhat unique. We were very much trusted. We could come and go almost as we pleased and were under no direct supervision, working alone and carrying the keys of the office with us. Apart from being the most comfortable job in the prison – for in the office we had a wireless and, during the winter, a roaring fire – ....'

staff – a condition of privacy and control to be appreciated only against the background of usual hospital conditions.

The recreational building figured in another way as a group territory. About six patients were assigned to the building to help with domestic and janitorial tasks. In a tacit exchange for their work, they were accorded special rights. On Sunday, after they and washed down the floors and tidied up from the night before, and before the late-morning opening of doors, the place was theirs. They would brew coffee and take from the refrigerator the cakes and cookies saved from the previous occasion of helping out in the kitchen. From the manager's desk they were able to borrow, for a few hours, both of the Sunday papers which were regularly delivered to the building. For a couple of hours after clean-up, while other paroled patients were crowded around the door waiting to get in, these workers could luxuriate in an experience of quietness, comfort, and control. If one of them arrived late for work, he could press through the group at the door, and he alone would be let in by one of his fellow workers on the inside.

Although the guardhouse tended to be a free place for any patient with parole, there were places that similarly drew from the whole hospital but were not open to all patients. One of these was the little office of the staff member who managed the building in which the theatre was housed. During rehearsals for plays, pageants, and the like – at which time the backstage of the theatre and the 'house' itself became a free place for the patient participants – this office was used by a small set of 'campus wheels' as a well-protected place in which to eat lunch and gossip. The building caretaker, being much in contact with patients and little in contact with colleagues, as in the case of the guards, tended to play a marginal role between staff and patients and was accorded, at least by the campus wheels, the respect and intimacy of not being treated as a staff person.

On a few of the wards, the group territory maintained by some patients came to be tacitly upheld by the ward staff. On these wards, where almost all the patients were regressed, senile, or organics, the few patients who were in contact were, in exchange for mopping the floor and keeping order, unofficially allotted a

whole wing of the porch, which was closed off to the other
patients by a barrier of chairs.

Some of the territorial jurisdictions developed by patients had
a phased character. For example, the work assignment of five
patients on a male chronic service was to help serve food to some
patients incapable of the routine trip from ward to cafeteria.
After serving these patients, the working patients would retire
with the empty plates to a wash-up room attached to the ward.
Just before or after doing this, however, they would be allowed
a plate of food and a jug of milk, to be consumed on their own, at
their own pace, in the ward kitchen. From the refrigerator in this
room they would take some black coffee saved over from breakfast, reheat it, light up a tailor-made, and for about half an hour
sit and relax in control of their own milieu. Even more fleeting
claims to territories were to be found. For example, in the male
admission service, on the ward to which depressed, excited, and
brain-injury cases were brought, a few of the patients in relatively
good contact would segregate themselves by a barrier of chairs in
an effort to keep a corner of the day room free of grossly symptomatic fellow inmates.[92]

III

I have mentioned two kinds of places over which the patient has
unusual control: free places and group territories. He shares the
first with any patient and the second with a selected few. There
remains private claim on space, where the individual develops
some comforts, control, and tacit rights that he shares with no
other patients except by his own invitation. I shall speak here of
personal territory. A continuum is involved, with a veritable
home or nest[93] at one extreme, and at the other a mere location

92. This kind of territory formation is, of course, very common throughout civil life. It can be observed in the enclosure arrangements at Ascot and
the chair barriers improvised by musicians who have to play at weddings (see
Howard S. Becker, 'The Professional Dance Musician and His Audience',
American Journal of Sociology, LVII [1951], p. 142).

93. On the concept of 'nesting', see E. S. Russell, *The Behaviour of
Animals* (2nd ed., London: Arnold, 1938), pp. 69–73; Hediger, op. cit.,
pp. 21–2.

The line between personal territories of the nestlike variety and group or refuge site[94] in which the individual feels as protected and satisfied as is possible in the setting.

In mental hospitals and similar institutions the basic kind of personal territory is, perhaps, the private sleeping room, officially available to around five or ten per cent of the ward population. In Central Hospital such a room was sometimes given in exchange for doing ward work.[95] Once obtained, a private room could be stocked with objects that could lend comfort, pleasure, and control to the patient's life. Pin-up pictures, a radio, a box of paperback detective stories, a bag of fruit, coffee-making equipment, matches, shaving equipment – these were some of the objects, many of them illicit, that were introduced by patients.

Patients who had been on a given ward for several months tended to develop personal territories in the day room, at least to the degree that some inmates developed favourite sitting or standing places and would make some effort to dislodge anybody who usurped them.[96] Thus, on one continued treatment ward, one elderly patient in contact was by mutual consent accorded a free-standing radiator; by spreading paper on top, he managed

territories is sometimes hard to draw. For example, in the social world of American boys, a tree house, fort, or cave constructed in a boy's yard is likely to be his personal territory, his friends participating by invitation that can be withdrawn should relations deteriorate; the same edifice constructed on unclaimed land is likely to be collectively owned.

94. Refuge sites are one of the specialized localities often within an animal's home range.

95. Aside from the work price of a private room, there were other drawbacks. In most wards, private-room doors were kept locked during the day, so that the patient had to ask each time he wanted to be let in, and he had to suffer the refusal or look of impatience this often brought forth from the staff person with the key. Further, some patients felt these rooms were not as well ventilated as the large sleeping dormitories and subject to greater extremes of temperature, so that during the hottest months some patients made an effort to transfer temporarily out of their private rooms.

96. Seating territories, famous from the light literature on clubs, are reported in mental-hospital material, for example, Johnson and Dodds, op. cit., p. 72: 'I occupied these sleeping quarters for several months. In the daytime, we occupied a pleasant day room, large and well-polished with easy chairs. Sometimes we sat here for hours with no one speaking. There was no sound other than an occasional scuffle, when one of the older inhabitants took exception to the fact that some newcomer was occupying the chair which was her customary right.'

to be able to sit on it, and sit on it he usually did. Behind the radiator he kept some of his personal effects, which further marked off the area as his place.[97] A few feet from him, in a corner of the room, a working patient had what amounted to his 'office', this being the place where staff knew they could find him when he was wanted. He had sat so long in this corner that there was a soiled dent in the plaster wall where his head usually came to rest. On the same ward, another patient laid claim to a chair that was directly in front of the T V set; although a few patients would contest this place, he generally could sustain his claim upon it.

Territory formation on wards has a special relation to mental disorder. In many civilian situations an equalitarian rule such as 'first come, first served' prevails, and some disguise conceals another organizing principle, 'strongest takes what he wants'. This last rule operated to some extent on bad wards, just as the first rule did on good wards. Another dimension must be introduced, however. The alignment to ward life that many back-ward patients took, for whatever voluntary reason or from whatever involuntary cause, led them to remain silent and un-protesting and to move away from any commotion involving themselves. Such a person could be dislodged from a seat or place regardless of his size or strength. Hence, on the bad wards, a special pecking order of a sort occurred, with vocal patients in good contact taking favourite chairs and benches from those not in contact. This was carried to a point where one patient might

97. Wherever individuals have an anchored work place, such as an office desk, a ticket window, or a lathe, they tend, with time, to exude arrangements of comfort and control, speckling the immediate area with the stuff that homes are made of. I cite an example again from life in the orchestra pit, Ottenheimer, op. cit.: 'Once a show has settled into a run, the pit takes on a cozy, lived-in atmosphere. The men put up hooks on which to hang their horns during intermission, and racks and shelves for music, books, and other paraphernalia. One common practice is to fasten a small wooden box to the music stand with coat-hanger wire, as a convenient repository for paper, pencils, chewing gum, and eyeglasses. A particular homey touch was supplied in the string section of the "West Side Story" orchestra by pin-ups fastened (out of the audience's sight) to the inner side of the curtains that hung from the pit railing. Some men even brought little portable radios – usually to follow a favorite sport.'

force a mute one off a footrest, leaving the vocal patient with a chair *and* a footrest, and the mute patient with nothing at all – a difference that is not negligible considering the fact that except for breaks at mealtime some patients spent the whole of the day on these wards doing nothing but sitting or standing in one place.

Perhaps the minimum space that was built into a personal territory was that provided by a patient's blanket. In some wards, a few patients would carry their blankets around with them during the day and, in an act thought to be highly regressive, each would curl up on the floor with his blanket completely covering him; within this covered space each had some margin of control.[98]

As may be expected, a personal territory can develop within a free place or group territory. For example, in the recreation room of a chronic male service one of the two large wooden armchairs favourably situated close to the light and the radiator was regularly taken by an elderly respected patient, both patients and staff recognizing his right to it.[99]

One of the most elaborate illustrations of territory formation in a free place in Central Hospital occurred in the disused basement of one of the continued-treatment buildings. Here a few of the more intact rooms had been taken over by lower-echelon staff to use as supply rooms; thus there was a paint room

98. Ecological niches such as doorways and blanket tents can also be found among autistic children, as reported, for example, by Bruno Bettleheim, 'Feral Children and Autistic Children', *American Journal of Sociology*, LXIV (1959), p. 458: 'Others, again, build themselves dens in dark corners or closets, sleep nowhere else, and prefer spending all day and all night there.'

99. As an experiment, I waited for an evening when the second good chair had been moved to another part of the room and then, before this patient arrived, sat in his chair, attempting to give the appearance of someone innocently reading. When he arrived at his usual hour, he gave me a long, quiet look. I attempted to give the response of someone who didn't know that he was being looked at. Failing in this way to remind me of my place, the patient scanned the room for the other good chair, found it, and brought it back to its usual place next to the one I was in. The patient then said in a respectful, unantagonistic tone: 'Do you mind, son, moving over into that chair for me?' I moved, ending the experiment.

and a room where grounds care equipment was stored. In each of these rooms a patient helper held semi-official dominion. Pin-ups, a radio, a relatively soft chair, and supplies of hospital tobacco were to be found. A few of the remaining less usable rooms had been appropriated by aging long-term parole patients, each of whom had managed to stock his nest with something, if only a broken chair and stacks of old *Life* magazines.[1] In the rare event of any of these patients being needed during the day by a member of staff, a message would be sent directly to his basement office, not his ward.

In some cases, an assignment provided a personal territory. For example, the working patients who looked after their ward's clothing and supply room were allowed to stay in this room when no chores were to be done; and there they could sit or lie on the floor away from the alternations of commotion and pall in the day room.

Facilities

I want now to consider two additional elements of under-life, which again involve physical arrangements.

I

In everyday life, legitimate possessions employed in primary adjustments are typically stored, when not in use, in special places of safekeeping which can be gotten to at will, such as foot-lockers, cabinets, bureau drawers, and safe-deposit boxes. These storage places protect the object from damage, misuse, and misappropriation, and allow the user to conceal what he possesses from others.[2] More important, these places can represent an

1. A few patients attempted to construct such nests in wooded parts of campus grounds, but apparently grounds staff quickly disassembled these structures.

2. Personal places of safekeeping are, of course, known in cultures not our own. See, for example, John Skolle, *Azalaï* (New York: Harper & Bros., 1956), p. 49: 'The Tuareg carried all their possession in leather bags. Those containing valuables they would lock with their native *cadenas*, three keys sometimes being required to work the combination. The system seemed singularly ineffectual as a measure of precaution because every man carried a

extension of the self and its autonomy, becoming more important as the individual forgoes other repositories of selfhood. If nothing can be kept only for oneself, and everything one uses is used by others, too, then little protection from social contamination by others is possible. Further, some of the things one must give up are those with which one has become especially identified and which one employs for self-identification to others. It is thus that a man in a monastery may be concerned about his one privacy, his letterbox,[3] and a man on a frigate about his canvas clothes bag.[4]

Where such private storage places are not allowed, it is understandable that they will be illicitly developed. Further, if one is to possess an object illicitly, then the place in which it is stored may itself have to be concealed. A personal storage space that is concealed and/or locked not merely to thwart illegitimate interlopers but also legitimate authority is sometimes called a *stash* in the criminal and near-criminal world, and will be called this here.[5] It may be noted that these illicit storage places represent a more complex matter, organizationally, then do simple make-do's, since a stash can ordinarily safeguard more than one kind of illicit possession. I would like to add that one important object that may be stashed is the human body (dead or alive),

---

dagger and anyone who so desired could ignore the lock and slash the leather bag. But no one thought of doing this. The lock was universally respected as a symbol of privacy.'

3. Thomas Merton, *The Seven Storey Mountain* (New York: Harcourt, Brace and Company, 1948), p. 384.

4. Melville, op. cit., p. 47.

5. An American prison example may be cited from Hassler, op. cit., pp. 59–60: 'Directly across from me is the dormitory's most illustrious tenant – "Nocky" Johnson, erstwhile political boss of Atlantic City and, if my memory serves, concessionaire for most of the more sordid activities in that resort. Nocky is a tall, heavily built man in his sixties. His standing in the prison hierarchy is evident, at first glance, in the half-dozen fine woollen blankets stacked on his cot (the rest of us have two of much poorer quality) and the lock on his tin cabinet – definitely *de trop* among the lesser fry. My embezzler neighbor tells me the hacks never examine Nocky's possessions as they do everyone else's. The glimpse I had of the interior of his cabinet showed it to be jammed with cartons of cigarettes – the principal medium of exchange in this moneyless sanctuary.'

giving rise to special terms such as hideout, stowaway, laying low, and to one of the inevitable scenes of detective fiction.

When patients entered Central Hospital, especially if they were excited or depressed on admission, they were denied a private, accessible place to store things. Their personal clothing, for example, might be stored in a room that was beyond their discretionary use. Their money was kept in the administration building, unobtainable without medical and/or their legal agents' permission. Valuables or breakables, such as false teeth, eyeglasses, wrist watches, often an integral part of body image, might be locked up safely out of their owners' reach. Official papers of self-identification might also be retained by the institution.[6] Cosmetics, needed to present oneself properly to others, were collectivized, being made accessible to patients only at certain times. On convalescent wards, bed boxes were available, but since they were unlocked they were subject to theft from other patients and from staff, and in any case were often located in rooms locked to patients during the day.

If people were selfless, or were required to be selfless, there would of course be a logic to having no private storage place, as a British ex-mental patient suggests:

> I looked for a locker, but without success. There appeared to be none in this hospital; the reason soon abundantly clear; they were quite unnecessary – we had nothing to keep in them – everything being shared, even the solitary face cloth which was used for a number of other purposes, a subject on which my feelings became very strong.[7]

But all have some self. Given the curtailment implied by loss of places of safekeeping, it is understandable that patients in Central Hospital developed places of their own.

It seemed characteristic of hospital life that the most common form of stash was one that could be carried around on one's person wherever one went.[8] One such device for female patients

6. It should be clearly stated that there are many strong clinical and administrative arguments for denying particular patients their personal possessions. The question of the desirability of such denials is not here at issue.

7. Johnson and Dodds, op. cit., p. 86.

8. In the light literature on criminal activity there are well-known portable stashes: false heels, false-bottomed suitcases, anal suppositories, etc. Jewels

was a large handbag; a parallel technique for a man was a jacket with commodious pockets, worn even in the hottest weather. While these containers are quite usual ones in the wider community, there was a special burden placed upon them in the hospital: books, writing materials, washcloths, fruit, small valuables, scarves, playing cards, soap, shaving equipment (on the part of men), containers of salt, pepper, and sugar, bottles of milk – these were some of the objects sometimes carried in this manner. So common was this practice that one of the most reliable symbols of patient status in the hospital was bulging pockets. Another portable storage device was a shopping bag lined with another shopping bag. (When partly full, this frequently employed stash also served as a cushion and back rest.) Among men, a small stash was sometimes created out of a long sock: by knotting the open end and twisting this end around his belt, the patient could let a kind of moneybag inconspicuously hang down inside his trouser leg. Individual variations of these portable containers were also found. One young engineering graduate fashioned a purse out of discarded oilcloth, the purse being stitched into separate, well-measured compartments for comb, toothbrush, cards, writing paper, pencil, soap, small face cloth, toilet paper – the whole attached by a concealed clip to the underside of his belt. The same patient had also sewn an extra pocket on the inside of his jacket to carry a book.[9] Another male patient,

---

and narcotics are the favourite items stashed in this manner. More fanciful stashes are described in espionage fiction.

9. Brendan Behan, in *Borstal Boy* (London: Hutchinson, 1958), p. 173, describing the response of an inmate in a British prison to the food available to those attending prison Mass, provides a parallel example: '"I'll say one thing," said Joe, topping his dog-end and putting it in his hiding-place, a piece of mailbag canvas sewed to the tail of his shirt, "you don't get this in the C. of E."'

A fine source here, as for so many aspects of underlife, is Herman Melville, op. cit., p. 47: 'You have no place whatever but your bag or hammock in which to put anything in a man-of-war. If you lay anything down, and turn your back for a moment, ten to one it is gone.

'Now, in sketching the preliminary plan, and laying out the foundation of that memorable white jacket of mine, I had had an earnest eye to all these inconveniences, and resolved to avoid them. I proposed, that not only should my jacket keep me warm, but that it should also be so constructed as to

an avid newspaper reader, invariably wore a suit jacket, apparently to conceal his newspapers, which he carried folded over his belt. Still another made effective use of a cleaned-out tobacco pouch for transporting food; whole fruit, unpeeled, could easily be put in one's pocket to be taken back to the ward from the cafeteria, but cooked meat was better carried in a grease-proof stash.

I would like to repeat that there were some good reasons for these bulky carryings-on. Many of the amenities of life, such as soap, toilet paper, or cards, which are ordinarily available in many depots of comfort in civil society, are not thus available to patients, so that the day's needs had to be partly provided for at the beginning of the day.

Fixed stashes, as well as portable ones, were employed, too; they were most often found in free places and territories. Some patients attempted to keep their valuables under their mattresses but, as previously suggested, the general hospital rule making dormitories off-limits during the day reduced the usefulness of this device. The half-concealed lips of window sills were sometimes used. Patients with private rooms and friendly relations with the attendant used their rooms as stashes. Female patients sometimes hid matches and cigarettes in the compacts they left in their rooms.[10] And a favourite exemplary tale in the hospital was

---

contain a shirt or two, a pair of trowsers, and divers knick-knacks – sewing utensils, books, biscuits, and the like. With this object, I had accordingly provided it with a great variety of pockets, pantries, clothes-presses, and cupboards.

'The principal apartments, two in number, were placed in the skirts, with a wide, hospitable entrance from the inside; two more, of smaller capacity, were planted in each breast, with folding-doors communicating, so that in case of emergency, to accommodate any bulky articles, the two pockets in each breast could be thrown into one. There were, also, several unseen recesses behind the arras; insomuch, that my jacket, like an old castle, was full of winding stairs, and mysterious closets, crypts, and cabinets; and like a confidential writing-desk, abounded in snug little out-of-the-way lairs and hiding-places, for the storage of valuables.

'Superadded to these were four capacious pockets on the outside; one pair to slip books into when suddenly started from my studies to the main-royal-yard; and the other pair, for permanent mittens, to thrust my hands into of a cold night-watch.'

10. The record of nicely planned stashes in total institutions, especially

of an old man who was claimed to have hidden his money, $1,200, in a cigar box in a tree on the hospital grounds.

It should be plain that some assignments also provided stashes. Some of the patients who worked in the laundry availed themselves of the individual lockers officially allocated only to non-patient workers. The patients who worked in the kitchen of the recreation building used the cupboards and the refrigerator as places in which to lock up the food and drink they saved from the various socials, and other indulgences they had managed to acquire.

II

If a fixed stash is to be used, then obviously means have to be devised for getting the object to the stash and for removing it from the stash to the place of use. In any case, if secondary adjustments are to be efficiently worked out, an unofficial, usually undercover, means of conveying relevant objects has to be established, in short, a *transportation system*. All legitimate transportation systems can be employed as part of underlife, since for each system there will be rules about who may use it and for what, and hence the possibility of misuse. Where an individual has some freedom of movement, as in the case of a paroled patient, then a portable stash of course also functions as a means of transportation. At least three differently defined objects can be

---

prisons, is inspiring. An example comes from a conscientious objector in solitary confinement (Cantine and Rainer, op. cit., p. 44): 'The men smuggled me food from the officers' mess – officers' eggs, officers' cheese. They slipped me pastry, candy. On several occasions a guard smelled the odour of strong cheese and shook the cell down. A built-in shelf under the table-top held the cheese. The perplexed guard sniffed, hunted. The hidden shelf and the cheese were never found.'

A prisoner in a British jail describes the attempted escape by a drummer turned locksmith (Dendrickson and Thomas, op. cit., p. 133): 'Jacobs ran for the workshop and thrust his key into the lock. The screw gave chase. As Jacobs was turning the key a heavy hand descended on his shoulder. He was marched ignominiously back to his cell.

'A turnover of unprecedented thoroughness followed, and a long-standing mystery of Dartmoor was solved at last – the mystery of his hiding-place. Files, hacksaw-blades, chisels, key-blanks, a hammer and many other articles were all discovered suspended on lengths of string inside his drum.'

conveyed in a transportation system: bodies, artifacts or things, and written or verbal messages.

The famous cases of illicit body transportation are to be found in prisoner-of-war camps[11] and (relative to a society as a whole) escape undergrounds; in both cases a regular escape route may be established rather than a one-shot effort. Everyday examples of illicit human transportation have to do not with escape but with routine movement. An example may be cited from Central Hospital: since the walled-in campus of the hospital covered more than 300 acres, buses were employed to transfer patients intramurally – from and to places of work, from and to the medical-surgical buildings, and so forth. Parole patients who were familiar with the bus schedule would sometimes wait for a bus and attempt to cadge a ride to another part of the campus to avoid having to walk.[12]

Illicit transportation systems for *objects* are of course common and could hardly be omitted from any study of secondary adjustments. The venerable arts of smuggling provide the leading examples, and whether the point of reference is the national state[13] or a social establishment,[14] many mechanisms of concealed transportation can be cited.

11. See, for example, Reid, op. cit., and Eric Williams, *The Wooden Horse* (New York: Berkley Publishing Corp., 1959).

12. I do not suppose there are many systems of transportation which are not used by someone as an illegitimate source of transport. The great American institution of 'riding the freights' is a vast example; another important example is 'hitchhiking'. During winter in northern Canada, before the widespread rural use of tracks, the main means of extended transportation for boys was to 'hitch' a ride on a horse-drawn sleigh wagon. An interesting feature of all of these widespread forms of transportation parasitism is the largeness of the social entity involved in the secondary adjustment: a town, a region, and even a whole nation.

13. For example, see the recent monograph by Neville Williams, *Contraband Cargoes* (Toronto: Longmans, 1959).

14. On techniques for smuggling liquor aboard a frigate, see Melville, op, cit., pp. 175–6. Prison illustrations of course abound. For example, Dendrickson and Thomas, op. cit., p. 103: 'The tense situation concerning reading matter in Dartmoor is, however, slightly relieved by a little army of books known as "floaters". These are books which have somehow escaped from the library without having been charged to the responsibility of any particular prisoner. And some have been smuggled into the prison from out-

Mental hospitals provide their own characteristic instances, including devices that are widely tolerated unofficially. For example, in Central Hospital, wards that were relatively far away from the canteen had worked out an informal system of order-placing and delivery. Two or more times a day, those on such a ward – both staff and patients – would make up a list and collect the money needed; a parole patient would then walk over to the canteen to fill the orders, carrying them back in a cigar box that was standard unofficial ward equipment for this purpose.

In addition to such relatively institutionalized collective practices, there were many individualistic ones. On almost every locked ward there were one or more patients with ground parole; and on every open ward there were patients with town parole. These privileged patients were in an excellent position to act as runners and they frequently did so, whether from sympathy, obligation, threat of trouble, or promise of reward. The patient canteen and the neighbourhood shops were therefore indirectly accessible to many patients. It should be added that while some of the objects transported seem insignificant, they could, in a context of deprivation, loom very large. Thus, the hospital had a suicidal patient, restricted to the ward and in a deep depression, who felt he could get through the day providing he had his favourite candies to suck on; and he felt very grateful indeed to the person who did this buying for him. Stamps, toothpaste, combs, etc., could also be easily bought at the canteen and easily transmitted, and they were often a very great boon to the recipient.

side. These books – mostly the works of the late Peter Cheyney – pursue a furtive, underground existence, rather like crooks on the run. They are passed from hand to hand, under the cover of shirts or jackets. They fly mysteriously into one's cell as the landing orderly is passing; they creep beneath the tables at mealtimes; they hide on top of the cistern in the recess. And, in the event of a surprise turnover, they frequently leap precipitously from cell windows rather than face discovery and arrest. A state of affairs which would probably have amused and delighted their creator.'

Similarly, Howard Schoenfeld in Cantine and Rainer, op. cit., p. 23, describes his experience in an isolation cell: 'I began to look forward to mealtimes when an inmate, prevented from talking to me by the presence of a guard, deposited a tray inside the cell. One evening I found a cigarette and match neatly taped on the underside of the tray.'

As important as the circulation of bodies and material objects is the circulation of *messages*. Undercover systems of communication seem to be a universal aspect of total institutions.

One type of undercover communication is face to face. In prisons, inmates have developed a technique of talking without either moving their lips or looking at the person they are talking with.[15] In religious institutions, some of which share with prisons and schools the distinction of having a rule of silence, a gestural language apparently develops that is versatile enough for inmates to use for purposes of kidding.[16] Here mental hospitals provide interesting material.

As previously suggested, on back wards of Central Hospital, many patients maintained the line of not receiving and giving communication overtures of the standard overt kind. Response to a statement either was slow or was handled in such a way as to suggest that the statement had not really been received. For these patients, withdrawn muteness was the official stand – a defence, presumably, against both importuning attendants and fellow patients that was grudgingly accepted as a legitimate mental symptom. (Acceptance seemed due to the very great difficulty of distinguishing this alignment to the ward from the appearance involuntarily presented by patients with massive irreversible neurological impairment.) Of course, this withdrawn stance, once assumed, became a commitment with its own restrictions. Mute patients had to submit to medical attentions without verbally expressing fear; they had to receive abuse without remonstrating; and they had to conceal interest in and orientation to what was going on in the ward. Many of the small transactions, the give-and-take, of daily social living had to be forgone.

In order to maintain the option of acting deaf and blind and still get around the concomitant communication restrictions, some backward patients seemed to employ a special set of communication conventions amongst themselves. In wanting to get or give something to a fellow patient, they first looked into his eyes, then down at the thing that was in question, such as a newspaper

15. A British example is given in Jim Phelan, *The Underworld* (London: Harrap & Co., 1953), pp. 7, 8, 13.
16. See Merton, op. cit., p. 382; Hulme, op. cit., p. 245.

or a deck of cards or an adjacent piece of ward bench, then back to their fellow patient's eyes. He could then cut off the communication, signifying no, or move away from the object, signifying a willingness to give it up, or, when not his own, toward the object, signifying a desire and willingness to receive it. A request or offer, and an acceptance or denial, could thus be exchanged without dropping one's front of being involved in no communication. While this system of communication seems very limited, more than one communication and commodity could be distributed through it. It should be added that occasionally a patient in the role of someone out of contact would preferentially select a particular person as someone not to be out of contact with.[17] This possibility, incidentally, seemed to lie behind some of the exemplary tales of 'making contact' staff persons were usually able to tell about their own therapeutic capacity or that of their favourite psychiatrist.

In addition to exploiting disguised means of direct communication, inmates in total institutions develop mediated systems[18] –

17. An anonymous autobiographical report printed in Johnson and Dodds, op. cit., p. 62, carries a similar implication: 'There were over forty patients in that ward and, of these only two were capable of carrying on a sustained conversation. They were an alcoholic, who had been there for thirteen years, and a cripple who had been institutionalized all her life. I realized immediately that the two sisters were competent and well-intentioned women. Within two days they dropped the habit of giving silly answers to my questions, and, thereafter, both treated me on an equality and chose to converse with me as though I were sane.'

18. An example is provided in James Peck's chapter in Cantine and Rainer, op. cit., p. 68, in discussing how prison strikers communicated to each other: 'But the most amusing notation [in the guards' daily record book which Peck by chance saw] was this: "I discovered an ingenious device which they used for passing periodicals from cell to cell and I seized it."

'Until then we had referred to these gadgets as carriers but we promptly changed the name to ingenious devices. We had invented them the first day of the strike. Clipped around the radiator pipes, where the pipes entered the wall, were the metal discs found in every private home with plumbing. Since they were thin enough to pass under the doors, we pulled them loose and attached 8-foot lengths of string. At first we built our string from the loops on Bull Durham tobacco bags (called Stud in Danbury), distributed free by the prison. Later we got hold of an old map which supplied us for the duration.

'At the other end of the string we would tie the papers or notes to be

the American prison term for which is 'kiting' – and the official systems already in use are sometimes exploited.[19]

In Central Hospital, patients made some effort to exploit the established communication systems. A patient who had worked in the staff cafeteria, or had friends who did, was sometimes able to use the intramural phone in the kitchen to inform his own ward, some distance away across the campus, that he was not coming in for dinner – a parole patient having the right to skip a meal providing his ward was informed in advance. Patients who participated in dance therapy could use the phone in the small office attached to the basement in which the therapy was held, and those who participated in the various stage productions could use the backstage intramural phone at will. Of course, the person receiving the call would have had similarly to stretch a

---

passed. Then we would get on the floor and zip the metal gadget underneath the door, across the hall and into the cell opposite – or the cell on either side of the opposite one. The man in that cell would pull the string until the message came into his cell. By zigzagging the length of the hall we could reach every striker.'

19. In prisons, where letters are often restricted as to frequency, content, and recipient, codes may be employed. Don Devault, a McNeil Island prisoner, provides an illustration (Cantine and Rainer, op. cit., pp. 92–3): 'Mostly letters were censored only when they specifically infringed one of about ten specific items printed on the rejection slip. For example, I had a letter rejected because I asked in it that my mother copy my letters and send them around to my friends. The censor said this disobeyed the regulation about trying to communicate with unauthorized correspondents thru authorized ones. However, when I rewrote the letter I said in it to my mother that I had found out, via the route of writing it in a letter and having it rejected, that I was not supposed to have her copy my letters over to send to others, and that I did not want to break the rules, etc. That passed the censor all right! Furthermore, my mother continually quoted letters addressed to me and written to her and did it completely openly and all were allowed in. I would answer by simply talking about the unauthorized correspondent rather than saying "Write to . . .". For reasons of this sort we at McNeil did not take the letter censorship very seriously. . . .'

Another kind of dodge is reported by Hulme, op. cit., p. 174, in her discussion of how the year was marked out: 'Or, there were the four letters she was permitted to write annually to her family, of four pages each and not a sentence more except with special permission which she seldom sought: instead, she shrunk her bold square handwriting down to the spidery lace that gave more lines to the page and saw herself finally writing just like all the other missionary sisters.'

rule to gain access to a phone, so that a completed intramural call between two patients, or between a patient and a willing attendant or other official, consituted something of a claim to fame as a sign of 'making out' in the hospital. Public pay phones on the grounds were also sometimes exploited or 'worked'. By being at a particular pay phone every day at the same time, one parole patient was able to receive daily phone calls from his girl friend no matter where she chanced to find a phone.[20]

Illicit transmission systems, whether employed for the circulation of persons, objects, or messages, have some noteworthy general features. Once a system of transmission has been worked out, there is some chance that those who use it will be able to transmit more than one kind of item. As Gresham Sykes has suggested, this means, from the point of view of the establishment's managers, that what starts out as a simple enough minor infraction of the rules can become the operating basis for conveying strongly tabooed contraband.[21]

Another general aspect of transmission systems is that any inmate whose assignment requires him to make the rounds of the institute is likely to be a natural choice as a carrier and end up working his assignment in this way, whether from desire or inmate pressure.[22] Similarly, lower-echelon staff whose situation

20. This is a modest secondary adjustment regarding use of a phone booth. A. J. Liebling, in his well-known study of the Jollity Building, a marginal New York Office building on midtown Broadway, describes the very extensive use made of lobby pay phones as offices capable of handling incoming business. See his *The Telephone Booth Indian* (New York: Penguin Books, 1943), pp. 31–3. He suggests that by mutual agreement these booths became time-phased personal territories for the indigent promoters that were sheltered in them.

21. Gresham Sykes, 'The Corruption of Authority and Rehabilitation', *Social Forces*, XXXIV (1956), p. 259.

22. See, for example, Bernard Phillips in Cantine and Rainer, op. cit., pp. 103–4: 'Message giving and general coordination devolve as tasks for the range-man who serves several cells in a single range and arranges barter and exchange. Highly socialized persons seek these jobs, and others such as library delivery boy and mail and commissary delivery. One does not need many close friends: almost anyone who is free enough to reach one's cell will run errands and do jobs which "outside" would be entrusted only to close friends. If he does not, he cannot last long on his pleasant assignment before getting into trouble.'

requires them to go regularly to the environing community settlements, and outsiders who have regular contact with inmates, are likely to find themselves under pressure to become carriers of contraband.[23]

SOCIAL STRUCTURE

In considering undercover transportation systems we found that the consumer of what is transported without authorization can also be the person who transports it. But in many cases the recipient of the unauthorized delivery makes regular use of the effort of another. By regularly fitting another's efforts into his own designs, the individual can greatly increase the range and scope of his secondary adjustments, including those which do not primarily rely on transportation systems. Since this use of another constitutes an important aspect of the underlife of the inmate, an attempt must be made to examine its forms and the elements of social organization that underlie them.

Hayner and Ash, op. cit., p. 367, provide a similar illustration from Washington State Reformatory at Monroe: 'A pool may be formed to which many inmates can contribute. The winner makes a substantial sum, but the promoter also profits. Boys who are members of the education crew may easily act as promoters. Since they must make the round of all the tiers each evening to deliver "home study papers" or to give aid on school problems, they are in a position to see every inmate and to find out if he desires to participate in the pool. Payments to winners may be made in a similar fashion.'

For a British prison example, see Dendrickson and Thomas, op. cit., p. 93: 'The job of landing orderly was quite separate from the ordinary daily routine of work....It was largely a matter of fetching and carrying for the landing officer, making up lists and collecting applications to see the governor and chaplain, etc. With it went a certain amount of freedom along the landings, the opportunity to pass snout and books into other cells and a general lightening of the monotonous routine.'

23. For example, Hayner and Ash, op. cit., p. 367: 'Men in this group [prisoner farm workers who remain overnight on the farm] have an opportunity to pick up articles from the side of the road – articles left by motorists during the night. The location of the cache is determined in advance during a visit with a prisoner at the Reformatory. A member of the permanent farm crew may pick up the money and pass it on to a member of the crew that works at the farm only during the day.'

I

One way in which an individual may incorporate another's effort into his own plans is based on unrationalized force or what might be called *private coercion*: here the helper helps not because his present condition will improve but because failure to comply will be costly enough to make him perceive compliance as involuntary; and here the person demanding help provides no pretext for the legitimacy of his demand.[24] Without considering here the admixture of this coercion in otherwise 'voluntary' cooperation, I want to suggest that in total institutions private coercion unadorned can be important in the underlife of inmates; open expropriation, blackmail, strong-arm techniques, forced sexual submission – these are methods that can be employed without rationalization as a means of bringing the activities of another into one's own line of action.[25] When such coercion becomes routine, how long it can remain naked and how soon it is regularized by a show of reciprocation or moral justification are other, and interesting, questions.

In Central Hospital, as suggested in regard to seating, the out-of-contact stance maintained by many backward patients created a situation open to private coercion; such patients often could be counted on not to remonstrate and hence could be exploited freely. For example, if, for whatever reason, one patient defined his legs as not a part of the self to be concerned with, then he was open to having a fellow inmate brush them aside to take the stool they were on, or for another inmate to use them, without permission, as a cushion. Understandably, then, attendants sometimes joked about the 'Svengali' role, pointing to a patient who specialized in the cold use of another, as when, in

24. Use of physical force by staff in mental hospitals for purposes presented as legitimate is a basic feature of patient life; some of its forms, such as forced feeding, prevention of suicide, or protecting one patient from another's attack, are not easily criticized.

25. A useful statement of this issue may be found in Gresham Sykes, *The Society of Captives* (Princeton: Princeton University Press, 1958), pp. 91–3, where he suggests that one of the informal roles found in prisons, the 'gorilla', is based on the possibility of acts of coercive exploitation.

order to save a good television seat and also get a drink of water, one patient in Central Hospital was reported to have used another patient as a seat keeper – putting him in the good chair while getting a drink and pushing him out of it upon returning.

II

A major way in which an individual may make use of another is by engaging with him in frankly economic exchange involving a sale or a trade. One person contributes to the designs of another solely by virtue of a prior explicit stipulation about what he will get in return; whom he gets it from is not relevant – a vending machine or a mail-order house would do as well as a person. The social conditions required for this kind of cooperation include some degree of mutual trust regarding the reality behind the appearance of what each offers, some consensus regarding what would be an unfairly high price, some mechanism for conveying and committing oneself to a bid and an offer, and a belief that it is all right to use persons and goods in this fashion. Consummation of an economic exchange can be said to 'express' these social conditions, in the sense of providing signs or evidence of their existence. I will consider later the fact that in any actual social situation the process of economic exchange will be modified by the influence of additional social arrangements, only suggesting here that in the case of unauthorized or undercover exchanges, trust in the other may have to be relatively great, since the other may turn out to be an official in disguise or someone who later gives evidence to officials, or someone who fails to deliver properly, relying on the undercover nature of the transaction to avoid official corrective action.

In Central Hospital, as in most other modern total institutions, it was permissible for inmates to spend money at the patient canteen and the various candy vending machines. As in other total institutions, however, there were greater limits placed on this consumer buying than on the outside. First, source and amount of money were prescribed. A patient was supposed to give up, on admission, all his cash and also the right to draw at will on savings; in exchange he was allowed to receive a small regulated amount from the hospital office in charge of his funds.[26] An official order signed by one's head of service was required of obtain extra amounts from one's hospital credit or, in the case to veterans, to increase one's monthly allotment from ten to twenty dollars. Since all his 'needs' were presumably being met by the hospital, patients were officially barred from earning money by hospital work.[27] Second, relative to the free market on the outside, the range of articles for sale was restricted: the patient canteen was not allowed, for example, to sell matches, or liquor, or razor blades, or contraceptives, and apparently found too little market for major pieces of clothing to stock them. Finally, for patients without ground parole, the canteen was officially accessible only when a group was taken to it or allowed to combine going to the canteen with attendance at an entertainment in the recreation building next door.

As we might expect from what is known of other situations, ways around such restrictions on the use of money[28] were developed by patients. Patients made some effort to keep their funds out of the control of the administration building, in part because officials were thought to use a kind of means test whereby, depending on their capacity to pay, patients were charged a portion of the cost of their care. A patient with a monthly V.A. check claimed he managed to keep it out of hospital hands for a

26. In some total institutions, notably prisons, regulations may require that inmates use scrip, or a credit arrangement with the canteen, instead of money; either of these arrangements is usually experienced as deprivational.

27. Patients with experience in prisons sometimes claimed that one great virtue of prisons was that there one could usually earn and save small amounts of money. A few mental hospitals have experimented with payments, and there is some belief in the psychiatric trade (which I strongly share) that this would greatly increase the tolerability of hospital life.

28. At the community level this is nicely documented by E. W. Bakke, *The Unemployed Worker* (New Haven: Yale University Press, 1940), in his discussion of how the unemployed during the great depression got around the grocery-order method of relief dispensation. See 'Loss of Function of Spending', pp. 355–9. Dostoevski, in his *Memoirs from the House of the Dead*, trans. Jessie Coulson (London: Oxford University Press, 1956), provides interesting material on the ways in which inmates in a Siberian prison managed to acquire and use money (pp. 15–17), suggesting (p. 16) that 'Money is coined freedom, and thus is ten times as dear to a man deprived of all other freedom.'

time by having his ex-landlady hold it for him. Some patients used postal savings to build up an account over which they alone had control. Some new patients quietly disregarded hospital rulings and continued to write, from the hospital, cheques on local banks. Patients claimed that some persons had attempted to bury money on the hospital grounds for safekeeping. A patient would sometimes use another patient for a bank, sometimes at a fee.

In Central Hospital the objects and services illicitly bought by patients, and the sources of funds illicitly employed, were illicit in varying degrees.

There was the quite forbidden act of buying or selling liquor, which had been smuggled onto the grounds. Patients claimed that liquor could regularly be had for a price, and while I drank a few times on the grounds both with attendants and with patients, I have no personal knowledge of a market in this commodity. So, too, it seemed that a few young ladies occasionally prostituted themselves for something less than a dollar, but I have no final evidence of this. I have no evidence that there was a market for drugs. A few patients were well known among fellow inmates and staff for lending money to patients and attendants at relatively high interest, reputed to be twenty-five per cent for a short period; in these cases it seemed that the lender was as much concerned with the social role derived from his business as with the monetary return.

Other services available for a price were less tabooed. Patients claimed they could get a pair of pants ironed for twenty-five cents. Several professional ex-barbers gave 'good' haircuts for cigarettes or money, this market being created by the very 'bad' haircuts normally given patients.[29] A watchmaker in one of the services had so well established himself in his trade that many members of staff, as well as patients, paid for his services, at approximately half the charge prevailing on the outside. A couple

29. One extremely popular patient who was a professional barber claimed he could make up to eighty dollars per month in the hospital at his trade. Having come from the maximum-security penal compound, he would occasionally be sent back to it for some delinquency while on ground parole. He claimed that an occupational contingency of this periodic banishment was that he lost his clientele each time and would have to build it up again when he won his way back to the hospital proper.

of patients had on-campus paper routes, and at least one hired patient helpers. A patient without town parole paid thirty-five cents to a patient with town parole to take a suit to the cleaner's and bring it back (a service for which there was a demand but perhaps no standard price), and he paid a worker in the shoe shop to put new heels on his non-issue shoes.

Although all of these services were bought and sold, they were not bought and sold by all patients. One of the most widespread sales activities involved matches, which were formally outlawed but whose possession was winked at except for patients felt to be untrustworthy with fire. One patient was known to the whole hospital as the seller of matches – a penny per pack – and throughout the day patients he did not know would come up to him, penny in hand, to buy matches.

The chief source of money income for patients, apart from what was authorized or brought in by relatives, appeared to be the car-washing trade. All levels of staff were customers, either on a 'regular' basis of about two dollars a month, or a wash at a time, at fifty or seventy-five cents. (The prevailing commercial rate for a single wash was $1.25 to $1.50.) Occasionally visitors to the grounds would be accosted as potential customers by would-be car washers. Some patients also waxed cars, but this required capital to pay for wax in advance and also an outside contact to buy the wax. The car trade, unlike most others in the hospital, had given rise to some entrepreneurial division of labour: one patient sold large cans of water to washers for five cents; another claimed he hired other patients to wash cars he had contracted for; another claimed he usually received fifty cents kickback for locating a waxing job.

Patients came to feel that car washing was their legitimate prerogative and that hospital work could unjustly interfere with the earning of money. Sometimes unofficial accommodations were worked out so that a patient could do his hospital job and still have time for what he sometimes called his 'real work'. It may be added that although a few female patients did wash cars, this source of income, like most unauthorized ones in the hospital, was considered appropriate only for men.

There were some minor ways of making money. Some patients

shined shoes, both for attendants and for other patients. At interservice ball games, some patients sold soft drinks at a profit. On a few wards, patients bought Kool-aid powder from the canteen and sold a made-up drink. One or two patients picked berries on campus bushes and sold the fruit, when they could, to resident staff wives.

Material given to patients by various hospital agencies was sometimes sold to fellow inmates. Patients sometimes sold prizes won at bingo when they returned from the recreation building where the games were held. Tailor-made cigarettes, given out at the end of hospital-wide socials, were sometimes sold, as were those earned by the kitchen helpers on the night that a particular welfare organization of the neighbouring city held its regular patient dance in the recreation building. Patients sometimes sold hospital-issue clothing; hospital-issue tobacco sometimes fetched five cents.

A few patients apparently obtained money from a source that would be illicit on the outside as well as the inside, the practice therefore qualifying as a petty racket. It was claimed that campus pay phones had in the past been fixed with gum so as to return coins only to the fixer. It was also claimed that library books had been stolen and sold, and that a few pieces of athletic equipment had been sold to persons in the neighbouring community.[30]

When an inmate of an institution improperly pays money for certain goods or services to someone who, as a representative of the organization, officially controls and manages access to those goods and services, we may speak of bribery. This was said to occur occasionally in connexion with a patient's obtaining a private room, but I have only hearsay evidence, and I do not think it was a regular practice. In prisons, of course, bribing guards is very widely reported.[31]

30. In European prisoner-of-war camps, sale of camp supplies to outsiders was sometimes of importance, especially when Red Cross food parcels contained items such as coffee, which had very high black-market value. See R. A. Radford, 'The Economic Organisation of a P.O.W. Camp', *Economica*, XI (1945), p. 192.

31. British prison argot is instructive here. See Dendrickson and Thomas, op. cit., p. 25: 'The word "bent" deserves separate explanation. It is used only in the past-participle form, to denote crooked. A bent screw [turnkey or

So far I have described the role in hospital underlife of the paper and metallic currency officially employed in the wider society. This medium of exchange has well-known fiduciary virtues; it takes up little room; it can be handled and stored without deterioration; it is hard to counterfeit, and within one denomination one token is as acceptable as another; it can be used for purposes of accounting and for measuring value; its intrinsic or commodity value is not great enough to cause disruptive runs on supply. For patients, official currency, while not easily stored, had an additional value: with money in his pocket the inmate could exert claims on goods beyond the hospital – he could talk a language understood on the outside, even though officially he was not allowed to speak.

In total institutions an unofficial substitute medium of exchange often develops. There is a reported case of a paper or 'fiat' currency developing in a P.O.W. camp;[32] ordinarily, however, the undercover medium is a widely desired commodity in itself and has marked limitations as a form of money. Typically, as in the many cases where cigarettes come to be employed as a medium of exchange,[33] storage can be a problem; equivalence

guard] is one who will co-operate with lags in getting joeys out of snout into the nick. You do not bend a screw – just to complicate matters, you "straighten" him, possibly with a bribe. Thus if you straighten a straight screw he becomes a bent one!'

On pp. 91–4, Dendrickson and Thomas describe some of several uses that can be made of a bent screw.

32. Radford, op. cit., p. 196 ff. This paper traces step by step the development of a closed 'shadow' economy, and I draw on it heavily. The paper is a model for students of underlife.

33. This means that a wide range of goods and services must be available for cigarettes, and that persons who do not smoke are still prepared to accept this form of payment because of what they can in turn buy with it. For example, Radford, writing of German P.O.W. camps (op. cit., p. 193), states: 'Actually there was an embryo labour market. Even when cigarettes were not scarce, there was usually some unlucky person willing to perform services for them. Laundrymen advertised at two cigarettes a garment. Battle dress was scrubbed and pressed and a pair of trousers lent for the interim period for twelve. A good pastel portrait cost thirty or a tin of "Kam". Odd tailoring and other jobs similarly had their prices.

'There were also entrepreneurial services. There was a coffee stall owner who sold tea, coffee or cocoa at two cigarettes a cup, buying his raw

among brands is an issue; debasing through thinning is easy; and consumption as a commodity can introduce wide fluctuations in the value of the money.

Hospital underlife nicely illustrates some of the characteristic imitations of substitute media of exchange. At some poker games, both coins and cigarettes were used as chips; but the winner of cigarettes tended to keep them to smoke. During the community dances in the recreation building a patient might go to the canteen for another patient, fetching a soft drink or a package of cigarettes in exchange for a couple of cigarettes. Similarly, on some back wards a patient with a tailor-made cigarette could avoid having to beg a light from the attendant by getting another patient to take the cigarette up to the attendant for a light, and in exchange the person doing the work would receive his promised couple of puffs. In these cases the persons involved in the transaction maintained the spirit of those consummating a coldly bargained agreement, not exchanging favours. But only a few patients seemed to want to buy such services, and only a few patients were known as persons willing to serve in this way.

The use of substitute money (and the development of a special value for the official currency of the wider society) could not become very extensive in Central Hospital because the supply of both currency and goods was not nearly as restricted as in some

---

materials at market prices and hiring labour to gather fuel and to stoke.'

Heckstall-Smith, op. cit., p. 193, writing about the British prison Wormwood Scrubs, states: 'Now that prisoners are no longer paid their earnings in cash, but in goods from the canteen, tobacco and cigarettes are used as currency. In prison, if one wants one's cell cleaned one pays a man so many roll-ups to do the job. With these, too, one can buy extra rations of bread and sugar. One can have one's shirt washed, or one's prison suit altered in the tailor's shop.

'The thin, hand-rolled cigarette will buy anything – even a fellow prisoner's body. So it is small wonder that in every prison in the country there is a flourishing Black Market in tobacco, or "snout", as it is called, run by the "Barons".'

The situation in Dartmoor where book is made with tobacco on radio reports of horse races is described by Dendrickson and Thomas, op. cit., pp. 95–6. For an American prison version, see Hayner and Ash, op. cit., p. 366.

prisons and prisoner-of-war camps.[34] So many visitors came and went that money and supplies constantly flowed in, in the form of kinship indulgences. Also, town-parole patients could bring in supplies with little fear of being searched at the gate, just as patients with only grounds parole could easily avoid detection in making forays off the grounds.[35] Additional restrictions applied to the cigarette economy, since the hospital issued paper and tobacco relatively freely to those engaged in steady work or to those with any other claim to 'helping out'. In some cases, these 'makings' were distributed periodically whether or not patients had worked in exchange. Although no one appeared to like much the cigarettes made from these materials, these roll-your-own cigarettes did place a ceiling on the value of tailor-mades, for tailor-mades could mean not *a* smoke, but only a good and prestigeful one.

One final undercover source of money and goods should be mentioned – gambling.[36] The small circles devoted to this activity

34. Radford, op. cit., describes the development of a unified market, stable price structure, regular changes on price levels, futures trading, arbitrage, currency issue, middlemen roles, fixing of price to avoid haggling, and other refinements of an economic system. Where prisoner-of-war economies were bound in with the local free economy, daily market postings apparently also developed. The shadow economy of Central Hospital could boast of none of these embellishments.

35. Central Hospital had a humane policy regarding gate guarding Patients without town parole could in fact stroll out and return without much chance of being stopped by the guards. When it was quite apparent that a patient was leaving without town parole, guards sometimes quietly approached him on return and discreetly questioned him about his status. A patient desiring to escape could in addition find several places to climb over the stone wall and also several places where the wall did not extend and where the wire-fence substitute could be easily breached. One route, known to patients and staff, consisted of a well-trod path leading through woods to a large hole in the fence. In these ways, the hospital was markedly different from some prisons. Interestingly enough, some patients claimed that even when they did achieve town parole and could rightfully pass out of the main gate they felt extremely unsure and guilty about doing so. I myself experienced this feeling.

36. In some total institutions, betting and gambling can form a basic way in which life is structured. See, for example, Hayner and Ash, op. cit., p. 365: 'Gambling in the Reformatory is especially popular....Inmates will gamble on any pretext:...The medium of exchange for this betting may be

in the hospital have already been described. Here I want only to stress again that for such use-of-another to be possible, social understandings of the kind that underlie a market had to be present. It need only be added that a readiness to accept an individual as an acceptable participant in a game of poker or blackjack was sometimes quite independent of his simultaneous manifestation of psychotic symptoms (especially if the stakes were appreciably relative to the resources of the participants).

The use of 'real' or substitute money is merely one form of economic activity, although perhaps the most effective form for large groups. At the other extreme we find 'direct barter'; here what the individual gives up may be desired only by the person who gets it, and what he is given in return may have little value to anyone else. What we have is a trade, not trade. This kind of barter, without the introduction of something like cigarettes that could be, if desired, retraded in turn, was common in Central Hospital. For example, fresh fruit, obtained as dessert after some meals, was sometimes traded for other desired items; hospital-issue clothing was also sometimes bartered.

III

I have suggested that sale or barter, and the elements of social organization these economic activities imply, provided an important unofficial means through which use-of-the-other occurred among inmates. However, as is probably true of many total institutions, there was a more important means through which objects and services changed hands, a more important way in which the unofficial efforts of the individual were multiplied by the incorporation of usable unofficial actions on the part of others.

Because of identification with the plight or life situation of another, one individual may voluntarily assist another or proffer him a ceremonial demonstration of regard, in the first instance providing the student with a sign of solidarity, in the second with a symbol of it. Such signs and symbols of concern for another are

---

any service or commodity capable of transfer from one inmate to another. A cell partner will often pay off a gambling debt by performing the necessary cleaning of the cell for a stipulated period.'

typically reciprocated in some way, since a person to whom one stands in this kind of supportive relation often stands in a supportive relation to oneself. An exchange of desirables *in effect* therefore emerges and, where the relation is an equalitarian one, the exchange is often nicely balanced.[37] Analytically speaking, however, this two-way transfer, or what might be called *social exchange*, is quite different from a frankly commercial exchange. Agreement in advance about what is to be exchanged is characteristic of an economic exchange, but might be compromising in a social exchange, for what can be frank purpose in one must be merely incidental consequence in the other. A person defaulting in an economic exchange may be made to repay what he owes; a person failing to return a favour or a gesture of regard often can only be accused of bad spirit and withdrawn from in disgruntlement. (Should the offended party want to take more direct action he will often cover the real cause of his complaint and hit upon another offence, one that can be pressed in jural-economic terms, thereby protecting both frames of reference.) Something given in exchange must be immediately paid for, or the extension of payment itself paid for; but while a social indulgence must be returned when the relationship calls for it, it need only be returned *if* the relationship calls for it, that is, when the putative recipient comes to be in need of a favour, or when he is ritually stationed for a ceremonial expression of regard. In social exchange the necessity is to stabilize the relationship, and a substantial favour given by one person can be adequately balanced by a purely ceremonial gesture from the other; for both acts can equally attest that proper concern for the other is present.[38] In economic

37. A discussion of these problems of reciprocity may be found in Marcel Mauss, *The Gift*, trans. Ian Cunnison (London: Cohen and West, 1954); C. Lévi-Strauss, *Les structures élémentaires de la parenté* (Paris: Presses Universitaires, 1949); G. Homans, 'Social Behaviour as Exchange', *American Journal of Sociology*, LXIII (1958), pp. 597–606; and Alvin Gouldner (to whom I am indebted in these matters), 'The Norm of Reciprocity', *American Sociological Review*, XXV (1960), pp. 161–78. See also M. Deutsch, 'A Theory of Cooperation and Competition', *Human Relations*, II (1949), pp. 129–52.

38. One of the interesting dilemmas in social exchange is that in equalitarian relationships a failure to give a nice equivalent to what one has

exchanges, on the other hand, no amount of mere thanks can presumably satisfy the giver; he must get something of equivalent material value in return. Characteristically, an economic claim upon another can sometimes be sold to a third person, who then has a right to exert the claim; but a claim for expressions and signs of solidarity from another can be transferred to a third only in a very limited way, as in letters of introduction. As regards calling for cooperation from another, we must therefore distinguish between economic payments and social payments.

The difference between economic payments and social ones is nicely illustrated by the double use made of money in Central Hospital. The pay received for car washing was an appreciable portion of what the same job would cost on the outside and was very often construed simply in monetary terms, as part of the market system. Thus, one of the rewards of hospital work for some of the staff was cheap car cleaning. However, money was also used in a purely ritual way. A patient who worked for a staff person expected to be occasionally given a quarter, not as a reasonable market payment for any service, but merely as an expression of appreciation. So, also, patients would sometimes not only buy a friend a soft drink at the canteen but also give him a nickel or dime outright, on their own initiative, saying, 'Here, buy a coke.' Like a tip, these rewards ordinarily could be expected, but not demanded, and were meant to measure *appreciation* or a relationship, not *exchange value* of work done.

In every social establishment bonds of solidarity develop among sets of members. In domestic and convivial establishments some of these bonds may be specifically prescribed as part of the primary adjustment of the participants. In other cases, as in the mildly involving freetime cliques found in some commercial offices, primarly adjustment will entail an option as to whether or not

---

received is an expression of disregard for the relationship and bad character; yet an avowed effort to give precisely the equivalent to what one has received, or to demand the precise equivalent to what one has given, violates the presumed basis of activity and places matters on an economic plane. Somehow one must get the equivalent of what one gives and yet this must be an unintended consequence of freely supporting others and freely being supported by them.

one becomes involved in these structures. In many cases, however, bondedness functions as part of the underlife of the establishment, and in two ways. First, the mere emotional support and sense of a personal tie provided thereby may not be something established in the official design of the organization. Perhaps the clearest form of this is the so-called office affair or, in hospital terms, 'bughouse romance', for such involvements, as previously suggested, can absorb a great deal of the participants' time, filling out much of the world in which they live. Second, and more important here, these substructures can provide the basis for both economic and social exchanges, of the kind that result in the unauthorized transfer of goods and services. To consider the role of social exchanges in Central Hospital, we must consider, then, the types of solidarity found there.

In Central Hospital, as in many other total institutions, some standard types of bond formation occurred. There were 'buddy' relations, in which two individuals exhibited what was felt to be a non-sexual relationship to each other, identifying to some degree with the other's concerns.[39] There were dating relationships, whereby two persons, usually of opposite sex, sustained a special kind of sexually tinged mutual concern.[40] There were clique

39. The distinctive element about the buddy relation in some total institutions is that it is an exclusive reciprocal relationship (as in the case of the matrimonial relationship): one has but one buddy and one is his only buddy. In the British cockney world the rhyming slang term 'china plate' (for mate), usually reduced to 'china', is widely used in this sense. In British prisons, the buddy relation is so heavily institutionalized in prisoner society that an unwary inmate may find himself compromised by being nice to a fellow prisoner who happens to talk to him during the day. Heckstall-Smith, op. cit., p. 30, may be cited: 'So you part at the end of the exercise period with a genial: "See you tomorrow." And tomorrow he will be back at your side. Tomorrow and the day after tomorrow and the day after that. By then he will have come to be looked upon by the other prisoners as your "mate". Worse still, they will, according to prison custom, avoid intruding upon this newly-formed friendship and you will find yourself paired off.'

Useful material on the buddy relation may be found in Behan, op. cit.

40. Most total institutions not only segregate the sexes during the night but admit as inmates only males or only females. In large institutions, then, what many students would call homosexual interest is very likely to exist if not homosexual activity. The leading documentation here, I think, is still

relationships, in which three or more persons, or two or more couples, exhibited preference for one another's company and exchanged some mutual aid. There were categoric relations, in which any two inmates, by virtue of knowing one another to be inmates, exhibited certain signs of mutual regard. Finally, there were patron relations, extending from a staff person to a patient whom he employed.

I propose to treat buddy, courting, and clique relations together under the general category of 'private relationships'. These were by and large not prohibited in the hospital, although courting couples, not being allowed to get married, were cautioned about 'getting in too deep', and homosexual relationships were officially forbidden, although cliques of paroled homosexuals quietly sustained their special solidarity on the grounds.

Inmates privately related loaned each other money, cigarettes, clothing, and paperback books; they helped each other move from one ward to another; they brought each other mildly contraband materials from outside the hospital; they tried to smuggle comforts to any of their number who had 'messed up' and been placed on a locked ward; they gave each other advice on how to get the various kinds of privileges, and they listened to each other's exposition of his case.[41]

In Central Hospital, as in mental hospitals in general, there seemed to be one interesting variety of buddy relation: the 'helper' pattern. A patient, often himself considered by others to be quite sick, would take on the task of regularly helping a certain other patient who, by staff standards, was even sicker than his helper. The helper would dress his buddy, roll and light his cigarettes, occasionally protect him from fights, guide him to the cafeteria, help him eat, and so forth.[42] While many of the services the helper supplied were ones that patients were authorized to

Clemmer, op. cit., Ch. x, 'Sexual Patterns in the Prison Community'.

41. Patient mutual aid is well described in William Caudill's early article. See William Caudill, F. Redlich, H. Gilmore, and E. Brody, 'Social Structure and Interaction Processes on a Psychiatric Ward', *American Journal of Orthopsychiatry*, XXII (1952), pp. 314–34.

42. For an additional treatment of this relationship, see Otto von Mering and Stanley King, *Remotivating the Mental Patient* (New York: Russell Sage Foundation, 1957), 'The Sick Help the Sicker', pp. 107–9.

receive, they were often ones that the particular patient would not have received as fully without his helper. The interesting point is that to the occasional observer the relationship was one way: the person helped did not make a visible return.[43] Furthermore, since both participants were likely to be relatively withdrawn, the period between specific services was not filled with sociable buddy-like interaction, although there was much opportunity for it.

Social exchanges in the hospital were characterized by the meagre resources the patients had for expressing mutual regard and extending mutual aid. This was one important hardship of the reduced circumstances of hospital living, officially acknow-ledged by making Christmas cards and Valentine-making mater-ials available to patients through the recreation building so that they would have something to send to others. As expected, then, some of the secondary adjustments practised in the hospital were designed to produce goods that could in turn be given to others – in short, *ritual supplies*.[44] The patient dining-halls and cafeterias served as one source of ritual supplies, for when port-able fruit was available – oranges, apples, or bananas – patients would take it back to the ward uneaten, not only for personal supplies and as a means of effecting economic exchange but also as something to give to friends. So, also, at bridge in the recrea-tion building, a man might accept a tailor-made cigarette and return the compliment with an orange, a fair economic exchange but performed in the spirit of persons in no way concerned with such picayune fairness. Similarly, in going to the serving line for seconds, a patient might ask his eating companions if he could get them anything; and in exchange they might offer around some salt, pepper, or sugar they might have brought along. So, too, in receiving cake and cookies at the recreation-building evening socials, a patient would wrap up some of this food and take it back to a friend who had not been allowed to leave the ward. Hospital-issue tobacco was also used in this fashion.

43. In a couple of cases, I observed that the helper attempted to obtain homosexual favours from the person helped, but I have no other evidence that this was common.

44. It is perhaps in connexion with the want of ritual supplies that we can partly understand the practice, already mentioned, of giving one's friends small amounts of money.

In brief, the hospital system was worked for ritual supplies.

The ritual role of cigarettes was particularly interesting. Some patients, especially those newly come to the hospital, were well enough situated to proffer tailor-mades as people do on the outside, although this entailed problems: a patient with his own pack would often accept a cigarette if they were being passed around. (I knew one young man who took pride in being able to work others for cigarettes, putting out a cigarette of his own at the approach of an easy mark.)[45] Bestowing a couple of puffs or 'drags' was a common courtesy to a buddy, as was giving him one's cigarette butt. (Butts were also one of the important ritual supplies through which attendants indulged patients.)

On regressed wards of ageing patients, the measure of ritual value changed. Here it was quite unlikely that anyone, with the possible exception of an attendant, would give a patient a whole tailor-made cigarette. Some of the patients could not roll their own cigarettes, and depended on more able patients to roll them one; rolling was an indulgence, sometimes beseeched by presenting oneself with the 'makings' before one's helper, and sometimes volunteered without being first requested. A butt from a rolled cigarette was sought by some patients, and proffered by others, this being a ceremonial coin rarely of value in other parts of the hospital. In general, a tailor-made butt displaced a rolled cigarette, the latter being discarded when the former was obtained. A type of charity relationship was found, whereby attendants and patients developed favourite recipients for their cigarette indulgences. A mute protégé, wanting a smoke, would come and stand before his patron when the latter lit up a tailor-made

45. This is to be contrasted to the social fate of cigarettes in some P.O.W. camps. Compare Radford, op. cit., pp. 190–91: 'Very soon after capture people realized that it was both undesirable and unnecessary, in view of the limited size and the equality of supplies, to give away or to accept gifts of cigarettes or food. "Goodwill" developed into trading as a more equitable means of maximizing individual satisfaction.'

I may add that the civilian habit of asking for a match or proffering one tended to be very much curtailed in the hospital; a light from a lit cigarette was ordinarily as much as one would ask for, even though there was a strong likelihood on some wards that the individual asked would have matches.

cigarette or was already engaged in smoking one. The suppliant would then wait until the cigarette was smoked down far enough to be given to him. He himself sometimes patronized another patient, passing on the butt he had received after smoking it down as far as he felt proper. The third recipient was likely to have to use a pin holder of some kind to keep the butt from burning him. Thrown on the floor, the butt was then sometimes picked up by a patient who would find it too small to smoke but large enough to strip for tobacco. Some back wards were organized so that a single cigarette would *routinely* pass through three or four hands.

A full treatment of the role of cigarettes, however, takes us beyond the private bonds of buddies and clique mates to a consideration of patient status as such, and especially to a consideration of the claims that two persons could make on each other simply by virtue of both being patients. Almost all patients in the hospital, with the exception of the few pre-adolescents, formed a single cigarette system involving the right to request and the obligation to grant a light from a lighted cigarette.[46] Very surprisingly, patients on the worst wards, sick enough to be mute for years, hostile enough to decline the offer of a cigarette, and distracted enough to forget to extinguish a lighted cigarette which had begun to scorch their hands, observed this system. A function of this system, of course, was that it saved patients from having to beseech an attendant for a light.

46. This giving and receiving of lights entailed a special relationship because the gesture through which evidence came that there was a relationship seemed to be the sole substance of the relationship, constituting thereby a kind of ritual relationship. Somewhat smaller than the cigarette circle was the network of patients that 'offered eyes' in passing each other on the hospital grounds. When patients of either sex and any age grade passed each other on the grounds, and when each could tell by appearance that the other was a patient, then a greeting would sometimes occur – a nod, or a hello, or an oriented smiling look. This nodding arrangement is typical in rural places in Western society, except that in rural places all categories of persons may participate, whereas in the hospital only patients tended to participate. When two unacquainted patients met off the hospital grounds and one knew the other to be a patient because of having seen him on the grounds, a question arose as to whether the two had the right and obligation to greet each other. The decision reached seemed to be partly determined by whether or not others were present who might wonder at the basis of the greeting.

Like the hospital system, hospital assignments were worked not merely for something that was to be personally consumed or traded, but for something that was to be given out of feelings of solidarity. The men who worked in the flower nursery were able to give their favourite staff persons flowers; those who worked in the kitchen were able to bring food back to the ward for friends; the man who obtained good tennis balls in exchange for looking after the tennis court was able to give some of them to favourite friends. On the wards where coffee was served with the milk already mixed in it – an appreciable deprivation for those who liked it black – patients working in the kitchen were in a position to provide their 'buddies' with coffee to their taste. Patients helping to divide up peanuts into bags to be given each patient attending the off-grounds ball game could be prevailed upon by their friends for supplies the day after the game.

One further source of ritual supplies may be mentioned: the food, cigarettes, and money brought patients by relatives. On the few wards that had a high internal esprit, indulgences from relatives were often disbursed to fellow inmates immediately, briefly flooding the ward with cookies or chocolate bars.

I have suggested that the mean conditions of life for patients in Central Hospital involved a loss of ritual supplies and led to the creation of these supplies from the stuffs at hand. Here a paradox must be stated. It has been said by criminologists that rulings create the possibility of infractions and therefore of bribes. So it can be said that restrictions can create active desire, and active desire can lead one to create the means of satisfying it. These means may be consumed privately and they may be traded; but they also may be given as an expression of regard to others. For example, on many locked wards at least one or two patients received a daily paper. After reading it, the owner was likely to carry it around under his arm or stash it on the ward; throughout the morning he could then vouchsafe a brief loan of it to friends. What was the ward's lack of reading matter was his ritual supply. Similarly, a patient who managed to gain permission to shave himself with the ward's equipment on an off-schedule day could often manage to keep the equipment out long enough to allow a buddy to shave, too.

An example of the indulgence-generating character of restrictions can be found in courtship practices at Central Hospital. When one member of the couple was locked up, the free member could effect the delivery of messages, cigarettes, and sweets by enlisting the aid of a paroled ward mate of the unfree partner. Also, by quietly sneaking into a building adjacent to one's locked-up partner, it was sometimes possible to make visual contact from the window of one building to the window of another. Through knowledge of the group-outing privileges of the unfree partner, it was sometimes possible to walk alongside the unfree member as he or she was being moved from the ward to another building. But it was when both partners had lost their parole privileges, or not yet obtained them, that really intricate chains of contact could be observed. For example, I once saw a locked-in male patient employ the standard device of dropping some money in a paper bag out the window to a paroled friend below. On instruction, the friend took the money to the patient canteen, bought some potato chips and coffee, and took these in a bag to a ground-level screened window through which the originator's girl friend was able to reach them. As one can see, for the few patients in this position the hospital provided a kind of game situation in which one could pit oneself against the authorities, and some of the relationships that flourished seemed to do so partly because the participants enjoyed the intrigue of sustaining them.

Although the passage of an indulgence between one person and another might be mediated by the assistance of one or even two other persons, the chains of mediation at Central Hospital did not seem to get any longer than this. Although small sets of friends might act as transportation systems, and most parole patients might be participants, still the patients as a whole did not form a *single* informal system in this regard, since, except for a cigarette light, one's claim was on a few particular fellow patients, rather than on any fellow patient as such.

I have suggested that restrictions create the possibility of getting not only oneself around them, but also one's friends. There is a further way in which restrictive life conditions generate their own supplies for social and economic exchange: where persons are deprived of knowledge of what is likely to happen to them, and where they are uninformed about how to 'make out' in a situation where making out may mean psychological survival, information itself becomes a crucial good, and he who can dispense it finds himself in a favourable position in the economic and social exchange systems.[47] It is understandable, then, that buddies in all total institutions give mutual aid by 'wising' each other up; it is similarly understandable that in Central Hospital, as in prisons, there is a desire on the part of the staff to keep new inmates away from old ones, lest the new, through friendship or economic exchange, learn the tricks of the trade.

IV

The private bonds that have been considered were one important class of relationships providing the bases of unofficial social exchange. The other important type, *patron relationships*, remains to be considered. In most cases, I think, these patron relationships were more stable than the private ones.

In Central Hospital there were two basic official types of organization in which the patient was located. One of these was the 'ward system', consisting of place of residence, the supervision received there, and relations to other and differentiated wards from which the patient came and to which he might be sent. The other was the 'assignment system' through which a patient left the ward and for all or part of the day came under the supervision of the staff person for whom he was working or from whom he was receiving one of the various kinds of therapies.

As previously suggested, hospital theory was that since the establishment cared for all the needs of the patients there was no reason for patients to be paid for the hospital work that they did. Willingness to work for nothing for the hospital was in fact defined as a sign of convalescence, a sign of interest in socially constructive activity, just as the work itself was defined as therapeutic. But whether from a desire to act according to civilian standards, or in order to achieve discipline and motivation, staff persons to whom

47. This theme is stated and systematically developed in a very useful paper by Richard McCleery, 'Communication Patterns as Bases of Systems of Authority and Power', in S.S.R.C. Pamphlet No. 15, op. cit., pp. 49–77.

patients were seconded did feel obliged to 'show their appreciation' of 'their' patients. And a functionary who did not show this kind of regard for his clients might have to report at the end of the year a declining number of patients engaged in his activity.

The chief indulgence provided to those who worked was the right to leave the ward each day for the period of time worked – from one half to six hours – and the right of occasional time off during working hours to go to the canteen or to recreation-building socials. The traditional rule in the hospital was that ground parole was given only to those who paid for it by work. (At the time of the study this rule was changing – much to the displeasure of some functionaries who felt they would no longer be able to discipline their charges. Admission service patients seemed to be able to obtain ground parole without having to engage in any but token labour, and chronic service patients were increasingly managing to stay on parole without a hospital job.)

The hospital management provided an official base for the system of patronage that emerged by allocating tobacco and cigarette paper to personnel managing patients, who doled out these supplies once or twice a week to their charges. Furthermore, at Christmas, party materials and small gifts were sometimes made available to functionaries, and assigned patients fully expected that the person for whom they worked would have at least one annual party involving refreshments and presents. For such occasions the staff member could officially order ice cream, fruit-punch concentrate, and cake from the hospital bakery without charge to himself, but almost always the patron felt obliged to supplement this offering by buying additional supplies of his own. Patients became keen judges of the quality of these provisions: richer ice cream or larger cakes from outside the hospital were likely to bring a high comparative rating by these critical consumers; the standard hospital fruit punch might lose points for the patron who served it.

In addition to these semi-official indulgences, the patron provided additional ones which were expected by the patients. A patron's especially good workers would expect occasional packages of tailor-made cigarettes, treats from the coke machine, handed-down clothing, the penny change from canteen purchases, and sometimes dimes and quarters.[48] In addition to these material indulgences, steady workers or steady therapy patients would occasionally expect their patron to run interference for them, helping them to get a wanted residence assignment, a day in the town, a lessened penalty for having been caught breaking some rule. Getting one's name put on the list for local dances and movies and for off-grounds baseball games was another favour anticipated. (The very knowledge that a staff person relied heavily upon a given patient for the carrying on of a job presumably affected the way in which other staff persons dealt with this patient.) Finally, patients sometimes also expected a reduction in the social distance between themselves and their patrons, a greater amount of directness and equality than they could obtain from other similarly placed staff persons.

The automobile complex was significant here. One of the surest status symbols differentiating staff from parole patients was that of driving a car. This was very rigorously prohibited to anyone of patient status. Consequently, anyone seen at the wheel could be taken, on this ground basis, to be not a patient. In part in response to this, in part perhaps as a cause of it, the staff tended to walk very little, using their cars for all but the shortest trips on the grounds.[49] Now one of the special indulgences a staff person

48. A patient with one of the 'best' jobs in the hospital, delivering messages from the central administration building to other parts of the hospital, was reputed to make as much as eight dollars a month from tips, but I have no firm evidence of this.

49. Every place and every thing within the grounds of a mental hospital seems to share with the worst wards an appreciable sense of isolation, banishment, and ritual disease. A car seems to represent a piece of secular equipment that is not much tainted by place and that clearly points to the sureness of one's connexion with the outside normal world. Perhaps the remarkable staff interest at Central Hospital in keeping their cars brightly clean is to be fully understood neither by the bargain rates prevailing on the grounds nor the staff's sympathetic desire to see patients receive some money. I may add that one of the release fantasies sometimes found among patients was to obtain a new, good car after discharge and drive back in it through the grounds to visit old buddies and patrons. This fantasy was occasionally realized but it seemed to me not nearly as frequently as it could have been. I should further add that while there was an association between high-priced cars (other than Cadillacs) and the four or five topmost adminis-

could give a patient was to drive him from one point to another on the grounds; this provided not only greater leeway of time before the patient's next scheduled obligation but also evidence that he was trusted by staff and intimate with them. This evidence could be very broadly conveyed from the front seat of a car since there was a very low adhered-to speed limit on the grounds and a tendency for paroled patients to take note of who was going where with whom.

Some of the patronage obtained by the patient was, of course, a by-product of the control that had to be invested in him to facilitate his helping with his patron's job. Thus, the patient in charge of the basement room that was unofficially used to store grounds-care supplies not only had his own chair and desk, but kept, under his own key, tobacco supplies that he doled out to the patient crew that unofficially worked under him. He was, therefore, in a position to be a patron in his own right. Similarly, the trusted patient helper who managed the serving kitchen during socials in the recreation building carried keys, and with them the task of keeping unauthorized patients out of the kitchen. He was, therefore, in a position to allow a friend into the kitchen for a taste preview. Involved here, of course, was a special way of working one's assignment.[50]

Although there were always some indulgences that patients reasonably anticipated would arise from working with a particular staff person,[51] some patients managed to 'work' these usual ways. Around Christmas time, some hospital-wise patients suddenly became ardent participants in a number of assignments, combining several jobs and several therapies. When the festive season came around, they could be sure of many presents and a whole round of parties – in truth, a Season, in the débutante sense of that term. (Patrons were of course not entirely opposed to this

---

trative heads, and light joking by some higher staff with old cars about the newer, better cars of some attendants, still there was no apparent general association between staff rank and newness or make of car.

50. Sykes, 'Corruption of Authority', op. cit., pp. 260–61, analyses this issue under the title 'Corruption by Default'.

51. Compare the system of 'toting' characteristic of the bond between American mistress and maid, especially southern mistress and Negro maid.

exploitation of their largesse, because a Christmas party with too few participants was an embarrassment to the function presumably performed by the work or therapy, and in addition, as already suggested, an extra name added to the list of persons occasionally attending created a good impression in the administrative office.) So, too, some chronic patients, feeling that they could obtain ground parole only by volunteering for steady work, would take a job, establish parole status, and then gradually stop coming to work on the assumption that they would not be reported immediately, or, if reported, would not be immediately put back on the wards. Others would work for a time at one job, establish good relations with the staff person in charge, and then go to work for someone else, but they would periodically go back to their former patron to request 'makings' or small change, thereby attempting to work the man rather than the assignment.

On the back wards, where many of the patients exhibited pronounced resistance to ordinary social intercourse, attendants had one or two 'working patients' who could be used as a steady source of help in running the ward. In such cases, the two systems, the ward system and the assignment system, converged, and the patient worked for the same person who had residential surveillance over him. In such situations the working patient was sure to receive a steady flow of favours, because the restrictions of back-ward life created a multitude of potential dispensations.[52] Private and semi-private rooms tended to be the right of working patients; purchases made at the canteen for attendants would be rewarded by a cigarette or, in the case of fetching drinks, the empty bottles, worth two cents apiece at the canteen; attendants could bestow on a patient the right to keep a razor and matches in his room and to keep his clothing each night; when asked for a light, the attendant could act promptly and, as a special act of trust, toss his cigarette lighter to the patient, thus minimizing the submissive aspects of getting a light; control of clothing supplies and recreational lists also provided attendants with patronage to dispense.

It must be added that the patron relationship was not the only

52. A good statement of ward dispensations can be found in Belknap op. cit., pp. 189–90.

basis of favours between staff and patient; private 'buddy' relationships unconnected with a work assignment did occur, especially, it seemed, among some young male attendants and young male patients, the combined solidarity of age group, sex, and working class at times tending to cut through organizational distinctions.[53] Most male attendants had to accept being firstnamed by some patients and 'no-named' by others, and, along with athletic workers, caretakers, firemen, guards, and police, were often willing to engage in a certain amount of profane kidding with many paroled male patients. I cite an instance from my field notes:

Movie night. The police patrol car drives slowly past the theatre building as the patients come out, in order to ensure an orderly dispersal. The car slows to a stop, the policeman watches the crowd of male patients looking over the female patients, and singles out a well-known well-liked parole patient. The patient turns and greets the policeman as he would a friend.
Patient: Hi'a man.
Policeman: I seen you last night [at the patient dance]; if y'd danced any longer y'd shake them balls right off.
Patient (dismissingly): Go away, man.

Given the fact that the attendant had discretionary control over most of the supplies that patients used, it was to be expected that patient-attendant solidarity (apart from the patron relationship) provided a basis for transmitting favours, of which I cite one example from field notes:

Am eating with a patient-friend in one of the large patient cafeterias. He says: 'The food is good here but I don't like [canned] salmon.' He then excuses himself, dumps his plateful of food into the wastebucket, and goes to the dietary section of the steamtray line, coming

53. These are the claims of what John Kitsuse has called 'the male alliance'. A useful statement of the issue can be found in Sykes, 'Corruption of Authority', op. cit., 'Corruption through Friendship', pp. 259–60. See also Harold Taxel, 'Authority Structure in a Mental Hospital Ward' (Unpublished M.A. thesis, Dept. of Sociology, University of Chicago, 1953), who reports (pp. 62–3) that patients turn to attendants to get around rules, whereas nurses function to uphold rules, and (p. 83) that there is a tacit agreement that attendants will break rules for patients when possible.

back with a plate of eggs. He smiles in a mocking conspiratorial way and says: 'I play pool with the attendant who looks after that.'[54]

While many of these favours, patron or private, were mildly illicit, it should be noted that some, such as the courteous giving of a light or the quick unlocking of a door, were merely the patient's official due, albeit rarely received. For example, in those wards where patients were required to go to a central cafeteria for food three times a day, the attendants found they could best schedule the flow of people by having the patients lined up at the ward doorway ready to go fifteen minutes before the dinner call, even though this caused many patients to stand bunched up for fifteen minutes with hardly anything possible to do. Working patients, or those with special private ties with attendants, would be excused from this obligation and would go in to dinner after everyone had gone, or would precede the rest, thereby saving themselves the wait.

V

I have mentioned three arrangements through which one individual can make use of the goods or services of another: private coercion, economic exchange, and social exchange. Each of these arrangements has its own set of assumptions and its own required social conditions. But this is an analytically simplified picture. Each of these arrangements has a strong constraining claim on the way the individual presents his activity to others. In actual practice, however, several bases for the use of another are often simultaneously and routinely exploited, the obligation being merely to constrain the appearance of the activity so that some single one among the three models will appear to determine what occurs.

For example, in the context of the patron relationship, it was usually easy to distinguish between economic and social payments, but cases arose that introduced interesting difficulties. I

54. The same patient claimed he could appear well-dressed in khaki hospital issue when he went into the city on town parole by getting a new issue of pants each time, since these pants before their first washing had a sheen that made them passable as higher-quality pants and a stiffness that ensured their keeping a crease.

have heard an attendant bargain with a patient over how much daily work was a fair exchange for the right to shave oneself every day, the bargaining occurring before the parties entered into the agreement, yet this is just the kind of exchange that after a time became an uncalculated expression of mutual regard. Furthermore, when a patron wanted a service performed that was new or was not considered appropriate, special indulgences and payments might be bargained for and settled in advance, grafting an impersonal economic contract onto a non-market relationship.[55]

The distinction between economic and social payments involves some further problems. A patient's expectation that his patron would enter with him into a purely economic contract regarding car cleaning led some staff persons into paying for the washing of clean cars, thereby affecting an economic practice for bond-supportive reasons. The male patients who were felt to have purchased the sexual favours of female patients were somewhat disapproved of, as were the presumed sellers, since it was felt that sexual activity was supposed to signify exclusive bondedness,[56] not open sales.[57] Further, a certain amount of instability seemed to be involved: what was given once as a special gesture of regard could become in time a standard expectation, quite taken for granted, so that something like a regressive process occurred – each new means of showing regard became routinized and hence

55. The opposite issue, that of economic exchange being restricted to participants in a supportive relationship, has frequently been reported in studies of folk societies. See, for example, C. M. Arensberg, *The Irish Countryman* (New York: Peter Smith, 1950), pp. 154–7; Service, op. cit., p. 97. In Shetland Island communities some residents carefully do at least some buying at every shop in order not to give personal offence to the shopkeeper. To buy *nothing* at a local shop implies that one has 'fallen out' with the owner.

56. It might be added that in mental hospitals, prostitution and what is perceived as 'nymphomania' can have an equivalent disorganizing influence on the validity of sex as a symbol of a reciprocally exclusive relationship: in both cases a socially inappropriate person can obtain the sexual favour of a particular woman and for the wrong reasons.

57. Sykes, *Society of Captives*, pp. 93–5, suggests that in prison there is a wide range of things that could well be sold undercover that inmates felt ought not to be sold, and that indulgence in this misuse of marketing led an inmate to being socially typed: '...the prisoner who sells when he should give is labelled a *merchant* or *pedlar*.'

ineffective as a sign of consideration, and would have to be supplemented by additional indulgences. And once an indulgence became fully taken for granted, its withdrawal might cause direct and open comment. For example, when a dance crowd in the recreation building ate up all the cookies and cake prepared for the occasion, the kitchen helpers would openly complain to staff about being robbed of their due; to keep peace, therefore, kitchen workers were allowed to put aside leftovers before the food itself was served.

Other tacit combinations of coercion, economic exchange, and social exchange were to be found. Corresponding to the fact that money was given in a ritual, not merely an economic,way was the phenomenon of begging – a practice very important in the exchange systems of some societies. Patients did not merely wait to be indulged with small change and cigarettes but themselves initiated the process. A patient would go up to a favourite attendant or, sometimes, to another patient and beg for the 'loan' of a dime or nickel for a coke, or even for a couple of pennies to make up what was needed for a purchase. The style in which this begging was often done, implying that the person asked was somehow 'square' and guilty of hopeless respectability, suggested that this was a means of expressing distance from one's situation and of elevating one's dispossessed condition into an honourable one. Whatever its meaning, such begging was an instance of persuading others to show sympathy before they themselves seemed ready to do so.

Different bases for making use of another were combined in still other ways. One issue in Central Hospital, as in other such institutions, was that in according an attendant the selfless obligation physically to constrain and coerce patients who were deemed a danger to themselves or others, a convenient cover was provided for private coercion. Economic and social payments also came to cover arrangements nominally foreign to both. When one patient bought the service of a small errand from another by means of a cigarette or a 'drag', the buyer occasionally handled the transaction in an imperious way, giving the appearance of getting more pleasure from making the other patient perform a menial act than from the service itself. Paternalistic old-line attendants on back wards, in getting ready to give a patient sweets bought with the patient's canteen funds, would sometimes teasingly hold off granting the indulgence until the patient had made some abject begging signs or affirmed that he did indeed want what the attendant was about to give him. Butt-giving, by both attendants and patients, was also sometimes used to humble the recipient. So, too, when a visiting charity organization gave community-wide socials for patients in the recreation building, and at intermission had a few of its members go around the hall giving out a couple of tailor-made cigarettes to each patient, the recipient found himself in a position of receiving pure alms from someone unknown who owed him nothing. Great desire for tailor-made cigarettes made almost all the patients present accept these offerings; but in the case of new patients, or ones in the company of visitors, the looks of resentment, half-concealed derision, or embarrassment suggested that there was no apt framework, at least of a self-respecting kind, in which to place this activity.[58]

Finally, it is evident that any avowed means of making use of another's goods or services could be, and was, employed at times with complete guile and chicanery, so that a gambler might find himself cheated, a purchaser defrauded, and a friend made a convenience of. (Theoretically, of course, even a person who thinks he is not contributing in any way to the ends of another, and would not do so were he aware of it, can find himself an unwitting contributor to another's designs.)

The issue is that every sector of social life and, more specifically, every social establishment provide the setting in which characteristic faces are placed on the arrangements through which use of another is possible, and characteristic combinations of these arrangements are sustained behind appearances.[59] It is

58. I knew two long-term female patients not in need of cigarettes who were gracious enough to accept this handout deferentially so as not to embarrass the giver.

59. The stable combinations of coercive, economic, and social payments are in great need of special study so that we can employ one framework to look at the similarities and differences among such payments as: prebends, tithes, bribes, gratuities, tributes, favours, gifts, courtesies, honorariums, bounty, lagniappe, booty, bonuses, ransoms. It should be borne in mind

these structural units of appearance and reality that we must study.[60] I would like to add that given a particular social entity as a point of reference – a relationship, a social establishment, a group – we can examine any particular participant's total unofficial claim on others, what in America is sometimes called one's *clout*, and in the U.S.S.R. one's *blat*.

I want to raise two general questions about underlife in Central Hospital.

First, it should be clear that a description of underlife in an institution can provide a systematically biased picture of life in it. To the degree that members confine themselves to primary adjustments (whether out of satisfaction or incapacity to build a different world), underlife may be unrepresentative and even unimportant. Moreover, the secondary adjustments most easily observed may be ones that are elaborate and colourful, and these, as in the case of Central Hospital, may be practised mainly by a handful of well-connected informal leaders. Their conduct may be of great importance to the student if he wants to learn how the particular institution can be worked and how institutions in general might be worked; but in searching for the range and scope of secondary adjustments, the student may fail to see how the average member lives. This report necessarily focuses on the activity of manipulative paroled patients, giving an over-rosy view both of the life of patients as a whole in Central Hospital and of the efficiency of their techniques for unofficially altering their life conditions.

The second general question I want to raise has to do with social control and bond formation.

The social arrangements which make economic and social

that in most societies economic exchange is not the most important way in which moneys, goods, and services are transferred.

60. A useful case-history report regarding the several bases of social exchange may be found in Ralph Turner, 'The Navy Disbursing Officer as a Bureaucrat', *American Sociological Review*, XII (1947), pp. 342–8. Turner distinguishes among three bases for the distribution of favours: friendship patterns, simulated friendship, and, thinnest in sentiment of all, simple favour exchanges; in all three patterns, however, the notions of formal claim, impersonal payment, and bribe had to be overtly disclaimed. See also Sykes, 'Corruption of Authority', op. cit., p. 262 fn.

exchange possible obviously function to ensure that the individual will be able to incorporate into his own plan of action the efforts of others, increasing many times the efficacy of secondary adjustments he makes by himself on his own behalf. Now it is plain that if these social arrangements are to be sustained, some form of social control will have to be exerted to keep people in line, to make them live up to their bargains and their obligation to perform favours and ceremonies for others. These forms of social control will constitute secondary adjustments of a very special class – a class of adjustments which underlie and stabilize a vast complex of other unofficial, undercover practices. And from the point of view of inmate underlife in total institutions, these controls will have to be exerted over both inmates and staff.

Inmate control of staff in total institutions takes traditional forms, for example: arranging for 'accidents' to occur to a staff person,[61] or the massed rejection of a particular item of food,[62] or the slowing-down of work production, or the sabotaging of plumbing, lighting, and communication systems, all of which are readily vulnerable to inmate action.[63] Other inmate sanctions of staff may take the form of 'collective' or individual teasing and more subtle forms of ritual insubordination, such as the military technique of saluting a troublesome officer from too great a distance, or with too much precision, or with too slow a tempo. A staff threat to the whole system of undercover arrangements may be answered with extreme action such as strikes or riots.

There is a popular view that the inmate group's social control of its members is well organized and strong, as in the case of 'kangaroo courts'. And apparently in prisons the trustworthiness of an inmate regarding other inmates' secondary adjustments is an important basis of social typing.[64] But evidence in general suggests that inmate social control of other inmates is weak.

61. For example, Dendrickson and Thomas, op. cit., p. 130.

62. Cantine and Rainer, op. cit., p. 4.

63. ibid., p. 10.

64. See, for example, the discussion by Morris G. Caldwell, 'Group Dynamics in the Prison Community', *Journal of Criminal Law, Criminology and Police Science*, XLVI (1956), p. 651, of 'Right Guys', and Gresham Sykes and Sheldon Messinger, 'The Inmate Social System', S.S.R.C. Pamphlet No. 15, op. cit., especially pp. 5–11.

Certainly lack of undercover policing action seemed characteristic of underlife in Central Hospital,[65] with the partial exception of Prison Hall.[66]

When a ward patient misbehaved, all the patients on the ward might well suffer extra deprivations, and certainly when a parole patient escaped and committed an infamous crime on the outside, parole conditions were temporarily tightened for many patients; and yet in these cases where the action of the one made it harder for the many to effect any 'deals' with staff there did not seem to be any evident patient reprisal against such offenders.[67] Furthermore, underlife 'security' seemed weak. An inmate deciding to escape might tell one or two of his friends with safety, but a clique of five or six seemed quite unreliable as a repository of secret information. This was partly due to the fact that staff psychiatrists took the position that the patient ought to tell all in

65. I do not consider the social control exerted by attendants relative to their own secondary adjustments. For example, an ex-Prison Hall patient claimed that attendants there could accept bribes for special services and not fear squealers because they prepared the ward chart of anyone with whom they did illicit business; an informer would then have to face a case record in which his own guilt had been prepared. Certainly the patients in both parts of the hospital often expressed the sentiment that if they brought charges against an attendant for cruelty or theft, the ward staff would 'stick together' no matter what. It is interesting to compare here the material on another group required to exert direct coercion, the police, and the findings that point to the great amount of mutual secrecy support that police give one another. See William Westley, 'Violence and the Police', *American Journal of Sociology*, LIX (1953), pp. 34–41, and 'Secrecy and the Police', *Social Forces*, XXXIV (1956), pp. 254–7.

66. Prison Hall in Central Hospital was claimed by some patients to be 'organized' in the more extensive manner of prisons for the sane. Here, it was claimed, an attendant could be bribed to 'kite' a letter or bring in contraband, a book was operated, 'stir politics' thrived, a clique of inmates 'ran the place', and a patient strike would be employed to deal with officials who got out of hand. I have no first hand information on these matters.

67. During the research an alcoholic patient, felt by many patients to be 'snotty', talked two very well-liked student nurses into going drinking with him in the local community. The girls were caught and sent home before their course ended, and the patient was returned to a demotion ward. I predicted to myself that he would be ostracized for this act by other patients; while there were in fact many inmate voices raised against him out of his presence, no actual action seems to have been taken against him by his fellow patients.

the interests of his own therapy; and by a peculiar extension of this principle, many patients felt they could improve their own psychiatric status by squealing on their friends. Thus, it was no surprise to hear a recreational official say, with resignation and some kindness in her voice,

You know, they're just like babies. As soon as one does something wrong, the others come and tell me.

Nor to hear one of the most successful patient entrepreneurs say:

During the [World] Series anybody can get anything covered right here in front of the canteen. I never play around here because there are too many police spies, both white and coloured, and you just don't know. If I want to place a number I just phone up and in the afternoon someone will be in to take it up.

Lack of informal social control and the previously described lack of broad-span patient cooperation ought to be taken together as evidence of weak informal social organization on the part of patients. Psychiatry can explain this by the argument that mental patients by definition are incapable of sustaining ordinary order and solidarity, an explanation that does not account as well for the anomie in prisons and some concentration camps. In any case, it is interesting to look at possible additional explanations. One is that patients in Central Hospital exhibited little reactive solidarity: instead of clinging together to uphold their patient status against the traditional world, they sought in cliques and dyads to define themselves as normal and to define many of the other patients present as crazy. Very few patients, in short, were or came to be proud of being patients.[68] Reactive solidarity was further weakened by the fact that it was difficult to define all staff as being restrictive and harsh, even though conditions of life on the ward might be consistently so.

VI

In describing the range of secondary adjustments employed by patients in Central Hospital, I have tried to develop concepts

68. Suggested by William R. Smith, who has done unpublished work on inmate solidarity.

with which the secondary adjustments of other establishments could also be described. The unit of description was determined by a concern for comparative analysis, not drama. As a result, the flow of patient activity in Central Hospital has been chopped into small and jagged pieces for purposes of sorting. The impression may be given, therefore, that patients throughout the day fitfully engaged in childish tricks and foolhardy gestures to better their lot, and that there is nothing inconsistent between this pathetic display and our traditional notions of mental patients being 'ill'. I want to state, therefore, that in actual practice almost all of the secondary adjustments I have reported were carried on by the patient with an air of intelligent down-to-earth determination, sufficient, once the full context was known, to make an outsider feel at home, in a community much more similar to others he has known than different from them. There is an old saw that no clear-cut line can be drawn between normal people and mental patients; rather there is a continuum with the well-adjusted citizen at one end and the full-fledged psychotic at the other. I must argue that after a period of acclimatization in a mental hospital the notion of a continuum seems very presumptuous. A community is a community. Just as it is bizarre to those not in it, so it is natural, even if unwanted, to those who live it from within. The system of dealings that patients have with one another does not fall at one end of anything, but rather provides one example of human association, to be avoided, no doubt, but also to be filed by the student in a circular cabinet along with all the other examples of association that he can collect.

PART THREE: CONCLUSIONS

I

In every social establishment, there are official expectations as to what the participant owes the establishment. Even in cases where there is no specific task, as in some night-watchman jobs, the organization will require some presence of mind, some awareness of the current situation, and some readiness for unanticipated events; as long as an establishment demands that its participants not sleep on the job, it asks them to be awake to certain matters. And where sleeping is part of the expectation, as in a home or a hotel, then there will be limits on where and when the sleeping is to occur, with whom, and with what bed manners.[69] And behind these claims on the individual, be they great or small, the managers of every establishment will have a widely embracing implicit conception of what the individual's character must be for these claims on him to be appropriate.

Whenever we look at a social establishment, we find a counter to this first theme: we find that participants decline in some way to accept the official view of what they should be putting into and getting out of the organization and, behind this, of what sort of self and world they are to accept for themselves. Where enthusiasm is expected, there will be apathy; where loyalty, there will be disaffection; where attendance, absenteeism; where robustness, some kind of illness; where deeds are to be done, varieties of inactivity. We find a multitude of homely little histories, each in its way a movement of liberty. Whenever worlds are laid on, underlives develop.

69. When stagecoach travellers in Europe in the fifteenth century might be required to share an inn bed with a stranger, courtesy books laid down codes of proper bed conduct. See Norbert Elias, *Über den Prozess Der Zivilisation* (2 vols.; Basel: Verlag Haus Zum Falken, 1934), Vol. II, pp. 219–21, '*Über das Verhalten im Schlarfraum*'. On the sociology of sleep I am indebted to unpublished writings of Vilhelm Aubert and Kaspar Naegle.

II

The study of underlife in restrictive total institutions has some special interest. When existence is cut to the bone, we can learn what people do to flesh out their lives. Stashes, means of transportation, free places, territories, supplies for economic and social exchange – these apparently are some of the minimal requirements for building up a life. Ordinarily these arrangements are taken for granted as part of one's primary adjustment; seeing them twisted out of official existence through bargains, wit, force, and cunning, we can see their significance anew. The study of total institutions also suggests that formal organizations have standard places of vulnerability, such as supply rooms, sick bays, kitchens, or scenes of highly technical labour. These are the damp corners where secondary adjustments breed and start to infest the establishment.

The mental hospital represents a peculiar instance of those establishments in which underlife is likely to proliferate. Mental patients are persons who caused the kind of trouble on the outside that led someone physically, if not socially, close to them to take psychiatric action against them. Often this trouble was associated with the 'prepatient' having indulged in situational improprieties of some kind, conduct out of place in the setting. It is just such misconduct that conveys a moral rejection of the communities, establishments, and relationships that have a claim to one's attachment.

Stigmatization as mentally ill and involuntary hospitalization are the means by which we answer these offences against propriety. The individual's persistence in manifesting symptoms after entering the hospital, and his tendency to develop additional symptoms during his initial response to the hospital, can now no longer serve him well as expressions of disaffection. From the patient's point of view, to decline to exchange a word with the staff or with his fellow patients may be ample evidence of rejecting the institution's view of what and who he is; yet higher management may construe this alienative expression as just the sort of symptomatology the institution was established to deal with and as the best kind of evidence that the patient properly belongs where he now finds himself. In short, mental hospitalization out-manoeuvres the patient, tending to rob him of the common expressions through which people hold off the embrace of organizations – insolence, silence, *sotto voce* remarks, uncooperativeness, malicious destruction of interior decorations, and so forth; these signs of disaffiliation are now read as signs of their maker's proper affiliation. Under these conditions all adjustments are primary.

Furthermore, there is a vicious-circle process at work. Persons who are lodged on 'bad' wards find that very little equipment of any kind is given them – clothes may be taken from them each night, recreational materials may be withheld, and only heavy wooden chairs and benches provided for furniture. Acts of hostility against the institution have to rely on limited, ill-designed devices, such as banging a chair against the floor or striking a sheet of newspaper sharply so as to make an annoying explosive sound. And the more inadequate this equipment is to convey rejection of the hospital, the more the act appears as a psychotic symptom, and the more likely it is that management feels justified in assigning the patient to a bad ward. When a patient finds himself in seclusion, naked and without visible means of expression, he may have to rely on tearing up his mattress, if he can, or writing with faeces on the wall – actions management takes to be in keeping with the kind of person who warrants seclusion.

We can also see this circular process at work in the small, illicit, talisman-like possessions that inmates use as symbolic devices for separating themselves from the position they are supposed to be in. What I think is a typical example may be cited from prison literature:

Prison clothing is anonymous. One's possessions are limited to toothbrush, comb, upper or lower cot, half the space upon a narrow table, a razor. As in jail, the urge to collect possessions is carried to preposterous extents. Rocks, string, knives – anything made by man and forbidden in man's institution – anything – a red comb, a different kind of toothbrush, a belt – these things are assiduously gathered, jealously hidden or triumphantly displayed.[70]

70. Cantine and Rainer, op. cit., p. 78. Compare the things that small boys stash in their pockets; some of these items also seem to provide a wedge between the boy and the domestic establishment.

But when a patient, whose clothes are taken from him each night, fills his pockets with bits of string and rolled up paper, and when he fights to keep these possessions in spite of the consequent inconvenience to those who must regularly go through his pockets, he is usually seen as engaging in symptomatic behaviour befitting a very sick patient, not as someone who is attempting to stand apart from the place accorded him.

Official psychiatric doctrine tends to define alienative acts as psychotic ones – this view being reinforced by the circular processes that lead the patient to exhibit alienation in a more and more bizarre form – but the hospital cannot be run according to this doctrine. The hospital cannot decline to demand from its members exactly what other organizations must insist on; psychiatric doctrine is supple enough to do this, but institutions are not. Given the standards of the institution's environing society, there have to be at least the minimum routines connected with feeding, washing, dressing, bedding the patients, and protecting them from physical harm. Given these routines, there have to be inducements and exhortations to get patients to follow them. Demands must be made, and disappointment is shown when a patient does not live up to what is expected of him. Interest in seeing psychiatric 'movement' or 'improvement' after an initial stay on the wards leads the staff to encourage 'proper' conduct and to express disappointment when a patient backslides into 'psychosis'. The patient is thus re-established as someone whom others are depending on, someone who ought to know enough to act correctly. Some improprieties, especially ones like muteness and apathy that do not obstruct and even ease ward routines, may continue to be perceived naturalistically as symptoms, but on the whole the hospital operates semi-officially on the assumption that the patient ought to act in a manageable way and be respectful of psychiatry, and that he who does will be rewarded by improvement in life conditions and he who doesn't will be punished by a reduction of amenities. Within this semi-official reinstatement of ordinary organizational practices, the patient finds that many of the traditional ways of taking leave of a place without moving from it have retained their validity; secondary adjustments are therefore possible.

III

Of the many different kinds of secondary adjustment, some are of particular interest because they bring into the clear the general theme of involvement and disaffection, characteristic of all these practices.

One of these special types of secondary adjustment is 'removal activities' (or 'kicks'), namely, undertakings that provide something for the individual to lose himself in, temporarily blotting out all sense of the environment which, and in which, he must abide. In total institutions a useful exemplary case is provided by Robert Stroud, the 'Birdman' who, from watching birds out his cell window, through a spectacular career of finagling and make-do, fabricated a laboratory and became a leading ornithological contributor to medical literature, all from within prison.[71] Language courses in prisoner-of-war camps and art courses in prisons[72] can provide the same release.

Central Hospital provided several of these escape worlds for inmates.[73] One, for example, was sports. Some of the baseball players and a few tennis players seemed to become so caught up in their sport, and in the daily record of their efforts in competition, that at least for the summer months this became their overriding interest. In the case of baseball this was further strengthened by the fact that, within the hospital, parole patients could follow national baseball as readily as could many persons on the outside. For some young patients, who never failed to go, when allowed, to a dance held in their service or in the recreation building, it was possible to live for the chance of meeting someone 'in-

71. Gaddis, op. cit.

72. J. F. N., op. cit., pp. 17–18.

73. Behind informal social typing and informal group formation in prisons there is often to be seen a removal activity. Caldwell, op. cit., pp. 651–3, provides some interesting examples of prisoners on such kicks: those involved in securing and using drugs; those focused on leatherwork for sale; and 'Spartans', those involved in the glorification of their bodies, the prison locker room apparently serving as a muscle beach; the homosexuals; the gamblers, etc. The point about these activities is that each is world-building for the person caught up in it, thereby displacing the prison.

teresting' or re-meeting someone interesting who had already been
met – in much the same way that college students are able to survive their studies by looking forward to the new 'dates' that may
be found in extracurricular activities. The 'marriage moratorium'
in Central Hospital, effectively freeing a patient from his marital
obligations to a non-patient, enhanced this removal activity. For a
handful of patients, the semi-annual theatrical production was an
extremely effective removal activity: tryouts, rehearsals, costum-
ing, scenery-making, staging, writing and rewriting, performing –
all these seemed as successful as on the outside in building a
world apart for the participants. Another kick, important to
some patients – and a worrisome concern for the hospital chaplains – was the enthusiastic espousal of religion. Still another,
for a few patients, was gambling.[74]

Portable ways of getting away were much favoured in Central
Hospital, paperback murder mysteries,[75] cards, and even jigsaw
puzzles being carried around on one's person. Not only could
leave be taken of the ward and grounds be taken leave of through
these means, but if one had to wait for an hour or so upon an
official, or the serving of a meal, or the opening of the recreation
building, the self-implication of this subordination could be dealt

74. Melville, op. cit., devotes a whole chapter, ch. lxxiii, to illicit gambling aboard his frigate.

75. The getaway role of reading in prison is well described in Behan, op.
cit.; see also Heckstall-Smith, op. cit., p. 34: 'The prison library offered a
fairly good selection of books. But as time went by I found myself reading
merely to kill time – reading everything and anything I could lay my hands
on. During those first weeks, reading acted as a soporific and on the long
early summer evenings I often fell asleep over my book.'

Kogon, op. cit., pp. 127–8, provides a concentration-camp example: 'In
the winter of 1942–3 a succession of bread thefts in Barracks 42 at Buchenwald made it necessary to establish a nightwatch. For months on end I
volunteered for this duty, taking the shift from three to six o'clock in the
morning. It meant sitting alone in the day room, while the snores of the
comrades came from the other end. For once I was free of the ineluctable
companionship that usually shackled and stifled every individual activity.
What an experience it was to sit quietly by a shaded lamp, delving into the
pages of Plato's *Dialogues*, Galsworthy's *Swan Song*, or the works of
Heine, Klabund, Mehring! Heine? Klabund? Mehring? Yes, they could
be read illegally in camp. They were among books retrieved from the
nation-wide wastepaper collections.'

with by immediately bringing forth one's own world-making equipment.

Individual means of creating a world were striking. One depressed, suicidal alcoholic, apparently a good bridge player, disdained bridge with almost all other patient players, carrying around his own pocket bridge player and writing away occasionally for a new set of competition hands. Given a supply of his favourite gumdrops and his pocket radio, he could pull himself out of the hospital world at will, surrounding all his senses with pleasantness.   •

In considering removal activities we can again raise the issue of overcommitment to an establishment. In the hospital laundry, for example, there was a patient worker who had been on the job for several years. He had been given the job of unofficial foreman, and, unlike almost all other patient workers, he threw himself into his work with a capacity, devotion, and seriousness that were evident to many. Of him, the laundry charge attendant said:

That one there is my special helper. He works harder than all the rest put together. I would be lost without him.

In exchange for his effort, the attendant would bring from home something for this patient to eat almost every day. And yet there was something grotesque in his adjustment, for it was apparent that his deep voyage into the work world had a slightly make-believe character; after all, he was a patient, not a foreman, and he was clearly reminded of this off the job.

Obviously, as some of these illustrations imply, removal activities need not be in themselves illegitimate; it is the function that they come to serve for the inmate that leads us to consider them along with other secondary adjustments. An extreme here, perhaps, is individual psychotherapy in state mental hospitals; this privilege is so rare in these institutions,[76] and the resulting contact with a staff psychiatrist so unique in terms of hospital status structure, that an inmate can to some degree forget where he is as he pursues his psychotherapy. By actually receiving what the

76. Of approximately 7,000 patients in Central Hospital, I calculated at the time of the study, that about 100 received some kind of individual psychotherapy in any one year.

institution formally claims to offer, the patient can succeed in getting away from what the establishment actually provides. There is a general implication here. Perhaps every activity that an establishment obliges or permits its members to participate in is a potential threat to the organization, for it would seem that there is no activity in which the individual cannot become over-engrossed.

Another property is clearly evident in some undercover practices and possibly a factor in all of them: I refer to what Freudians sometimes call 'overdetermination'. Some illicit activities are pursued with a measure of spite, malice, glee, and triumph, and at a personal cost, that cannot be accounted for by the intrinsic pleasure of consuming the product. True, it is central to closed restrictive institutions that apparently minor satisfactions can come to be defined as great ones. But even correcting for this re-evaluation, something remains to be explained.

One aspect of the overdetermination of some secondary adjustments is the sense one gets of a practice being employed *merely* because it is forbidden.[77] Inmates in Central Hospital who had succeeded in some elaborate evasion of the rules often seemed to seek out a fellow inmate, even one who could not be entirely trusted, to display before him evidence of the evasion. A patient back from an overlate foray into the local town's night life would be full of stories of his exploits the next day; another would call aside his friends and show them where he had stashed the empty liquor bottle whose contents he had consumed the night before, or display the condoms in his wallet. Nor was it surprising to see the limits of safe concealment tested. I knew an extremely resourceful alcoholic who would smuggle in a pint of vodka, put some in a paper drinking cup, and sit on the most exposed part of the lawn he could find, slowly getting drunk; at such times he took pleasure in offering hospitality to persons of semi-staff status. Similarly, I knew an attendant who would park his car just outside the patient canteen – the social hub of the patient universe – and there he and a friendly patient would discuss the most inti-

77. This theme is developed by Albert Cohen in *Delinquent Boys* (Glencoe, Ill.: The Free Press, 1955).

mate qualifications of the passing females while resting a paper cup full of bourbon on the differential covering, just below the sight line of the crowd, drinking a toast, as it were, to their distance from the scene around them.

Another aspect of the overdeterminism of some secondary adjustments is that the very pursuit of them seems to be a source of satisfaction. As previously suggested in regard to courtship contacts, the institution can become defined as one's opponent in a serious game, the object being to score against the hospital. Thus I have heard cliques of patients pleasurably discuss the possibility that evening of 'scoring' for coffee,[78] accurately employing this larger term for a smaller activity.[79] The tendency of prison inmates to smuggle food and other comforts into the cell of someone suffering solitary confinement may be seen not only as an act of charity but also as a way of sharing by association the spirit of someone taking a stand against authority.[80] Similarly, the time-consuming elaborate escape planning that patients, prisoners, and P.O.W. internees engage in can be seen not merely as a way of getting out but also as a way of giving meaning to being in.

I am suggesting that secondary adjustments are overdetermined, some of them especially so. These practices serve the practitioner in ways other than the most evident ones: whatever else they accomplish these practices seem to demonstrate – to the practitioner if no one else, that he has some selfhood and

78. A detailed description of the conniving and sustained undercover effort required to score for coffee in prison is provided in Hayner and Ash, op. cit., pp. 365–6.

79. Traditionally, the value of pursuit itself is considered relative to the wider society, as when drug addicts are defined as playing an intensely meaningful daily game against society in obtaining the daily fix, and hustlers, grifters, and delinquents are seen as working hard at the intriguing, honourable task of making money without being seen working for it.

80. This theme is suggested by McCleery, S.S.R.C. Bulletin No. 15, op. cit., p. 60 fn.: 'The present study suggests that the display of goods and privileges among inmates serves to symbolize status that must be gained by other means. The symbols declare an ability to manipulate or resist power; and the inmate body betrays a compulsion to supply these symbols to men undergoing punishment, although their only function is to resist power bravely.'

personal autonomy beyond the grasp of the organization.[81]

IV

If a function of secondary adjustments is to place a barrier between the individual and the social unit in which he is supposed to be participating, we should expect some secondary adjustments to be empty of intrinsic gain and to function solely to express unauthorized distance – a self-preserving 'rejection of one's rejectors'.[82] This seems to happen with the very common forms of ritual insubordination, for example, griping or bitching, where this behaviour is not realistically expected to bring about change. Through direct insolence that does not meet with immediate correction, or remarks passed half out of hearing of authority, or gestures performed behind the back of authority, subordinates express some detachment from the place officially accorded them. An ex-inmate of the penitentiary at Lewisburg provides an illustration:

On the surface, life here appears to run almost placidly, but one needs to go only a very little beneath the surface to find the whirlpools and eddies of anger and frustration. The muttering of discontent and rebellion goes on constantly: the *sotto voce* sneer whenever we pass an official or a guard, the glare carefully calculated to express contempt without arousing overt retaliation . . .[83]

Brendan Behan provides a British prison illustration:

81. This point is nicely expressed by Dostoevski in his description of life in a Siberian prison camp, op. cit., p. 17: 'There were in the prison many who had been sentenced for smuggling, and there is therefore nothing surprising in the way vodka was brought in in spite of all the guards and inspections. Smuggling, by the way, is by its very nature a rather special crime. Can one imagine, for instance, that with some smugglers money and profit do not stand in the foreground, but play a secondary part? It really is so, however. The smuggler works for love of it, because he has a vocation. He is in some sense a poet. He risks everything, runs into terrible danger, twists and turns, uses his invention, extricates himself; sometimes he seems to act almost by inspiration. It is a passion as strong as that for cards.'

82. Lloyd W. McCorkle and Richard Korn, 'Resocialization Within Walls,' *The Annals*, CCXCIII (1954), p. 88.

83. Hassler, op. cit., pp. 70–71. For a military example of bitching, see Lawrence, op. cit., p. 132.

The warder shouted at him.

'Right, sir,' he shouted. 'Be right along, sir,' adding in a lower tone, 'You shit-'ouse.'[84]

Some of these ways of openly but safely taking a stand outside the authorized one are beautiful, especially when carried out collectively. Again, prisons provide ready examples:

> How to express contempt for authority? The manner of 'obeying' orders is one way.... Negroes are especially apt at parody, sometimes breaking into a goose-step. They seat themselves at table 10 at a time, snatching off caps simultaneously and precisely.[85]

When the sky pilot got up in the pulpit to give us our weekly pep talk each Sunday he would always make some feeble joke which we always laughed at as loud and as long as possible, although he must have known that we were sending him up. He still used to make some mildly funny remark and every time he did the whole church would be filled with rawcous [sic] laughter, even though only half the audience had heard what had been said.[86]

Some acts of ritual insubordination rely on irony, found in the wider society in the form of gallows gallantry and in institutions in the construction of heavily meaningful mascots. A standard irony in total institutions is giving nicknames to especially threatening or unpleasant aspects of the environment. In concentration camps, turnips were sometimes called 'German pineapples',[87] fatigue drill, 'Geography'.[88] In mental wards in Mount Sinai Hospital, brain-damage cases held for surgery would call the hospital 'Mount Cyanide',[89] and staff doctors were

typically misnamed, being referred to by such terms as 'lawyer,' 'white-collar worker,' 'chief of crew,' 'one of the presidents,' 'bartender,' 'supervisor of insurance' and 'credit manager.' One of us

84. Behan, op. cit., p. 45. Primary school children in American society very early learn how to cross their fingers, mutter contradictions, and grimace covertly – through all of these means expressing a margin of autonomy even while submitting to the teacher's verbal punishment.

85. Cantine and Rainer, op. cit., p. 106.

86. J. F. N., op. cit., pp. 15–16. See also Goffman, *Presentation of Self*, 'derisive collusion', pp. 186–8.

87. Kogon, op. cit., p. 108.

88. ibid., p. 103.

89. Edwin Weinstein and Robert Kahn, *Denial of Illness* (Springfield, Ill.: Charles Thomas, 1955), p. 21.

(E.A.W.) was called by such variations as 'Weinberg,' 'Weingarten,' 'Weiner' and 'Wiseman,' . . .[90]

In prison, the punishment block may be called the 'tea-garden'.[91] In Central Hospital, one of the wards containing incontinent patients was sometimes felt to be the punishment ward for attendants, who called it 'the rose garden'. An ex-mental patient provides another illustration:

> Back in the dayroom Virginia decided that her change of clothing represented Dressing Therapy. D.T. Today was my turn for D.T. This would have been rather amusing if you had had a good stiff drink. Of paraldehyde. The Juniper Cocktail, as we call it, we gay ladies of Juniper Hill. A martini, please, we more sophisticated ones say. And where, nurse, is the olive?[92]

It should be understood, of course, that the threatening world responded to with ironies need not be one sponsored by an alien human authority, but may be one that is self-imposed, or imposed by nature, as when dangerously ill persons joke about their situation.[93]

Beyond irony, however, there is an even more subtle and telling kind of ritual insubordination. There is a special stance that can be taken to alien authority; it combines stiffness, dignity, and coolness in a particular mixture that conveys insufficient insolence to call forth immediate punishment and yet expresses that one is entirely one's own man. Since this communication is made through the way in which the body and face are held, it can be constantly conveyed wherever the inmate finds himself. Illustrations can be found in prison society:

'Rightness' implies bravery, fearlessness, loyalty to peers, avoidance of exploitation, adamant refusal to concede the superiority of the official value system, and repudiation of the notion that the inmate is of a lower order. It consists principally in the reassertion of one's basic

90. ibid., p. 61. See especially ch. vi, 'The Language of Denial'.

91. Dendrickson and Thomas, op. cit., p. 25.

92. Mary Jane Ward, *The Snake Pit* (New York: New American Library, 1955), p. 65.

93. A useful report on ironies and other devices for dealing with life threat is provided by Renée Fox in *Experiment Perilous* (Glencoe, Ill.: The Free Press, 1959), p. 170 ff.

integrity, dignity, and worth in an essentially degrading situation, and the exhibition of these personal qualities regardless of any show of force by the official system.[94]

Similarly, in Central Hospital, in the 'tough' punishment wards of maximum security, where inmates had very little more to lose, fine examples could be found of patients not going out of their way to make trouble but by their very posture conveying unconcern and mild contempt for all levels of the staff, combined with utter self-possession.

V

It would be easy to account for the development of secondary adjustments by assuming that the individual possessed an array of needs, native or cultivated, and that when lodged in a milieu that denied these needs the individual simply responded by developing makeshift means of satisfaction. I think this explanation fails to do justice to the importance of these undercover adaptations for the structure of the self.

The practice of reserving something of oneself from the clutch of an institution is very visible in mental hospitals and prisons but can be found in more benign and less totalistic institutions, too. I want to argue that this recalcitrance is not an incidental mechanism of defence but rather an essential constituent of the self.

Sociologists have always had a vested interest in pointing to the ways in which the individual is formed by groups, identifies with groups, and wilts away unless he obtains emotional support from groups. But when we closely observe what goes on in a social role, a spate of sociable interaction, a social establishment – or in any other unit of social organization – embracement of the unit is not all that we see. We always find the individual employing methods to keep some distance, some elbow room, between himself and that with which others assume he should be identified. No doubt a state-type mental hospital provides an overly lush

94. Richard Cloward, 'Social Control in the Prison', S.S.R.C. Pamphlet No. 15, op. cit., p. 40. See also Sykes and Messinger, op. cit., pp. 10–11. Some minority groups have, relative to the society at large, a variant of this non-provoking but hands-off-me stance. Compare, for example, the 'cool stud' complex among urban American Negroes.

soil for the growth of these secondary adjustments, but in fact, like weeds, they spring up in any kind of social organization. If we find, then, that in all situations actually studied the participant has erected defences against his social bondedness, why should we base our conception of the self upon how the individual would act were conditions 'just right'?

The simplest sociological view of the individual and his self is that he is to himself what his place in an organization defines him to be. When pressed, a sociologist modifies this model by granting certain complications: the self may be not yet formed or may exhibit conflicting dedications. Perhaps we should further complicate the construct by elevating these qualifications to a central place, initially defining the individual, for sociological purposes, as a stance-taking entity, a something that takes up a position somewhere between identification with an organization and opposition to it, and is ready at the slightest pressure to regain its balance by shifting its involvement in either direction. It is thus *against something* that the self can emerge. This has been appreciated by students of totalitarianism:

> In short, Ketman means self-realization *against* something. He who practices Ketman suffers because of the obstacles he meets; but if these obstacles were suddenly to be removed, he would find himself in a void which might perhaps prove much more painful. Internal revolt is sometimes essential to spiritual health, and can create a particular form of happiness. What can be said openly is often much less interesting than the emotional magic of defending one's private sanctuary.[95]

I have argued the same case in regard to total institutions. May this not be the situation, however, in free society, too?

Without something to belong to, we have no stable self, and yet total commitment and attachment to any social unit implies a kind of selflessness. Our sense of being a person can come from being drawn into a wider social unit; our sense of selfhood can arise through the little ways in which we resist the pull. Our status is backed by the solid buildings of the world, while our sense of personal identity often resides in the cracks.

95. Czeslaw Milosz, *The Captive Mind* (New York: Vintage Books, 1955), p. 76.

THE MEDICAL MODEL
AND
MENTAL HOSPITALIZATION

SOME NOTES ON THE VICISSITUDES

OF THE TINKERING TRADES

I am grateful to Fred Davis and Sheldon Messinger for criticism and suggestions which have been incorporated without specific mention. Without specific reference I draw, too, on the fundamental paper in this area, Alfred H. Stanton and Morris S. Schwartz, 'Medical Opinion and the Social Context in the Mental Hospital', *Psychiatry*, XII (1949), pp. 243–9.

IN each society there are favoured ways in which two individuals can approach and have dealings with each other, for example, as kindred to kindred, or high caste to low. Each of these frameworks for contact can be at once a source of identity, a guide for ideal conduct, and a basis of both solidarity and divisiveness. Each framework involves a set of interdependent assumptions that fit together to form a kind of model. In every case we find that characteristic pressures prevent persons from fully realizing the ideal and that the resulting deviations have characteristic reverberations. The student of society can therefore use for his purposes the same models that members of society use for theirs.

In our Western society, an important way in which two individuals may deal with each other is as server and served. By exploring the assumptions and ideals behind this occupational relationship, I think we can understand some of the problems of mental hospitalization.

I

Specialized occupational tasks can be divided into two categories, one where the practitioner 'meets the public' through his work, a second where he does not, performing it only for the established members of his work organization. I assume that the problem of facing the public and of controlling it is sufficiently central to merit treating together all who experience it. This means that a hardware-store clerk and a factory tool-bin man are to be separated for purposes of study, in spite of similarities in what they do.

Among tasks requiring the performer to meet the public, two kinds may be distinguished, one where the public consists of a sequence of individuals, and another where it consists of a sequence of audiences. A dentist performs the first kind of task, a comedian the second.

Tasks which require the practitioner to meet the public (in either of its forms) vary in the degree to which they are presented to this public as a personal service, that is, as an assistance desired by the recipient. A *personal-service occupation* may be defined, ideally, as one whose practitioner performs a specialized personal service for a set of individuals where the service requires him to engage in direct personal communication with each of them and where he is not otherwise bound to the persons he serves.[1] By this definition the process of being served a summons, for example, is not a personal service for the person served. A psychologist who sells vocational testing to persons who want to learn about their aptitudes is performing a personal service, but if he tests the same persons for the employment office of an organization they are merely the subjects of his work and not his clients. So also, in spite of the language of census takers, I exclude domestic servants from the category of servers, since a maid has a mistress, not a public, and I exclude charwomen, since they do not routinely engage in direct communication with those who walk on their clean floors.

In this paper I want to consider personal-service occupations as here defined, but I shall include some practitioners who do not entirely fit my definition, since the ideal on which it is based draws people who are not in a position to conform to it. Deviations from an ideal imposed by self or others create problems of identity that the student must understand in terms of the ideal – and understand differently depending on the relation of the deviation to the ideal: a high-pressure car salesman and an insurance-company doctor both provide something less than a personal service, but for a different framework of reasons.

A traditional means of classifying personal-service occupations is by the honour accorded them, with the liberal professions falling at one extreme and the humble trades and crafts at the other. This can be an obscuring distinction, separating by rank those

1. Sociological interest in service occupations stems largely from Everett C. Hughes and is documented in the work of his students at the University of Chicago, especially Oswald Hall and Howard S. Becker. See especially the latter's 'The Professional Dance Musician and His Audience', *American Journal of Sociology*, LVII (1951), pp. 136–44.

who are similar in spirit. The division I want to employ places at one extreme those, such as ticket-takers or telephone operators, who perform a perfunctory technical service, and at the other those with an expertness that involves a rational, demonstrable competence that can be exercised as an end in itself and cannot reasonably be acquired by the person who is served. Perfunctory servers tend to have customers, 'parties', or applicants; expert servers tend to have clients. Both types of servers are likely to have some independence from the persons they serve, but only experts are in a position to build that independence into a solemn and dignified role. It is the social and moral assumptions underlying the practice of expert, rather than perfunctory, servicing that I want to consider in this paper.

I suggest that the ideals underlying expert servicing in our society are rooted in the case where the server has a complex physical system to repair, construct, or tinker with – the system here being the client's personal object or possession. Hereafter in this paper when I use the term service relation (or occupation) this pure case will be implied unless the context necessitates a more careful reference.

We deal with a triangle – practitioner, object, owner – and one that has played an important historical role in Western society. Every large society has expert servers, but no society has given such service more weight than has ours. Ours is a service society, so much so that even such institutions as stores come to follow this style in word if not in fact, responding to the need of both clerks and customers to feel that expert personal service is being provided even while they despair of realizing it.

The type of social relationship I will consider in this paper is one where some persons (clients) place themselves in the hands of other persons (servers). Ideally, the client brings to this relationship respect for the server's technical competence and trust that he will use it ethically; he also brings gratitude and a fee. On the other side, the server brings: an esoteric and empirically effective competence, and a willingness to place it at the client's disposal; professional discretion; a voluntary circumspection, leading him to exhibit a disciplined unconcern with the client's other affairs or even (in the last analysis) with why the client should want the service in the first place; and, finally, an unservile civility.[2] This, then, is the tinkering service.

We can begin to understand the service relation by examining the concept of the fee. There is a double sense in which a fee is not a price.[3] Traditionally a fee is anything other than what the service is worth. When services are performed whose worth to the client at the time is very great, the server is ideally supposed to restrict himself to a fee determined by tradition – presumably what the server needs to keep himself in decent circumstances while he devotes his life to his calling. On the other hand, when very minor services are performed, the server feels obliged either to forgo charging altogether or to charge a relatively large flat fee, thus preventing his time from being trifled with or his contribution (and ultimately himself) from being measured by a scale that can approach zero.[4] When he performs major services for very poor clients, the server may feel that charging no fee is more dignified (and safer) than a reduced fee.[5] The server thus avoids dancing to the client's tune, or even bargaining, and is able to show that he is motivated by a disinterested involvement in his work. And since his work is the tinkering kind, which has to do with nicely closed and nicely real physical systems, it is precisely the kind of work in which disinterested involvement is possible: a repair or construction job that is good is also one that the server can identify with; this adds a basis of autonomous interest to the job itself. Pre-

2. This description of the service relationship draws heavily on Parson's paper, 'The Professions and the Social Structure', which I feel is still the leading statement in this area. See also Talcott Parsons and Neil Smelser, *Economy and Society* (Glencoe, Ill.: The Free Press, 1956), pp. 152–3.

3. See, for example, A. M. Carr-Saunders and P. A. Wilson, *The Professions* (Oxford: The Clarendon Press, 1933), section 'Fees and Salaries' pp. 451–60.

4. The more lowly the tinkering trade, the more need the server may have to forgo charging for certain minor but skilled services. Among shoemakers these acts of *noblesse oblige* can become lordly indeed, just at a time in history when lords can no longer afford the original version.

5. Carr-Saunders and Wilson, op. cit., p. 452: 'In most other professions [*other than accountancy*] the associations attempt to induce their members not to undercut, though objection is never raised to the remission of fees when the client is poor.'

sumably the server's remaining motivation is to help mankind as such.

The server's attachment to his conception of himself as a disinterested expert, and his readiness to relate to persons on the basis of it, is a kind of secular vow of chastity and is at the root of the wonderful use that clients make of him. In him they find someone who does not have the usual personal, ideological, or contractual reasons for helping them; yet he is someone who will take an intense temporary interest in them, from their own point of view, and in terms of their own best interests. As one student of human affairs suggests:

As defined in this culture, the expert is one who derives his income and status, one or both, from the use of unusually exact or adequate information about his particular field, in the service of others. This 'use in the service of' is fixed in our industrial-commercial social order. The expert does not trade in the implements or impedimenta of his field; he is not a 'merchant,' a 'collector,' a 'connoisseur,' or a 'fancier,' for these use their skill primarily in their own interest.[6]

It therefore pays the client to trust in those for whom he does not have the usual guarantees of trust.

This trustworthiness available on request would of itself provide a unique basis of relationship in our society, but there is still another factor: the server's work has to do with a rational competence, and behind this a belief in rationalism, empiricism, and mechanism, in contrast to the more self-referential processes that plague people.

The interaction that occurs when client and server are together ideally takes a relatively structured form. The server can engage in mechanical, handwork operations on the client's possession, especially work of a diagnostic kind; he can also engage in verbal exchanges with the client. The verbal part itself contains three components: a *technical* part, namely the giving and getting of relevant repair (or construction) information; a *contractual* part, being a statement, often discreetly brief, regarding approximate costs, approximate time for the job, and the like; and finally, a *sociable* part, consisting of a few minor courtesies, civilities, and

6. Harry Stack Sullivan, 'The Psychiatric Interview', *Psychiatry*, XIV (1951), p. 365.

signs of deference. It is important to see that everything that goes
on between server and client can be assimilated to these components of activity, and that any divergences can be understood in
terms of these normative expectations. The full assimilation of the
interaction between server and client to this framework is often
for the server one of the tests of a 'good' service relation.

The technically relevant information that the server needs, in
order to repair or construct effectively, comes to him from two
sources: from the client's verbal statements, and from the object
itself, through the direct impression it makes on the server. Following the practice sometimes employed in medicine, we can call
the client's reported difficulties *symptoms*, and the data directly
obtained by the server *signs*, although there is no particular war-
rant for this usage in semiotics. The dignity of the service relation
is partly based on the capacity of the client to contribute usable
information, albeit filtered through lay language and lay sensi-
bility. The servicing can then take on something of the spirit of a
joint undertaking, with the server showing some respect for the
client's unschooled appraisal of the trouble.

The server has contact with two basic entities: a client and the
client's malfunctioning object. Clients are presumably self-
determining beings, entities in the social world, that must be
treated with appropriate regard and ritual. The possessed object is
part of another world, to be construed within a technical, not a
ritual, perspective, The success of the servicing depends on the
server keeping these two different kinds of entities separate while
giving each its due.

II

Let us now turn to the object that the server repairs or constructs.
I have described this object (or possession) as a physical system in
need of expert attention, and I shall focus on repairs, as more
usual than construction. Linked with the notion of repairs is a
conception of the repair cycle, the phases of which I would like
to describe briefly.

We can begin by considering our everyday conception of
etiology. The common nail can serve us as a starting point, for it
is an object that commonly begins a repair cycle. A nail on the

road can stop a car; a nail on a chair can tear trousers; a nail on a rug can ruin a vacuum cleaner; and a nail on the ground can pierce a foot. Note that a nail is not characteristic of the environment but is in a way an isolated haphazard occurrence in it; the environment is not fully responsible for it. The nail's contact with the possession is therefore a bad break, an accident, an unanticipated event. Once this contact occurs, a kind of causal transfer follows; the little evil is transplanted, taking on an intimate persistent causal status within the possession. We say: 'I sat down and I picked up a splinter'; or, 'I was driving and I picked up a nail.' Note, too, that although the nail and the car may be cursed for the trouble they cause, it is foreign to the service complex for the client, and especially for the server, seriously to impute intent or malice to the injuring agent or the injured possession. (It is only when the client fails to follow common-sense precautions or expert advice that the server inevitably begins to have a moral role.)

Now a foreign agent lodged in a physical system may be permanently dealt with by the internal corrective capacities of the system itself, by natural repair or natural compensation, and cease to constitute a problem for the object's possessor. But with many disruptive agents a different phase follows, namely, an increased malfunctioning over time. The little evil spreads out until the whole system is placed in jeopardy. Thus the tyre, once punctured, gets lower and lower, until the tube and rim are ruined and the car can no longer be driven.

There is a threshold point where the possessor himself finally sees that his possession has suffered damage or injury. If the possessor cannot make his own repairs and if he defines his problem as one that a server can help with, he becomes a client in search of a server, or in search of referral to a server through a set of intermediaries.

Once a server is found, the client brings him the total possession, or the total of what remains, plus, when possible, the broken parts. The central point here is that the whole complex of the possession, all that the server will need for his work, is voluntarily put at the disposal of the server by the client.

Now begins the famous process: observation, diagnosis,

prescription, treatment. Through the client's report, the server vicariously relives the client's experience of trouble; the server then engages in a brief run-through of what remains of the possession's functioning, but now, of course, the malfunctioning occurs under skilled eyes, ears, and nose. (It is remarkable how at this juncture a lab coat of some kind often appears, symbolizing not merely the scientific character of the server's work but also the spiritual poise of a disinterested intent.)

After the server has done his work, a period of convalescence may occur during which reduced demands are placed upon the object and there is a heightened attentiveness to signs of relapse or insufficient repair. This care and vigilance become gradually reduced to periodic spot checks during which the client himself, or sometimes the server, rechecks matters to make doubly sure that things are as desired.

The final phase of the repair cycle occurs when the possession is 'as good as new', or, if a little weak at the mend, none the less at a stage where attention may be safely withdrawn from the whole issue of the repair.

I would like to add an historical note that has relevance for the repair cycle. One of the basic changes we have witnessed in the tinkering services in the last hundred years is the movement away from pedlar carts and home visits and the development of the *workshop complex*. Instead of the server bringing himself and his tools to the client, the client comes to the server and leaves the disordered object with the server, returning later to retrieve the repaired possession.

There are many advantages to having a work place of one's own, of course, which no doubt figured in the rise of the workshop. Often clients prefer a fixed address that provides continuously available service to a single date on an annual, monthly, or weekly cycle of home visits. Another advantage derives from an increasing division of labour. With a workshop, the server can invest in heavy fixed equipment. In addition he can take on more than one repair job at the same time, breaking down the work so that costly skilled help will not be engaged in doing unskilled labour. He need not turn away work while engaged in one job, or have to wait idly between jobs, but can distribute his work by manipulating the time that objects for repair are held in the workshop.

Another set of workshop advantages are social in character, having to do with the increased status leverage servers acquire when they acquire a workshop. Owning or renting one's shop ensures that the client cannot turn the server out of the house and that police cannot make him 'move on'. It is the client who becomes the guest. Furthermore, since the client is not present while the actual work is done, mistakes at work and padding of expenses are easily concealed from him; at the same time, the length of time for which the server requires the client's possession allows the server to dignify his service and charge high for it.[7] Finally, the kind of clothing, posture, and grooming that is associated with handwork can be clearly segregated from the kind of personal front that best fits the verbal aspects of server-client relations. A specialist in cleanliness can be kept permanently 'up front', or the working shop-manager can wash his hands, take off his apron, and put his jacket on when he hears the doorbell ring in the front of the shop.

It is plain that the workshop could function to weaken the service complex. After all, the client must now give up possession of his object for days at a time – let alone the control of watching the server at work. But perhaps increased need to trust has led to increased trustworthiness. In any case, when a work place becomes fixed in a community, the server becomes subject to the people he serves in a new way. It is known where he can be found; he is therefore available to disgruntled clients and subject to the general attitude of the community towards him. Under these circumstances he will feel constrained to provide the kind of service that will not be complained about.

III

Let us now examine some of the conceptual assumptions that underlie the service relation and its repair cycle.

If a possession or object is to be of use to its owner, its various

7. See E. Goffman, *The Presentation of Self in Everyday Life* (New York: Anchor Books, 1959), pp. 114–15.

parts must be in proper functional order relative to one another. The gears must mesh, the blood must flow, and the wheels or hands must turn. Here there is a happy coincidence that should not remain implicit: the functioning of the object, when seen, as it were, from its own point of view, has some relation to whether or not the possessor will be able to make use of it. In some cases, as with mechanical objects, the coincidence has been purposely prearranged, the object being designed in the first place to be of a particular use when it is working well. In other cases, as with beasts of burden and our own bodies, the coincidence is not designed but is present none the less. If a horse is to be worked, it must not be too ill.

A second assumption of the service relation is that the client's possession is fully his and that he can by law do with it what he will.

Third, the possession itself is assumed to form not only a relatively closed system but also one small enough to be moved around by the possessor, or, if not this, at least to be seen as a simultaneous whole by both possessor and server.

Fourth, and most important, the possessions that are to be serviced form not only relatively closed and relatively manageable systems but also distinct and obvious classes of systems. Whether we deal with products of nature or of manufacture, we deal with products struck from a mould, with strict reproduction, and with the use of standardized solutions to constructional and repair problems even when the outward appearance of products within a class may differ. It follows that if the server knows about the workings of one member of a given class, he is automatically competent to deal with other members of this class.[8]

There are some assumptions underlying the development of the workshop complex that should be made explicit.

The first assumption is that the workshop milieu will be benign relative to the injury the possession has suffered; the workshop will stop the progressive course of the disorder although not effect any cure by itself. A car with a top that leaks is handled in a

8. Technological change does of course bring limits. A garageman able only to pull apart and rebuild a Model A Ford finds himself today with some automotive skills that he cannot use and some automotive problems that he cannot solve.

closed garage or placed under a tarp until work can be started on it; this precaution does not mend the top, but it ensures that the tear will not get any bigger or the upholstery even more damaged. A chair that is beginning to crack may not be repaired right away in the shop to which it is taken, but presumably no one there will sit on it and aggravate the damage.

A second assumption is that the possession is sufficiently independent of its original environment to allow temporary transplanting to the shop without introducing a new set of damages.

A third assumption is that the client is not inextricably tied to his possession and can withstand the wait that turning the possession over to a workshop is likely to entail. Often the client's use of his possession is intermittent, so that time without the possession is not entirely waste time;[9] it is possible for him to consider the full period without his possession as a period filled with servicing activity.

I have suggested some of the assumptions that we must make regarding serviceable objects and service workshops if the service relation is to be ideally sustained. A final set of these assumptions concerns the structure of clienteles.

The character of the service relationship seems to require that the clientele be a set of persons who voluntarily use the service in a way that precludes their taking concerted action regarding it, thus exerting power over the server only as an aggregate, not a collectivity. In these circumstances the server can be independent of the good favour of any one of them, politely turning away any client he feels he will not be able to serve properly, just as each of them can withdraw should the relation prove unsatisfactory. Ideally, there is a double voluntarism to the relationship, as with persons living in sin, and a limit to the reasonable complaints that either party can make about the relationship while remaining in it. Ideally, expert servicing expresses mutual respect between client and server and is designed to be a gentlemanly process.

9. Recently this delicate point in the service schema has been strengthened by the practice of 'loan out'. On leaving one's watch or radio or car for repair, one is given loan of a substitute by the server until repairs are completed.

IV

The character of the service relationship, as here described, has a
logic of its own. Given its various premises, the server will be in a
position to sustain a definition of himself as someone who, merely
for a fee, provides an expert service that the client is in real need
of, and the client will be able to believe that there are strangers of
good will in society who are highly competent and dedicated to
their competence in such a way as to lend themselves to one's
concerns for only a fee. Yet while the service relationship is cast
in this pure and noble mould, it lacks the institutional supports
that buttress some of our other highly valued relationships, such
as familial ones. We can expect, then, that the framework of rights
and duties on each side of the relationship can form a kind of
matrix of anxiety and doubt, even when each party to the relationship is behaving properly. The client thinks: 'Is this server
really competent? Is he acting in my own interests? Is he over-
charging? Is he discreet? Is he secretly contemptuous of me because of the state in which he finds my possession?' (Each of these
dimensions of potential defection may occur in the absence of the
others, so that the total number of possibilities is quite large.)
The server thinks: 'Does this client really have confidence in me?
Is he concealing the fact that he has "shopped around" before
coming here? Will he pay the fee?'

In addition to these general anxieties, we can expect that more
specific ones will arise; once we see the service complex for what
it is, an ideal and model, we can appreciate that each type of
service will provide its own special instances of issues that cannot
easily be managed within the service model, giving rise to characteristic difficulties.

For example, there are service needs, such as those a plumber
fulfils, that tend to be presented to the server as a crisis: the family
must have water right away, or someone must stop the flood of
water that has started. At the same time, the plumber cannot
bring the defective equipment into the protection of his shop but
must do his work under the eyes of the household.

Another difficulty arises with those services, such as radio and
TV repair, in which the fee complex has become considerably

weakened, clients often (rightly) feeling that they are being 'taken'. But the show of dignity associated with these services has not declined and is supported by an increasingly high minimum fee.

Furthermore, there are certain trends in modern society that weaken the service complex. Many service establishments find it is more profitable to sell only new merchandise rather than waste space and personnel on repair work. Those that do make repairs increasingly tend to introduce a whole new set of internal works – to replace major parts rather than skilfully to repair them[10] – and of course there is the trend to 'automatic merchandising', machine or cafeteria style, which considerably reduces the role of the server or does away with it entirely.

Another major problem in the validity of the service model is that servers inevitably make an effort to select a clientele on the basis of technically irrelevant factors, such as social class status or ability to pay; clients act similarly. So, too, the server is likely to give his clients differential treatment on the basis of extraneous variables, although perhaps more deviation from the ideal occurs in getting to a server than in treatment once one gets to him.

An important source of difficulty is that the double independence that ideally exists between server and served is often in jeopardy. Where the server is not a 'free' one, that is, not in business for himself, his relations with his clients can be constrained by the claims of management upon him. (Correspondingly, of course, management may encounter many problems from employees' efforts to take the role of server in regard to the company's customers.) A point can be reached where the manager of a service establishment such as a large shoe-repair shop arrogates to himself all contact with the public, thereby removing the other shoemakers from the service category as here defined – regardless of popular and census classifications. Similarly, there are the problems of those whose calling is generally defined as appropriate for independent practice, such as law or architecture,

10. On this and some other deviations from the service ideal, see F. L. Strodtbeck and M. B. Sussman, 'Of Time, the City, and the "One-Year Guaranty": The Relations between Watch Owners and Repairers', *American Journal of Sociology*, LXI (1956), pp. 602–9.

but who find themselves with staff positions in which they have a captive clientele, or are captives of a clientele, or have only one client; cast in the traditional form of the free server, these persons tend to embarrass themselves and others by affecting a stance which the facts do not support. Court physicians provided a classic example, reminding us that today the dignity of medical service requires that a physician to a royal person be other persons' physician, too. And of course where a server's clients come from the same settled community, they are likely to be in potential if not actual communication with one another, ever ready to coalesce into a 'lay referral system' with unanticipated power over the server.[11] If there are only a few lawyers or doctors in the community, then clients probably need this power.

Two final sources of difficulty in the application of the service model should be mentioned, both having to do with the social consequences of professionalization. The cultivation of trustworthy disinterestedness inevitably seems to overreach itself in two ways. First, the server's increasingly proficient attention to the interests of the client can lead him to form ideal conceptions of client interest, and this ideal, together with professional standards of taste, efficiency, and foresightedness, can sometimes conflict with what a particular client on a particular occasion considers to be *his* own best interests. Even an interior decorator may politely tell a client to go elsewhere, being loath to carry out the client's unseemly wishes.

Second, the more a server is concerned with giving good service, and the more his own profession is given a public mandate to control him, the more he is likely to be accorded the public task of maintaining community standards, which at times will not be in the immediate interests of a particular client. The code that a builder adheres to, for example, forces his client to underwrite certain considerations for neighbours, whether the client wants to or not. The obligation of lawyers to give only lawful legal advice is another case in point. Here is a basic breach in the notion we started with of an independent client and an independent

11. The term 'lay referral system' is from Eliot Freidson, 'Client Control and Medical Practice', *American Journal of Sociology*, LXV (1960), pp. 374–82.

server. We now have a triad – client, server, community – and this can strike at the heart of serving even more than the triadic feature that occurs when the server joins an establishment of some kind and divides his loyalty between the firm's clients and the firm's management.

V

We now turn to the medical version of the tinkering-services model.[12] Our giving our bodies up to the medical server, and his rational-empirical treatment of them, is surely one of the high points of the service complex. Interestingly enough, the gradual establishment of the body as a serviceable possession – a kind of physicochemical machine – is often cited as a triumph of the secular scientific spirit, when in fact this triumph seems in part to have been both cause and effect of the rising regard for all types of expert servicing.

The signs that medical men currently employ, especially signs involving refined laboratory work, are increasingly sophisticated, yet medical men still claim to rely on the patient for reporting symptoms; the client is still a participant to be respected in the service relationship. But, as with other competencies, there are special points of strain in fitting the treatment of the body into the service framework. I would like to mention some of these, with the understanding that the same problems also arise to some degree in other kinds of servicing.

The first issue is that the body is, as psychoanalysts say, highly cathected in our society; persons place great value on its appearance and functioning and tend to identify themselves with it. Individuals are uneasy about giving their bodies up to the rational-empirical ministrations of others, and hence need their 'confidence' in the server continuously shored up by bedside assurances. This problem must not be overstressed, however, not because persons are ceasing to identify with their bodies but because of what we are slowly learning about how much they

12. Compare T. S. Szasz, 'Scientific Method and Social Role in Medicine and Psychiatry', *A.M.A. Archives of Internal Medicine*, CI (1958), pp. 232–3, and his 'Men and Machines', *British Journal for the Philosophy of Science*, VIII (1958), pp. 310–17.

identify with quite non-corporal things, such as wrist watches and cars, seeing in a threat to these 'good objects' a threat to self.

The very willingness of clients to put their bodies' fate in the hands of their physicians carries its own problem for medical men: they may find that sympathy with the patient subjects them to emotional stress when they are uncertain of what is wrong or what can be done for the patient, or when they are certain that little can be done and must impart this information to the person (or his guardian) whose fate will be sealed by it.[13] But here, perhaps, we have a problem not for medical servicing as such but for the individuals who perform it.

Another problem is that the body is one possession that cannot be left under the care of the server while the client goes about his other business. Admittedly physicians show a remarkable capacity to carry on the verbal part of the server role while engaging in the mechanical part, without this segregation breaking down, but there are inevitable difficulties here, since the client is very interested in what is happening to his body and is in a good position to see what is being done. (Barbers, hairdressers, and prostitutes know of these troubles, too, of course, since poor mechanical activity on their part may be instantly perceived by the ever-present client.) One solution is anaesthesia; another is the wonderful brand of 'non-person treatment' found in the medical world, whereby the patient is greeted with what passes as civility, and said farewell to in the same fashion, with everything in between going on as if the patient weren't there as a social person at all, but only as a possession someone has left behind.[14]

13. An analysis of the pressures upon a physician to evade communicating a known bad prognosis and to offer an opinion when in fact he feels uncertain is provided in Fred Davis, 'Uncertainty in Medical Prognosis, Clinical and Functional', *American Journal of Sociology*, LXVI (1960), pp. 41–7.

14. The non-person solution seems especially effective when the examining physician is accompanied by colleagues and subordinates, as when making rounds, for then he will have participants available for a technical conversation about the case. So effective is this way of suppressing the social presence of the patient that his fate can be openly discussed around his bed without the discussants having to feel undue concern; a technical vocabulary presumably unknown to the patient helps in this regard.

Another issue in medicine has to do with the appreciable margin of merely palliative action, of 'elective procedures', and of unsuccessful treatment. With many mechanical objects, every possible disorder can be fixed, depending only on how much of the original object is replaced with new parts, and this may require no great skill. A radio mechanic of average ability can fix absolutely any broken radio by the simple expedient of checking out sections of the circuit and replacing the parts where the trouble seems to lie. It is the realistic boast of a well-supplied automotive-parts distributor that he can build a complete car in his supply rooms from the parts on hand. Not so in medicine. Some parts of the body cannot be replaced, and not all physical disorders can be corrected. Further, due to medical ethics, a physician cannot advise a patient to junk the badly damaged or very worn object his body may have become (as can those who service other types of objects), although the physician may tacitly give such advice to other interested parties.

Although this lowered probability of repair is characteristic of medicine, there are effective techniques for the management of doubt. Even in the case of a brain surgeon, who may expect to lose half his cases, clients can be made to see that this is merely a chancy, last-resort department of medicine, made tolerable by the probability of effectiveness achieved in many of the other departments. Further, there are expert services, albeit of a non-tinkering kind, such as those a lawyer or broker provides, where the probability of success may well be lower than in general medicine and a sense of ethical professional service can still survive. In all these cases the server can take the stand that, whether he succeeds or fails this time, he is applying the best techniques to the best of his abilities, and that in general it is better to rely on these techniques and abilities than to rely on pure chance. Respectful and continued relations between many brokers and their clients attest to the fact that, once a service definition of the situation is accepted, clients are willing to accept a probability very little greater than chance as justification for remaining within the relationship. The client finds that he must consider not how well he has done with the server, but rather how much worse he might have done without him, and with this understanding he is led to accord the ultimate tribute to esoteric skill: cheerful payment of the fee in spite of the loss of the object that the server was hired to save.

Another interesting difficulty in applying the tinkering-service model to medical practice is that the injurious agent is recognized in some cases to be not a randomly disposed improbable event in the environment, but the environment itself. Instead of there being one nail on the road, the road is covered with them. Thus, for certain physical disorders, a given climate or given type of work is exacerbating. If the patient can afford a complete change of scenery, the pathogenic environment can be looked upon as merely one of the many possible environments, and hence the improbable member of a generally healthy class. For many patients, however, change in life situation is not practical, and the service model cannot be satisfactorily applied.

Associated with the fact that the environment itself may be the pathogenic agent is the possibility of pursuing medicine at the community level, treating not a single individual but a large social unit, and reducing the probability of a specific illness within a whole set of persons rather than curing a specific patient. The whole emerging field of epidemiology is of this order, constituting not so much a threat to medical practice on individuals as a supplement to it.

While many individuals can be relied upon to act as responsible, self-willing agents in regard to their bodies, it is apparent that the very young, the very old, and the mentally ill may have to be brought to medical attention 'for their own good' by someone else, thus radically changing the usual relation between client, possession, and server. Often an attempt is made to assimilate such situations to the free-agent model by having the patient brought in by someone with whom he is socially identified, typically a kinsman who can stand in for him and as a guardian be trusted to represent his ward's best interests. Perhaps a factor here is that the seeking of medical service by free agents is often itself not so free, but a product of consensus, if not pressure, on the part of the patient's close kin group. It may be added that when dire news must be given a patient he may suddenly find that his capacities as object and as client are split apart. He retains his status as an object but his role as client is subtly transferred to someone close to him. Sometimes the issue is not that he is no longer competent as a social person but that the physician is disinclined to become embroiled as a participant-witness of someone's immediate response to a destruction of life chances.

The guardian problem can illustrate the conflict that may arise between what a server and his discipline feel is in the best interests of the client and what the client himself desires. This potential conflict is sharpened by a further factor, the tension between client interests and community interests. An obvious example is the case of communicable diseases, where the physician has the legal obligation to protect the community as well as his client. Other examples of this conflict are abortion and the treatment of unreported gunshot wounds, although in both cases there is an out, an abortion often being defined as not in the 'best' interests of the person seeking it, and gunshot wounds being treated, provided police authorities are informed at the same time. A third instance is the early restriction on the use of plastic surgery for purely cosmetic reasons, although what was at stake here was not so much the welfare of the community as the dignity and disinterestedness of the medical profession itself. And of course there are other instances, such as the Soviet physician's interesting problem of whether to grant to a worker what will be his only holiday although he doesn't have very much wrong with him,[15] or the American physician's problem of whether to 'write scrip' for drugs to confirmed addicts.

Another problem in managing medicine within the service framework is that patients often feel they can seek advice from their physician on non-medical matters, and the physician sometimes feels he has a special competence that justifies his accepting this diffusion of his role.[16] More important, and increasingly important, is another problem: in spite of the efforts of medical professional associations, in some countries medical practice as a whole is tending away from the ideal of the free practitioner with an unorganized clientele to one where a bureaucratic agency of

15. M. G. Field, 'Structured Strain in the Role of the Soviet Physician', *American Journal of Sociology*, LVIII (1953), pp. 493–502.
16. Szasz, 'Scientific Method ...' op. cit., p. 233 fn.

some kind provides service to clients who have little choice over which of the available physicians they get to see. This is a serious threat to the classic service relation, but I do not think we yet know about its long-range consequence for the service ideal.

From the point of view of this paper, the most relevant strain in the application of the service model to medicine resides in the workshop complex, in spite of the fact that on some occasions, as in certain surgical undertakings, a roomful of people may be intimately regulated by a multitude of detailed rules, almost all of which are rationally grounded in technical considerations. While typically presenting themselves as public service institutions run for the benefit of mankind, some hospitals have frankly operated for the profit of their owners, and all have shown concern about the social characteristics of their staff and patients. So, too, many hospitals are involved in training programmes that lead some treatment decisions to be influenced not merely by the needs of the patient in question but also by the techniques and medications in which the hospital specializes. Similarly, many hospitals are involved in research programmes that sometimes lead to treatment dictated not so much by the needs of the patient as by the requirements of the research design.

There are other difficulties, too. As already suggested, the client will find it difficult to treat his body, and have it treated, impersonally, and to overlook the fact that he cannot use it in the usual fashion while it is being repaired. Further, it is increasingly appreciated that even a brief sojourn in the hospital can create 'separation anxiety' in the very young; the implication is that the workshop in such cases is not a benign neutral environment, but a hurtful one. Furthermore, since the client must reside in the workshop during the active treatment phase of the repair cycle, he is well situated to see the difficulties of assimilating everything that occurs around and to him to the service model. The success of the patient in making this assimilation necessarily resides in his being deceived about certain procedures, because always some of the hospital routine will be dictated not by medical considerations but by other factors, notably rules for patient management that have emerged in the institution for the convenience and comfort of staff. (The same divergence from service-determined rules is true, of course, of every workshop, but in these other workshops the client is not usually present to see what happens.) The longer the required stay in the hospital, and the more chronic and lingering the disorder, the greater the difficulty the patient will have in seeing the hospital as a thoroughly rational service institution.

In spite of these and other difficulties in housing medical services within a hospital establishment, there are factors which are effective in allowing the patient to assimilate all his hospital experience to the service model – providing his stay is not too long. Obviously the hospital can provide the patient with the benefit of heavy capital equipment and specialized instruments that no doctor's office could provide. Further, to rest immobile in bed is, after all, defined as what one does in our society when one is sick, and in some cases the patient may feel physically incapable of doing anything else. Some technical aspects of medical attention add additional support: bone fractures and many post-operative states patently necessitate immobility, as do, occasionally, such post-operative procedures as draining; some therapies require a highly regulated diet; charting and lab work often require constant availability of the patient. All of this provides rational justification for the posture the patient must assume in the hospital.

An additional factor strengthens this assimilation of hospital experience to the service model. Often during hospitalization and post-hospital care there is a split introduced into the patient's environment: within a bandage or cast or otherwise bounded part of the body, a medically adjusted environment is intensively maintained; the condition in which everything outside this boundary is maintained can then be rationalized not on the direct grounds of its salubriousness, but as a basis for ensuring the maintenance of the inner environment. In this way the area over which patently useful medical actions are maintained can be greatly reduced without jeopardizing the possibility that the patient will be able to assimilate everything that is occurring to him to the medical model.

These bases of validity to the service claims made by hospitals make more secure the service stance assumed by the physician, who can move solemnly without fear of being taken unseriously by his clients or by himself. In a situation of great concern to the client and in the face of still appreciable ignorance, the physician can often enough deliver the goods, proving that he merits the respect his stance implies he expects. The client attests to the validity of the physician's claims, and through this to the viability of the medical model, by his willingness to follow the server in viewing the disorder impersonally – no one's desire, no one's intention, and no one's fault. Hospitalization will temporarily remove the individual from his social roles, but if he lives through his ordeal he is likely to return to the social place he left behind, a place that is kept open and warm for him through the institution of 'medical absence', by which others discount the importance of his departure.

Although the expert servicing model does seem to be the one that medical practice is patterned on, I want to conclude this discussion of the medical model by suggesting that this individual-oriented service framework is not the only one that medical action fits into (a qualification earlier implied in the reference to insurance company doctors and epidemiology); two other frameworks must be mentioned.

First, medical men can be employed not to service a particular individual but to ensure that a social undertaking involving a number of persons is managed in a way consistent with certain minimal standards of medical care, these standards being established and ultimately enforced by agents acting for the wider community. What was previously discussed as a limitation on orientation to a given client can become a practitioner's main function. Thus, certain sporting ventures, such as boxing matches, employ watchdog physicians, just as factories and mines are forced to operate in a way consistent with minimal standards of safety. We can speak here of the *normative* function of medicine; engineers, electricians, and architects may be employed in a similar fashion.

Secondly, medical men can be employed in a *maintenance* role for the purpose of treating a participant in an undertaking, not for himself, or to guard community standards, but simply to maximize the usefulness of the participant for the undertaking.

Pharmaceutical pepping-up of athletes and horses is an example; medical supervision of torture to ensure the prisoner will not die before he talks is another; the feeding of labour-camp inmates to keep up their strength for work is still another.[17] The normative function and the maintenance function are often found combined, as in the dental and medical services attached to large-scale social establishments, especially isolated ones like ships' companies and armies.

Besides personal-service medicine, then, we can have company medicine of various kinds. In suggesting these additional models for medical activity, I do not deny that the personal service received by some under-privileged patients is sometimes less adequate – from the patients' point of view – than that received by some employees as part of the maintenance and normative functions of medicine in their work establishment. The concern here is not what medical attention the individual receives but rather the organizational framework in which he receives it.

VI

Now, finally, we can turn to the issue posed by the title of this paper: the application of the expert servicing model, in its medical version, to institutional psychiatry.

The Western history of the interpretation of persons who seem to act oddly is a dramatic one: wilful or involuntary consort with the devil, seizure by the tendencies of wild animals, etc.[18] In Britain, in the latter part of the eighteenth century, the medical mandate over these offenders began in earnest. Inmates were called patients, nurses were trained, and medically styled case records were kept.[19] Madhouses, which had been retitled asylums for the insane, were retitled again, this time as mental hospitals. A similar movement was led in America by the Pennsylvania

17. An interesting treatment of the influence of this function in military medicine may be found in R. W. Little, 'The "Sick Soldier" and the Medical Ward Officer', *Human Organization*, XV (1956), pp. 22–4.

18. See, for example, Albert Deutsch, *The Mentally Ill in America* (2nd ed.; New York: Columbia University Press, 1949), pp. 12–23.

19. Kathleen Jones, *Lunacy, Law, and Conscience* (London: Routledge and Kegan Paul, 1955), pp. 55–6.

Hospital, beginning in 1756.[20] Today in the West there are differences in stress between practitioners with an 'organic' approach and those with a 'functional' one, but the assumptions underlying both approaches similarly support the legitimacy of applying the medical version of the service model to asylum inmates. For example, in many communities certification by a physician is a legal requirement for involuntary mental hospitalization.

When a patient-to-be comes to his first admissions interview, the admitting physicians immediately apply the medical-service model. Whatever the patient's social circumstances, whatever the particular character of his 'disorder', he can in this setting be treated as someone whose problem can be approached, if not dealt with, by applying a single technical-psychiatric view. That one patient differs from another in sex, age, race grouping, marital status, religion, or social class is merely an item to be taken into consideration, to be corrected for, as it were, so that general psychiatric theory can be applied and universal themes detected behind the superficialities of outward differences in social life. Just as anyone in the social system can have an inflamed appendix, so anyone can manifest one of the basic psychiatric syndromes. A uniform professional courtesy shown to patients is matched with a uniform applicability of psychiatric doctrine.

There are certainly cases of mental disorder (associated with brain tumours, paresis, arteriosclerosis, meningitis, etc.) that appear beautifully to fulfil all the requirements of the service model: a randomly distributed rare event injures the client's mental functioning without anyone intending it and without his being personally to blame. After a while he and or others sense that 'something is wrong'. Through a route of referrals he is brought, voluntarily or involuntarily, to the attention of psychiatrists. They gather information, make observations, provide a diagnosis, a prescription, and suggest a course of treatment. The patient then recovers, or the progress of his pathology is checked, or (a likelihood with 'organic reactions') the disease follows its known and inevitable course, ending in the patient's death

20. Deutsch, op. cit., p. 58 ff.

or his reduction to an incurable state of mere vegetative functioning. In the more benign cases, where the patient can benefit markedly from treatment, he is likely to re-evaluate his past experience so as to recognize that the psychiatric service was performed in his own interests and that he would have sought it out voluntarily had he realized what was wrong and what could be done for him. Everything ends happily ever after,[21] and if not happily then at least tidily. One can find framed case records in the hallways of the medical-surgical buildings of some mental hospitals that provide, in regard to an actual case, an outline of early ('prodromal') social signs and symptoms, documentation of the lay failure to assess these correctly, description of the behaviour of the patient while he was sick, and drawings of the autopsy findings confirming the correctness of the diagnosis and appropriateness of the treatment. Social misconduct and visible organic pathology are brought together in a perfect confirmation of the applicability of the medical model.

While some psychiatric cases may be neatly handled within the framework established by the medical model there are very evident sources of difficulty, especially in regard to the largest category of mental patients, those with so-called 'functional' psychoses. Many of these difficulties have been described in the literature and are well known in psychiatry. I would like to review them briefly here, starting with the more incidental kinds and working up to ones that are more fundamental.

One issue in the applicability of the service model to institutional psychiatry arises from the fact that part of the official mandate of the public mental hospital is to protect the community from the danger and nuisance of certain kinds of misconduct. In terms of the law and of the public pressures to which the mental hospital is sensitive, this custodial function is of major importance. Within the institution surprisingly little explicit reference is made to it, however, the focus being on the medical-like

21. A good illustration of this is provided in Berton Roueché's *New Yorker* article 'Ten Feet Tall', detailing an incident of manic-depressive side effects caused by cortisone treatment. This article is available in Roueché's collection, *The Incurable Wound* (New York: Berkley Publishing Corp., n.d.), pp. 114–43.

therapeutic services the hospital supplies patients. If we view the mentally ill as persons that others have had a special kind of trouble with, then the custodial role of the hospital (much like the custodial role of the prison) is understandable and, many would feel, justifiable; the point here, however, is that a service to the patient's kin, neighbourhood, or employer is not necessarily a service to the community at large (whatever that may be) and a service to any of these is not necessarily a service, especially not a medical service, to the inmate. Instead of a server and the served, we find a governor and the governed, an officer and those subject to him.[22]

During the patient's hospitalization he is very likely to pass from the jurisdiction of one medical person to another, and this shift is not a result of a referral system in which the practitioner suggests another server and the patient voluntarily follows the suggestion; the patient will pass from the jurisdiction of one medical person to another because of daily and weekly medical shifts, and because of the frequency with which patients are shifted from one ward to another and medical staff from one service to another. Being members of the same organization, the patient and the doctor are both subject to decisions they do not make concerning whom they will see.[23]

Further, we must see the mental hospital in the recent historical

22. See Talcott Parsons, 'The Mental Hospital as a Type of Organization', in M. Greenblatt, D. Levinson, and R. Williams, eds., *The Patient and the Mental Hospital* (Glencoe, Ill.: The Free Press, 1957), p. 115.

23. In research hospitals instructive attempts have been made to deal with this problem. The role of ward physician may be strictly segregated from the role of therapist, the therapist-patient relation remaining constant, regardless of a shift in ward residence of a patient. (See, for example, Stewart Perry and Lyman Wynne, 'Role Conflict, Role Redefinition, and Social Change in a Clinicial Research Organization', *Social Forces*, XXXVIII [1959], pp. 62–5). In private general hospitals which have one or two psychiatric floors, an even closer approximation to the service relation is found: a psychiatrist in private practice may have several 'beds' and will temporarily hospitalize a patient when he feels it is necessary. The house staff, typically residents, will then have the job of keeping the patient fed and quiet, and the psychiatrist will visit his patient once or twice a day, as do the doctors who make use of beds on other floors. Many of the forms of the service relationship are thereby retained; how much therapy results is a different question.

context in which it developed, as one among a network of institutions designed to provide a residence for various categories of socially troublesome people. These institutions include nursing homes, general hospitals, veterans' homes, jails, geriatrics clinics, homes for the mentally retarded, work farms, orphanages, and old-folks' homes. Every state hospital has an appreciable fraction of patients who might better be contained in some one of these other institutions (just as these other institutions have some inmates who might better be contained in a mental hospital), but who must be retained because no space is available, or can be afforded, in these other institutions. Each time the mental hospital functions as a holding station, within a network of such stations, for dealing with public charges, the service model is disaffirmed. All of these facts of patient recruitment are part of what staff must overlook, rationalize, gloss over about their place of service.

One of the most striking problems in applying the service model to mental hospitalization has to do with the largely involuntary character of admission to a mental hospital in America. As with the medical attention required by the very young and the very old, there is an effort to employ the guardian principle and assimilate action taken by a next of kin to action taken by the patient himself. It is true that treating the very young and very old as irresponsible does not seem to be violently inconsistent with or corrupting of our continued relations with them. But, though some involuntary patients do come to see the errors of their resistance to hospitalization, in general the unwilling patient's resentment seems to remain. He is likely to feel that he has been railroaded into the hospital with the help, or at least with the consent, of his close ones. While ordinarily an encounter with a server is likely to affirm the individual's belief in the rationality and good will of the society in which he lives, an encounter with hospital psychiatrists is likely to have an alienating effect.

The patient is not the only one, it seems, who declines to view his trouble as simply a type of sickness to be treated and then forgotten. Once he has a record of having been in a mental hospital, the public at large, both formally, in terms of employment restrictions, and informally, in terms of day-to-day social treatment, considers him to be set apart; they place a stigma on him.[24] Even the hospital itself tacitly acknowledges that mental disorder is shameful; for example, many hospitals provide a code mail address so that patients can send and receive mail without having their status advertised on the envelope. Although the extent of stigmatization is declining in some circles, it is a basic factor in the life of the ex-patient. Unlike much medical hospitalization, the patient's stay in the mental hospital is too long and the effect too stigmatizing to allow the individual an easy return to the social place he came from.[25]

In response to his stigmatization and to the sensed deprivation that occurs when he enters the hospital, the inmate frequently develops some alienation from civil society, sometimes expressed by an unwillingness to leave the hospital. This alienation can develop regardless of the type of disorder for which the patient was committed, constituting a side effect of hospitalization that frequently has more significance for the patient and his personal circle than do his original difficulties. Here again we deal with something that does not fit the service model.[26]

24. See, for example, Charlotte Green Schwartz, 'The Stigma of Mental Illness', *Journal of Rehabilitation* (July–August 1956).

25. It seems characteristic that in medical hospitals men who are laid up will joke with the nursing staff in a self-belittling hearty way, as if to say that the body lying supine for the nurses' ministrations is so uncharacteristic of the permanent self that anything can be safely said about it. In mental hospitals, on the other hand, this easy dissociation from one's current character and circumstances is much less feasible; hence, male mental patients tend to be serious, and where self-distancing expressions are introduced, these may have psychotic-like proportions.

26. In his article, 'The Social Dynamics of Physical Disability in Army Basic Training', *Psychiatry*, X (1947), pp. 323–33, David M. Schneider shows how withdrawal from duties, even on medical grounds, can lead to ever-increasing isolation on the part of the sick person and increasing confirmation of his being different. The effects of separateness can then become more important than the initial causes. Operating on a somewhat similar understanding, U.S. Army research psychiatrists at Walter Reed have recently developed the notion that the more a soldier is allowed to see that he has a major psychiatric problem needful of special psychiatric treatment, the less likely is he to be quickly reassimilated into the military group in which he originally experienced his trouble. See, for example, B. L. Bushard, 'The U.S. Army's Mental Hygiene Consultation Service', in *Symposium on Preventive and Social Psychiatry*, 15–17 April 1957, Walter Reed Army

Another difficulty lies in the nature of psychiatric skills themselves. It seems fair to say that the current assumption as regards functional psychotics is that the patient has developed faulty ways of relating to persons and needs to engage in therapeutic learning experiences to correct these patterns. But the capacity to provide a patient with this experience is not quite a technical skill, nor can it be imparted as assuredly as a technical one. Further, what skills of this kind a staff may have cannot easily be broken down into the skill-status hierarchy characteristic of other service establishments, where high-placed personnel perform the crucial brief tasks and unskilled lower levels perform routine preparatory work or merely ensure that the environment is kept benign. A ward attendant often seems to be as well equipped to offer a 'good' relation to a patient as a highly trained psychiatrist, and, whether good or bad, the contribution of the attendant will impinge continuously on the patient, instead of impinging very intermittently as does the hospital psychiatrist's.[27] Menials who prepare the patient to see the psychiatrist can presumably exercise through this preparation about as much psychiatric intervention as the psychiatrist himself, the domain of face-to-face social contact being one in which every participant is equally licensed to carry and use a scalpel. This is so even though hospital administrations, operating within the medical model,

---

Institute of Research, Washington, D.C., pp. 431–43, especially p. 442: 'These ends [*minimization of psychiatric disability*] can be accomplished through little actual, direct work with the patient himself, but do require extensive and working liaison with a variety of other agencies. Far more important than the verbal interchange with the patient is the non-verbal implication in his being seen early, listened to empathically, and restored to a duty status with dispatch. Any implication that the problem stems from remote or imponderable situations, is due to 'disease' or is based upon considerations which are not immediate and amenable to mastery, will frequently lead to the undermining of such defences as may be still intact.'

27. The milieu therapy movement presumably springs from a recognition that crucial hospital experience cannot be restricted to the therapeutic hour (when there is one) and that all personnel therefore can have an equal fatefulness for the patient. Sources here are Alfred H. Stanton and Morris S. Schwartz, *The Mental Hospital* (New York: Basic Books, 1954), and Maxwell Jones, *The Therapeutic Community* (New York: Basic Books, 1953).

give to psychiatrists the right to make crucial decisions concerning the disposition of the patient.

Operating to exaggerate the fact that little psychiatric skill is available anywhere, and where available not always distributed according to the staff hierarchy, is another issue: the usual circumspection or 'functional specificity' of the server is directly denied in psychiatric service. All of the patient's actions, feelings, and thoughts – past, present, and predicted – are officially usable by the therapist in diagnosis and prescription. Current conceptions about the psychogenic character of many physical disorders even bring into the psychiatrist's domain matters otherwise apportioned to medical practitioners, with the result that the psychiatrist can indeed claim to treat 'the whole person'.[28] The organization of auxiliary psychiatric servers in the hospital – internist, psychologist, neurophysiologist, social worker, nursing staff – attests to the psychiatrist's diffuse mandate, feeding information to him that he alone has an official right to put together into an over-all assessment of a patient. None of a patient's business, then, is none of the psychiatrist's business; nothing ought to be held back from the psychiatrist as irrelevant to his job. No other expert server with a system to tinker with seems to arrogate this kind of role to himself.

Corresponding to this diffuse diagnostic mandate of the psychiatrist is an equally diffuse prescriptive one. Incarcerating institutions operate on the basis of defining almost all of the rights and duties the inmates will have. Someone will be in a position to pass fatefully on everything that the inmate succeeds in obtaining and everything he is deprived of, and this person is, officially, the psychiatrist. Nor need the psychiatrist exercise this right according to uniform bureaucratic rulings, as a member of the civil service or the military might. Almost any of the living arrangements through which the patient is strapped into his daily round can be modified at will by the psychiatrist, provided a psychiatric explanation is given. Again we see that the psychiatric

28. A minor consequence of the psychogenic doctrine of physical disorders is that some mental patients are disinclined to present a claim for needed physical treatment because they fear they will be thought to be 'imagining things'.

role is unique among servers, no other being accorded such power.

In discussing the medical model in a general hospital, it was suggested that life conditions within the hospital could be divided into an inner and outer sphere: the inner sphere contains the injured area of the organism under conditions of medically indicated control that are highly responsive to the state of the injury; the outer sphere provides, in a rougher way, housing for the inner sphere. In mental hospitals this division between a therapeutic and a housing milieu can sometimes be sustained. Where medical (as opposed to psychological) intervention is employed, there can be some effort to administer the treatment under highly controlled conditions, allowing the times between treatments to be handled with less medical attention. And there are cases, as when a patient is actively suicidal or homicidal, when his whole daily round is closely managed and constitutes an inner sphere of medical control intimately adjusted to his circumstances; life conditions can thus be assimilated to treatment. Similarly, for patients of advanced neurophysiological deterioration, back-ward conditions seem closely adapted to the capacities of the organism: the patient's sitting all day in one place, with a vacuous expression on his face, is, in a way, an inevitable and irremedial extension of his state.

But during the earlier stages of cerebral deterioration, and during most of the life course of some organic disorders, such as epilepsy, the absolute assurance that an organic syndrome is present is by no means clearly related to the life conditions accorded the patient in the hospital. However ultimately hopeless a condition is, there are relatively few patients so deteriorated that typical back-ward life is an accurate reflection of and response to their capacities. As to how 'normal' their living arrangements could be, there is no present agreement. Diagnosis, then, may be medical, while treatment is not, the patient being treated merely with the life available for patients of his general kind. And when we turn to functional cases, ward life ceases to be a technical response to their capacities, in the sense that bed rest is an expression of the physical state of a post-operative patient. And yet, as we shall see, mental-hospital staffs do argue that the life conditions of the patient are both an expression of his capabilities and personal organization at the moment and a medical response to them.

Next I want to suggest that, compared to a medical hospital or garage, a mental hospital is ill-equipped to be a place where the classic repair cycle occurs. In state mental hospitals, and to a greater extent in private and veterans' hospitals, opportunity for observing the patient is available, but staff are often too busy to record anything but acts of disobedience. Even when staff time is available for this work, the patient's conduct on the ward can hardly be taken as a sample of his conduct off it: some conduct felt to be unacceptable on the outside does not occur here (especially when this conduct was a response to disliked persons in the patient's home environment), and other forms of misconduct overlay the old in response to the inmate's current involuntary situation. A refraction of conduct thus occurs, the walls of the institution acting like a thick and faulted prism. Unless one argues for the validity of testing persons under this particular kind of stress, the ward would seem to be the worst possible place for a server's observations.

Similarly, even where diagnostic conferences are held in regard to each patient, the effort of these meetings can be directed to agreeing on which of the legally required labels will be affixed to the case-record statement; and the timing of these meetings may have little to do with the presence or absence of an accumulation of data to act upon.

What is true of the difficulties of diagnosis in mental hospitals is even more true of treatment. As already suggested, the problem of easing the patient's attitude to the world is confused and exacerbated by the problem of easing his attitude to involuntary hospitalization. In any case, the treatment given in mental hospitals is not likely to be specific to the disorder, as it is, in general, in a medical hospital, garage, or radio repair shop; instead, if treatment is given at all, a cycle of therapies tends to be given across the board to a whole entering class of patients, with the medical work-up being used more to learn if there are counterindications for the standard treatments than to find indications for them.

At the same time, the patient's life is regulated and ordered according to a disciplinarian system developed for the management by a small staff of a large number of involuntary inmates. In this system the attendant is likely to be the key staff person, informing the patient of the punishments and rewards that are to regulate his life and arranging for medical authorization for such privileges and punishments. Quiet, obedient behaviour leads to the patient's promotion in the ward system; obstreperous, untidy behaviour to demotion. Interestingly enough, it is when the patient finds himself willing to improve his social conduct that the attendant is likely to bring him to the attention of the doctor as both worthy of consideration and able to profit from it, so that, as Ivan Belknap has described, the patient often gets a doctor's attention when he least needs it.[29]

29. Belknap, op. cit., p. 144. I would like to add that since mental patients are persons who on the outside declined to respond to efforts at social control, there is a question of how social control can be achieved on the inside. I believe that it is achieved largely through the 'ward system', the means of control that has slowly evolved in modern mental hospitals. The key, I feel, is a system of wards graded for degree of allowable misbehaviour and degree of discomfort and deprivation prevalent in them. Whatever the level of the new patient's misbehaviour, then, a ward can be found for him in which this conduct is routinely dealt with and to a degree allowed. In effect, by accepting the life conditions on these wards, the patient is allowed to continue his misbehaviour, except that now he does not particularly bother anyone by it, since it is routinely handled, if not accepted, on the ward. When he requests some improvement in his lot he is then, in effect, made to say 'uncle', made to state verbally that he is ready to mend his ways. When he gives in verbally he is likely to be allowed an improvement in life conditions. Should he then again misbehave in the old way, and persist in this, he is lectured and returned to his previous conditions. If instead of backsliding he states his willingness to behave even better, and retains this line for a suitable length of time, he is advanced further within the quick-discharge cycle through which most first admissions are moved up and out within a year. A point then is often reached where the patient is entrusted to a kinsman, either for walks on the hospital grounds or for town expeditions, the kinsman now being transformed into someone who has the incarcerating establishment and the law to reinforce the threat: 'Be good or else I'll send you back.' What we find here (and do not on the outside) is a very model of what psychologists might call a learning situation – all hinged on the process of an admitted giving-in. For this reason, patient morale on the rebellious wards seems stronger and healthier than on the discharge wards, where there is a slight air of persons having sold out to get out.

The period in the mental hospital is a difficult one for the patient to assimilate to the medical model. A very standard complaint is: 'Nothing is being done with me – I'm just left to sit.' And corresponding to this difficulty is the fact that current official psychiatric treatment for functional disorders does not, in itself, provide a probability of success great enough easily to justify the practice of institutional psychiatry as an expert service occupation, as here defined, especially since the probability that hospitalization will damage the life chances of the individual is, as already suggested, positive and high.

The problem, however, is not merely that of a low probability of successful service but, for some patients, a question of the validity of applying the whole service frame of reference in the first place.

First, we must see that the discreetness of the entity in which the disorder exists is questionable. True, in cases that are organic in character, the patient encloses within himself the world in which the damage is felt and the world in which repairs, if possible, can be made. This is not so in instances of functional psychosis. In so far as the patient's symptomatic behaviour is an integral part of his interpersonal situation, the server would have to import this whole situation into the hospital in order to observe the patient's difficulty and to treat it. Instead of there being a relatively benign and passive environment and an isolated point of trouble, the figure and ground of usual service conceptions merge into one, the patient's interpersonal environment being inseparable from the trouble he is experiencing. Theoretically, it might of course be possible for a slight therapeutic change in the patient to have a benign circular effect on his environment when he gets sent back to it, and it might be possible to arrange to return him to a new environment, but in practice the patient is usually returned, when he is discharged, back into the system of which his psychotic response is a natural part.

But there is a still more fundamental issue, which hinges on the applicability of the concept of 'pathology'. Ordinarily the pathology which first draws attention to the patient's condition is conduct that is 'inappropriate in the situation'. But the decision as to whether a given act is appropriate or inappropriate must often necessarily be a lay decision, simply because we have no technical mapping of the various behavioural subcultures in our society, let alone the standards of conduct prevailing in each of them. Diagnostic decisions, except for extreme symptoms, can become ethnocentric, the server judging from his own culture's point of view individuals' conduct that can really be judged only from the perspective of the group from which they derive. Further, since inappropriate behaviour is typically behaviour that someone does not like and finds extremely troublesome, decisions concerning it tend to be political, in the sense of expressing the special interests of some particular faction or person rather than interests that can be said to be above the concerns of any particular grouping, as in the case of physical pathology.[30]

For the patient, the application of the pathology concept to his conduct can have effects that are incompatible with the service ideal. In so far as he feels he has acted inappropriately at all, he may see his action as part of the normal social world of intention, responsibility, and culpability – much like the initial lay perception of his troublesome conduct. To have one's behaviour defined as involuntary, non-responsible, and non-culpable may be helpful in some cases, but this none the less involves a technical schema, not a social one, and ideally ought to disqualify the patient for any participation in the service relation even while qualifying him as an object of service. Szasz's description can be cited here:

More precisely, according to the common-sense definition, mental health is the ability to play whatever the game of social living might consist of and to play it well. Conversely, to refuse to play, or to play badly, means that the person is mentally ill. The question may now be raised as to what are the differences, if any, between social non-conformity (or deviation) and mental illness. Leaving technical psychiatric considerations aside for the moment, I shall argue that the difference between these two notions – as expressed for example by the statements 'He is wrong' and 'He is mentally ill' – does not necessarily lie in any observable *facts* to which they point, but may consist only of a difference in our *attitudes* toward our subject. If we take him *seriously,*

30. See T. S. Szasz, 'Psychiatry, Ethics, and the Criminal Law', *Columbia Law Review*, LVIII (1958), p. 188.

consider him to have human rights and dignities, and look upon him as more or less our equal – we then speak of disagreements, deviations, fights, crimes, perhaps even of treason. Should we feel, however, that we cannot communicate with him, that he is somehow 'basically' different from us, we shall then be inclined to consider him no longer as an equal but rather as an inferior (rarely, superior) person; and we then speak of him as being crazy, mentally ill, insane, psychotic, immature, and so forth.[31]

We should not overestimate this problem, however, because, in fact, there is no great danger in mental hospitals of having one's acts consistently defined in a neutral technical frame of reference. In medicine it is possible to act as if there were no right or wrong streptococci, merely dangerous ones. In psychiatry there is a formal effort to act as if the issue is treatment, not moral judgement, but this is not consistently maintained. Ethical neutrality is indeed difficult to sustain in psychiatry, because the patient's disorder is intrinsically related to his acting in a way that causes offence to witnesses. Further, the standard way of dealing with such offences in our society is to sanction the offender, negatively and correctively. Our whole society operates on this assumption in every item and detail of life, and without some functional equivalent it is hard to see how we could maintain a social order without it.

It is understandable, then, that even occasions set aside to demonstrate that professional non-moralistic psychotherapy is taking place in the institution will be invaded by a moralistic perspective, albeit a modified one. It is understandable that a large part of psychotherapy consists of holding the sins of the patient up to him and getting him to see the error of his ways. And in a sense, I do not see how it can or should be otherwise. The interesting point here is that psychiatric staff are in a position neither to forgo the fiction of neutrality nor actually to sustain it.

31. T. S. Szasz, 'Politics and Mental Health', *American Journal of Psychiatry*, CXV (1958), p. 509. See also his 'Psychiatric Expert Testimony – Its Covert Meaning & Social Function', *Psychiatry*, XX (1957), p. 315, and 'Some Observations on the Relationship between Psychiatry and the Law', *A.M.A. Archives of Neurology and Psychiatry*, LXXV (1956), pp. 297–315.

When applied to the mental hospital, the service model leads to a very characteristic ambivalence of action on the part of staff. Psychiatric doctrine requires ethical neutrality in dealing with patients, for what others see as misbehaviour the staff must see as pathology. The law even underwrites this position, a mental patient having the privilege of committing crimes without having to face legal action. And yet, in the actual management of patients, ideals of proper conduct must be held up as desirable, infractions inveighed against, and the patient treated as a 'responsible' person, that is, one capable of a personal effort to behave himself. Psychiatric staff share with policemen the peculiar occupational task of hectoring and moralizing adults; the necessity of submitting to these lectures is one of the consequences of committing acts against the community's social order.

VII

Given these many senses in which an expert service is not provided to the mental patient or the concept of expert service does not apply to the patient's plight, we can expect some difficulties in the interaction between institutional psychiatrist and patient, difficulties that are a necessary and natural product of mental hospitalization. The psychiatrist's training, orientation, and status commit him to approaching a mental patient civilly, in the guise of offering an expert service to a client who has voluntarily sought it. The psychiatrist must therefore assume that the patient wants treatment and has a rational mind that can come, albeit in an unskilled way, to the assistance of those who serve its possessor. The institution itself at every point affirms this service guise through the terminology used, the uniforms worn, and the terms of address employed.

If, however, the psychiatrist is to take the patient's words at face value as a report of symptoms, as in medical servicing, then the patient must be willing to respond in a very special way: a contrite admission of illness stated in modestly untechnical terms and a sincerely expressed desire to undergo a change of self through psychiatric treatment. In short, there is a psychiatric line the patient must follow if the psychiatrist is to be affirmed as a medical server.

The likelihood of an unschooled patient following the psychiatric line is not great. He may never in his life have had so many reasons obvious to him for seeing that he is not a voluntary client and for being disgruntled at his condition. He sees the psychiatrist as the person in power. In contact with the psychiatrist the patient is likely to make those kinds of demands and requests and take those stands that pull the relationship out of the service schema to, for example, that of a charge pleading with his master for more privileges, a prisoner remonstrating with an unlawful jailer, or a prideful man declining to exchange communications with someone who thinks he is crazy.

If the psychiatrist takes these complaints seriously, the relationship ceases to be the one for which he was trained. To defend his own professional role and the institution that hires him, the psychiatrist is under pressure to respond by treating these outpourings not as directly usable statements of information but rather as signs of the illness itself, to be discounted as direct information.[32] But to treat the statements of the patient as signs, not valid symptom reporting, is of course to deny that the patient is a participant as well as an object in a service relation.

The psychiatrist and patient tend to be doomed by the institutional context to a false and difficult relationship and are constantly funnelled into the contact that will express it: the psychiatrist must extend service civility from the stance of a server but can no more continue in that stance than the patient can accept it. Each party to the relationship is destined to seek out the other to offer what the other cannot accept, and each is destined to reject what the other offers. In many psychiatric settings, one can witness what seems to be the same central encounter between a patient and a psychiatrist: the psychiatrist begins the exchange by proffering the patient the civil regard that is owed a client, receives a response that cannot be integrated into a continuation of the conventional service interaction, and then, even while attempting to sustain some of the outward forms of

32. On the problem of discounted statements, see Stanton and Schwartz, op. cit., p. 200 ff.

server-client relations, must twist and squirm his way out of the predicament. All day long the psychiatric staff seems to be engaged in withdrawing from its own implicit overtures.

VIII

In discussing the application of the expert service model to various trades, I suggested some standard discrepancies or strains and argued that institutional psychiatric servicing faced a very extensive set of these problems. This situation is in itself not very noteworthy; many 'expert' services are sold that satisfy even less well than psychiatry the requirements of the model in whose guise they are presented, albeit few involving so many clients so sorely tried. What is analytically interesting about the mental-hospital case is that doctors are involved, and so are involuntary inmates. Medical doctors in our society are exemplars of the rational, tinkering approach and ordinarily are allowed to invest their performances with great dignity and weight. Having committed much time and expense to acquiring the medical role, and expecting their daily activity to support them in the role their training has vouchsafed them, they understandably feel compelled to maintain a medical approach and the medical version of the service model. Society at large seems to back them up in this, for it is a satisfaction to us all to feel that those we exile to madhouses are receiving treatment, not punishment, under a doctor's care. At the same time, involuntary mental commitment (and often even voluntary commitment) ordinarily entails for the individual a condition of life that is impoverished and desolate indeed, often generating a sustained hostility to his captors. The limited applicability of the medical model to mental hospitals brings together a doctor who cannot easily afford to construe his activity in other than medical terms and a patient who may well feel he must fight and hate his keepers if any sense is to be made of the hardship he is undergoing. Mental hospitals institutionalize a kind of grotesque of the service relationship.

While both doctors and inmates find themselves in a difficult institutional setting, the doctors, being in control of the institution, have the greater opportunity to evolve some mechanisms for coping with their problem. Their response to the situation provides us not only with an important aspect of hospital life but also with a case history of the interplay between social models of being – in this case the expert server – and the social establishments in which there is an attempt to institutionalize these role identities.

There are some features of the hospital situation that help the psychiatrist in the difficulties of his role. The physician's legal mandate over the fate of the patient and his institutional power over some elements of staff automatically provide the authority that other servers must in part win through actual interaction with the client. Further, while psychiatric knowledge often cannot place the psychiatrist in a position to predict the patient's conduct correctly, the same nescience provides the psychiatrist with interpretive leeway: by adding *post hoc* qualifications and adumbrations of his analyses, the psychiatrist can provide a picture of what has been happening with the patient that can no more be disproved than proved, as when an unanticipated psychotic break gives rise to the interpretation that the patient now feels secure enough or strong enough to express his psychosis. To this authority that cannot be discredited, the psychiatrist can add a force derived from medical tradition, 'clinical experience'. Through this magical quality, the formally qualified person of longest experience with the type of case in question is accorded the final word when there is doubt or ambiguity, this person also being apt to be the ranking practitioner present.

The psychiatrist, being medically trained, can provide minor medical services to patients and can refer more difficult medical cases to the hospital's hospital. This normative function (characteristic, as suggested, of what must be done in the Army, on a ship, in a factory, or wherever large numbers are gathered to contribute to an administrative end), instead of being seen as an ancillary housekeeping service, tends to be assimilated to the central functioning of the establishment, thereby strengthening the basis in reality of the notion that mental patients receive medical-like treatment in mental hospitals. Interestingly enough, state mental hospitals sometimes are so understaffed that medically qualified personnel could spend all their time making minor medical repairs on patients and must practise psychiatry – to the extent they do – at the expense of needed medical treatment.

An obvious way for the psychiatrist to solve his role problem is to leave the state mental hospital as soon as he can afford to, often with the claim that he is leaving in order to go where 'it will really be possible to practise psychiatry'. He may go, especially for the last year or two of his obligatory residency, to a private hospital, perhaps of the psychoanalytically oriented kind, where there is a patient load approaching that of private practice, and where a higher ratio of patients are voluntary and 'suitable' for psychotherapy. From such a hospital (or directly from the state hospital), he may go into private practice, an arrangement that may not bring his skill to many patients but will guarantee that activity is conducted in accordance with the service complex: an office, a secretary, hour-long appointments, voluntary appearance of the patient, sole control over diagnosis and treatment, and so forth.[33] For whatever reasons, this two- or three-stage job cycle is sufficiently common to constitute a standard career pattern in psychiatry.

Where the psychiatrist cannot, or does not want, to leave the state mental hospital, some other paths appear to have been established for him. He may redefine his role from that of a server to that of a wise governor, embrace the custodial aspects of the institution, and devote himself to enlightened administration. He can admit some of the weaknesses of individual therapy in the situation and move in the direction of the newer social therapies,

33. It is remarkable that the self-discipline required of the mental client if he is to allow his psychiatrist to act like any other professional man receives full and detailed justification in the psychoanalytical literature on the basis of technical therapeutic considerations. A wonderful pre-arranged harmony exists between what is good for the patient and what in fact the psychiatrist requires if an office profession is to be maintained. To paraphrase Mr Wilson, what is good for the profession is good for the patient. I have found especially refreshing the discussion of the psychological importance of the patient's appreciating that the therapist has a life of his own and that it would not be good for the patient if the therapist postponed his vacation, or saw the patient in response to midnight telephone calls, or allowed himself to be physically endangered by the patient. See, for example, C. A. Witaker and T. P. Malone, *The Roots of Psychotherapy* (New York: Blakiston Co., 1953), pp. 201–202.

attempting to involve the patient's kin in psychotherapy (on the assumption that the disorder resides in a family system),[34] or attempting to locate therapy in the full round of daily contacts that the patient has with all levels of staff.[35] He can turn to psychiatric research. He can withdraw from patient contact as much as possible, retreating into paper work, or into psycho-therapy with the lower levels of staff or with a small number of 'promising' patients. He can make a serious effort to warn the patients whom he treats that his knowledge is small, but this kind of candour seems destined to fail because the medical role is de-fined otherwise in our society, and because the power the psychia-trist has over the patient is not readily understood as something that would be given to anyone who knew little.[36] Occasionally the psychiatrist becomes a 'patients' man', agreeing with their claims as to what the institution is doing to them and voicing open criticism of the establishment to them. If he takes none of these tacks, the psychiatrist can at least become cynical about his role in the hospital, thereby protecting himself, if not his patients.[37]

In addition to these modes of adaptation involving career alignments, we find adaptations of a more diffuse and more ideological kind, in which staff levels participate. It is as if the service dilemma constituted a sore spot in the hospital social system, and that around this spot intellectual energies are expen-

34. Faced with the doctrine that the patient may merely be the 'symptom carrier' for his intimate circle, some research psychiatrists have made an effort to import whole families on to experimental residential wards. The side problems consequent upon such novel living arrangements, especially as re-gards the structure of family authority, are very great, and their masking effect has perhaps been underestimated.

35. Here the psychiatrist may explicitly admit that he must be therapist not to the individual but to the hospital social system. Psychiatric and medical training seem to equip doctors to accept the responsibility of governing a ward or hospital, freeing them from the trepidation an individual might have who had relevant training or experience for the task.

36. For a comment on the fate of verbal modesty in the context of high hospital office, see A. H. Stanton, 'Problems in Analysis of Therapeutic Implications of the Institutional Milieu', in *Symposium on Preventive and Social Psychiatry*, Walter Reed Army Institute of Research, Washington, D.C. (15–17 April 1957), p. 499.

37. Belknap, op. cit., p. 200.

ded to build up a protective skin of words, beliefs, and sentiments. Whatever its source, the resulting system of belief serves to bolster and stabilize the medical-service definition of the situation. We are thus provided with an illustration in miniature of the relation between thought and social position.

Perhaps the most obvious instance of institutional ideology is found in the public relations work that is currently fairly characteristic of mental hospitals. Hallway displays, orientation booklets, institutional magazines, displayable equipment, and newer therapies – these sources of definitions of the situation await patients, relatives, and visitors, establishing the obvious claims of the medical-service line.

Further, we have in mental hospitals a collection of traditional tales whose recounting illustrates the validity of the perspective employed by staff. These stories tell of times a patient was given privileges too early, or released against advice of physicians, and went on to commit suicide or murder. Attendants have jokes to tell illustrating the animal-like nature of patients. Those staff members who attend diagnostic conferences have humorous anecdotes about patients – for example, an inmate who made a dignified claim to sanity but finally allowed that he was an agent of the F B I. There are stories of patients who begged to be kept on a locked ward, or who engaged in obvious delinquencies in order to prevent their own discharge. There are other tales of 'pre-patients' who displayed increasingly florid and dangerous psychotic symptoms until others were finally convinced of the illness and provided hospitalization, at which point the patients were able to relax their symptomatology, having succeeded in communicating their need for help. Finally, there are heart-warming stories of impossible patients who finally came to form a good relationship with an understanding doctor and thereafter dramatically improved. As with the other of exemplary tales, these relationship stories seem to centre on proof of the rightness of the position taken by staff.[38]

The ideological or interpretative implications of management's activity seem to focus on two issues, the nature of patients and

38. Patients, of course, have their own set of exemplary tales almost equally discrediting of staff.

the nature of the hospital's activity, in both cases bolstering up
the medical-service definition of the situation.

The key view of the patient is: were he 'himself' he would
voluntarily seek psychiatric treatment and voluntarily submit to
it, and, when ready for discharge, he will avow that his real self
was all along being treated as it really wanted to be treated. A
variation of the guardian principle is involved. The interesting
notion that the psychotic patient has a sick self and, subordinated
to this, a relatively 'adult', 'intact', or 'unimpaired' self carries
guardianship one step further, finding in the very structure of the
ego the split between object and client required to complete the
service triad.

The case record plays a role here. It provides a means of systematically building up a picture of the patient's past that demonstrates that a disease process had been slowly infiltrating his
conduct until this conduct, as a system, was entirely pathological.
Seemingly normal conduct is seen to be merely a mask or shield
for the essential sickness behind it. An over-all title is given to the
pathology, such as schizophrenia, psychopathic personality, etc.,
and this provides a new view of the patient's 'essential' character.[39] When pressed, of course, some staff will allow that these
syndrome titles are vague and doubtful, employed only to comply
with hospital census regulations. But in practice these categories
become magical ways of making a single unity out of the nature
of the patient – an entity that is subject to psychiatric servicing.
Through all of this, of course, the areas of 'normal functioning'
in the patient can be discounted and disattended, except in so far
as they lead the patient willingly to accept his treatment.

The response of the patient to hospitalization can itself be
nicely handled by translating it into a technical frame of reference,
whereby the contribution of the hospital to the patient's trouble
becomes incidental, the important thing being the internally
generated mode of disturbance characteristic of the patient's
conduct. Interpersonal happenings are transferred into the
patient, establishing him as a relatively closed system that can be

39. The social psychology of perceived 'essential' character has recently
been developed by Harold Garfinkel in a series of unpublished papers, to
which I am much indebted.

thought of as pathological and correctable. Thus an action that the patient engages in with an official of the institution that may, to the official, have an aggressive cast is translated into a substantive term like 'aggressivity' that can be located well within the patient.[40] Similarly, a ward situation in which nurses do not bother to initiate contact with long-term patients (who in fact would respond to overtures) may be transferred into the patient by referring to him as 'mute'.[41] As Szasz has suggested, this view has similarities to the earlier view that the mental patient has a devil or evil spirit within him that must be and need only be exorcized.[42]

This translation process can be clearly seen in the process of group psychotherapy. In general this therapy – the principal verbal therapy patients in state hospitals receive – begins as a gripe session during which patients express demands and complaints in a relatively permissive atmosphere, with relatively direct access to a staff member. The only action on the part of the therapist that seems consistent with his obligation to the institution and his profession is to turn these demands aside by convincing the patient that the problems he feels he is having with the institution – or with kin, society, and so forth – are really *his* problems; the therapist suggests that he attack these problems by rearranging his own internal world, not by attempting to alter the action of these other agents. What we have here is a direct,

40. See John Money, 'Linguistic Resources and Psycho-dynamic Theory', *British Journal of Medical Psychology*, XXVIII (1955), pp. 264–6. Useful examples of this translation process are found in Edwin Weinstein and Robert Kahn, *Denial of Illness* (Springfield, Ill.: Charles Thomas, 1955). The authors cite such terms as 'akinetic mutism', 'Anton's syndrome', 'reduplicative paramnesia', 'anosognosia', which have been used traditionally to refer to a patient's failure to admit his injured condition; they then describe under categories such as 'displacement', 'misnaming', 'paraphasia' the various ways in which patients decline to respond to their situation in a civil and cooperative way, the intransigence being described as a psycho-physiological by-product of brain injury, not as a social response to involuntary threatening treatment. See also Belknap, op. cit., p. 170.

41. Robert Sommer, 'Patients who grow old in a mental hospital' *Geriatrics*, XIV (1959), p. 584.

42. T. S. Szasz, W. F. Knoff, and M. H. Hollender, 'The Doctor-Patient Relationship and Its Historical Context', *American Journal of Psychiatry*, CXV (1958), p. 526.

although no doubt not intentional, effort to transform the patient in his own eyes into a closed system in need of servicing. Thus, to cite a relatively extreme example, I have seen a therapist deal with a Negro patient's complaints about race relations in a partially segregated hospital by telling the patient that he must ask himself why he, among all the other Negroes present, chose this particular moment to express this feeling, and what this expression could mean about him as a person, apart from the state of race relations in the hospital at the time.[43]

One of the most intimate service redefinitions of the patient's nature is to be found in the idea of the 'danger mandate' characteristic of many of the tinkering services. It has been said that a medical student becomes a doctor when he finds himself in a position to make a crucial mistake.[44] Underlying this attitude is a belief that a serviceable system has organizational danger points and can therefore be greatly damaged if unskilled action is taken in these crucial, precarious matters. As already suggested, this tends to provide rational grounds for a technical hierarchy of skill and a social hierarchy of servers within any one servicing establishment.

There is a version of the danger mandate in mental hospitals. This is the view that a wrong action can greatly endanger the patient, and that the psychiatrist is in a position, due to training and skill, to take potentially dangerous actions regarding patients, actions that lesser persons in the medical hierarchy ought not to be allowed to take. Of course, in questions of prescribing drug dosage and weighing possible contra-indicating side effects of physical treatment, the model here holds well enough, but the

43. The techniques employed by group psychotherapists can be studied as part of small-group indoctrination methods. For example, one commonly finds that a few patients will be well versed in the psychiatric line and reliably willing to take it. A gripe raised by a patient may then be picked up by the therapist and referred back to these patients for their opinion. They translate for the complainer, showing that his own fellows see his complaint as part of his own personality, leaving the therapist to come in with the authoritative translation, but now with some of the group polarized against the complainer. A recent discussion of these issues may be found in Jerome D. Frank, 'The Dynamics of the Psychotherapeutic Relationship', *Psychiatry*, XXII (1959), pp. 17–39.

44. Personal communication from Howard S. Becker.

carry-over into the psychotherapeutic realm is more precarious, although often no less insisted on. It is sometimes suggested that lesser personnel, such as social workers, nurses, and attendants, ought not to engage in 'amateur therapy', and certainly not in amateur 'psychoanalysis'. A staff psychiatrist who takes on an inmate for special sessions of psychotherapy ought not to have his work tampered with by others, especially lesser others. The wrong move during psychotherapy, it is said, can 'precipitate' a psychosis, or cast the patient back into a regression from which he may never return, and exemplary tales provide evidence for this. Now while it is perfectly clear that this view fits in well with the traditional notion of a danger mandate, and while it is clear that the possession of this mandate confirms one's view of self as an expert server, it is much less clear that a purely verbal act can in fact have this effect. In any case, as previously suggested, any hospital inmate in personal therapy is likely to be undergoing, during the other twenty-three hours of each day, a barrage of potentially traumatic experiences, relatively uncontrolled in barbarity, that surely cloud any issue of a verbal probe going in the right or wrong direction. Moreover, given the state of psychiatric knowledge and skill, if a wrongly placed verbal shaft could cause this kind of damage, patients would be in danger indeed during the twenty-fourth hour.

Two further imputations about the patient's nature may be described, both of which again function to support the service model. When a patient is offered a discharge and declines to take it, sometimes engaging in activity calculated to assure his retention, it is commonly said that this proves he is still ill, that he is, in fact, too ill to leave. In this way a link is made between two massive aspects of the situation: being defined as ill or well, and being in or out of the hospital. There are of course many good reasons unconnected with the service model for a patient's diffidence about leaving. For example, he has already suffered the stigma of being a mental patient and in this reduced status has even poorer prospects on the outside than he did before he came in; furthermore, by the time he is ready to be discharged he is likely to have learned the ropes in the hospital and have worked himself up to a desirable position in the 'ward system'.

The other patient action that is rationalized in terms of the medical model is that of sudden alteration in propriety of conduct. Since the current conduct of the patient is supposed to be a profound reflection or sign of his personality organization – his psychic system – any sudden, apparently unprovoked, alteration in either a 'healthy' or a 'sick' direction must somehow be accounted for. Sudden changes for the worse are sometimes called relapses or regressions. Sudden changes for the better are sometimes called spontaneous remissions. Through the power of these words the staff can claim that, although they may not know what caused the change, the change can be handled within the medical perspective. Of course, this interpretation of the situation precludes one's employing a social perspective. In what is called sudden regression, the new conduct may involve no more or less illness or health than any other alignment to life; and what is accepted as spontaneous remission may be a result of the patient's not having been sick in the first place.

I am suggesting that the nature of the patient's nature is redefined so that, in effect if not by intention, the patient becomes the kind of object upon which a psychiatric service can be performed. To be made a patient is to be remade into a serviceable object, the irony being that so little service is available once this is done. And the great shortage of psychiatric staff can be seen as created not by the number of ill persons but by the institutional machinery that brings to this area the service definition of the situation.

I want now, finally, to consider the definitions that the staff maintain regarding the nature, not of the patient, but of the hospital's action upon the patient. Since the staff possess the voice of the institution, it is through these definitions that the administrative and disciplinary machinery of the hospital is presented to the patient and to the public. In brief, we find that the facts of ward management and the dynamics of the ward system are expressed in the language of psychiatric medical service.

The patient's presence in the hospital is taken as *prima facie* evidence that he is mentally ill, since the hospitalization of these persons is what the institution is for. A very common answer to a patient who claims he is sane is the statement: 'If you aren't sick, you wouldn't be in the hospital.' The hospital itself, apart from the therapeutic services administered by its trained staff, is said to provide a sense of security for the patient (sometimes only to be obtained by knowing that the door is locked)[45] and a release from daily responsibilities. Both of these provisions are said to be therapeutic. (Whether therapeutic or not, it is difficult to find environments which introduce more profound insecurities; and what responsibilities are lifted are removed at a very considerable and very permanent price.)

Other translations can be mentioned. Regimentation may be defined as a framework of therapeutic regularity designed to allay insecurity; forced social mixing with a multitude of heterogeneous, displeased fellow inmates may be described as an opportunity to learn that there are others who are worse off. Sleeping dormitories are called wards, this being affirmed by some of the physical equipment, notably the beds, which are purchased through hospital suppliers. The punishment of being sent to a worse ward is described as transferring a patient to a ward whose arrangements he can cope with, and the isolation cell or 'hole' is described as a place where the patient will be able to feel comfortable with his inability to handle his acting-out impulses.[46] Making a ward quiet at night through the forced taking of drugs, which permits reduced night staffing, is called medication or sedative treatment. Women long since unable to perform such routine medical tasks as taking bloods are called nurses and wear nursing uniforms; men trained as general practitioners are called psychiatrists. Work assignments are defined as industrial therapy or as a means through which the patient can express his reawakened capacity for assuming civil duties. Reward for good behaviour by progressively increasing rights to attend socials may be described as psychiatric control over the dosage and timing of social exposure. Patients housed where treatment is first given are said to be in the 'acute' service; those who fail to leave after the initial cycle of medical action are moved to what is called the 'chronic service'

45. Of the more than hundred patients I knew in the hospital I studied, one did allow that he felt too anxious to go more than a block or so from his ward. I knew, or knew of, no patient who preferred a locked ward, except patients described by staff.

46. See, for example, Belknap, op. cit., p. 191.

or, more recently, 'continued-treatment wards'; those ready to leave are housed in a 'convalescent ward'. Finally, discharge itself, which at the end of a year tends to be granted to most first-admission, averagely cooperative patients or to any other patient for whom kinfolk exert pressure, is often taken as evidence that 'improvement' has occurred, and this improvement is tacitly imputed to the workings of the institution. (Among the reasons for discharge of a particular patient may be ward population pressure, spontaneous remission, or the social conformity instilled in him by the disciplinary power of the ward system.) Even the concise phrases, 'discharged as cured' or 'discharged as improved', imply that the hospital had a hand in the curing or improving. (At the same time, failure to be discharged tends to be attributed to the difficulty of treating mental disorder and to the stubbornness and profundity of this kind of illness, thus affirming the medical model even in the face of not being able to do anything for the patient.) In fact, of course, a high rate of discharge might just as well be taken as evidence of the improper functioning of the hospital, for since little actual treatment is available, the improvement of the patient occurs in spite of hospitalization, and presumably might occur more frequently in circumstances other than the deprived ones within the institution.

Some of the verbal translations found in mental hospitals represent not so much medical terms for disciplinary practices as a disciplinary use of medical practices. Here the lore of state mental hospitals contains some exemplary tales for sociologists. In some mental hospitals, it has been said, one way of dealing with female patients who became pregnant on the hospital grounds was to perform hysterectomies. Less common, perhaps, was the way of dealing with those patients, sometimes called 'biters', who continued to bite persons around them: total extraction of teeth. The first of these medical acts was sometimes called 'treatment for sexual promiscuity', the second, 'treatment for biting'. Another example is the fashion, now sharply declining in American hospitals, of using lobotomy for a hospital's most incorrigible and troublesome patients.[47] The use of electro-shock, on the

47. I have been told of manic mental patients who were tubercular and for whom lobotomy was prescribed lest their hyperactivity kill them. This is

attendant's recommendation, as a means of threatening inmates into discipline and quietening those that won't be threatened, provides a somewhat milder but more widespread example of the same process.[48] In all of these cases, the medical action is presented to the patient and his relatives as an individual service, but what is being serviced here is the institution, the specification of the action fitting in to what will reduce the administrator's management problems. In brief, under the guise of the medical-service model the practice of maintenance medicine is sometimes to be found.

CONCLUSION

IX

In citing some senses in which mental hospitalization does not fit the medical-service model, I have not mentioned the difficulties in applying the model to outpatient private psychiatric practice, although these of course exist (such as: the length of time required for treatment, with consequent strain on the concept of the fee; the low probability of effective treatment; and the very great difficulty of knowing to what to attribute change in the patient's condition).

Further, in focusing on the difficulties of the application to the mental hospital of the medical-service model, I do not mean to imply that the application of the model has not sometimes proved useful to those institutionalized as patients. The presence of medical personnel in asylums has no doubt served to stay somewhat the hand of the attendant. There seems little doubt that doctors are willing to work in these unsalubrious, isolating environments because the medical perspective provides a way of looking at people that cuts across standard social perspectives and therefore provides a way of being somewhat blind to ordinary tastes and distastes. The availability of the medical version of one's situation has no doubt provided some patients with a claim on

---

a decision that does involve the personal service, not the maintenance, function of medicine. It may be repeated that the act itself is not the determining issue but rather the organizational context in which it is recommended.

48. See Belknap, op. cit., p. 192.

middle-class consideration within the hospital; the moratorium, on medical grounds, from family living has no doubt been of great help to some patients; the general medical notion of the 'curability' of 'mental disorder' consequent on the administration of 'treatment' has no doubt made re-integration into the free community easier for some patients and for those to whom they return; and the idea that one has been undergoing treatment for a lifelong wasting of one's previous years can provide some patients with a way of making some kind of acceptable sense out of the time spent in exile in the hospital.

Nor in citing the limitations of the service model do I mean to claim that I can suggest some better way of handling persons called mental patients. Mental hospitals are not found in our society because supervisors, psychiatrists, and attendants want jobs; mental hospitals are found because there is a market for them. If all the mental hospitals in a given region were emptied and closed down today, tomorrow relatives, police, and judges would raise a clamour for new ones; and these true clients of the mental hospital would demand an institution to satisfy their needs.

Professional psychiatric staff itself does not have an easy role. The members' medical licence gives them one of the firmest claims to deference and regard available in our society, and one of the firmest expert service occupations, yet in the mental hospital their whole role is constantly in question. Everything that goes on in the hospital must be legitimated by assimilating it or translating it to fit into a medical-service frame of reference. Daily staff actions must be defined and presented as expressions of observation, diagnosis and treatment. To effect this translation, reality must be considerably twisted, somewhat as it is by judges, instructors, and officers in other of our coercive institutions. A crime must be uncovered that fits the punishment, and the character of the inmate must be reconstituted to fit the crime.

But the staff is of course not the only group that finds difficulties in applying the service model; patients, too, have problems which cast light on the relation between stance and reality. The patient's round is harsh and barren. As such this has no sociological interest for us here; there are, after all, other situations even in American life that are almost as bad and a few that are worse. Our concern here is that the service model employed in mental hospitals brings a special twist and bite to these deprivations.

In a medical hospital, one's own physical incapacities are taken as a sign that treatment, however unpleasant or confining, is needed for one's own good and should be accepted. In a psychiatric hospital, failure to be an easily manageable patient – failure, for example, to work or to be polite to staff – tends to be taken as evidence that one is not 'ready' for liberty and that one has a need to submit to further treatment. The point is not that the hospital is a hateful place for patients but that for the patient to express hatred of it is to give evidence that his place in it is justified and that he is not yet ready to leave it. A systematic confusion between obedience to others and one's own personal adjustment is sponsored.

Further, when we inquire into the particularities of the way these establishments are staffed and run, and the beliefs that circulate in them, we find that, whatever else these institutions do, one of their central effects is to sustain the self-conception of the professional staff employed there. Inmates and lower staff levels are involved in a vast supportive action – an elaborate dramatized tribute – that has the effect, if not the purpose, of affirming that a medical-like service is in progress here and that the psychiatric staff is providing it.[49] Something about the weakness of this claim is suggested by the industry required to support it. (Perhaps a sentimental sociological generalization is suggested: the farther one's claims diverge from the facts, the more effort one must exert and the more help one must have to bolster one's position.)

Mental patients can find themselves in a special bind. To get

49. The wider community is engaged in this role support, too. There is an important sense in which the ideal therapeutic experience envisaged today is a prolonged immersion in individual psychotherapy, preferably psychoanalytic. In this view, the ideal way to improve state hospital service would be to increase psychiatric staff so that more individual therapy would be possible, and, barring this admittedly hopeless ideal, to provide a maximum amount of second-best therapy, such as group psychotherapy and counselling. It is possible that this kind of solution is more likely to help the role predicament of psychiatrists than to help the human situation in which mental patients find themselves.

out of the hospital, or to ease their life within it, they must show acceptance of the place accorded them, and the place accorded them is to support the occupational role of those who appear to force this bargain. This self-alienating moral servitude, which perhaps helps to account for some inmates becoming mentally confused, is achieved by invoking the great tradition of the expert servicing relation, especially its medical variety. Mental patients can find themselves crushed by the weight of a service ideal that eases life for the rest of us.